STOCK INVESTING FOR BEGINNERS: VALUE EDITION

FEATURING: 20 STOCKS & ETFS TO BUY AND HOLD
FOR THE NEXT 21 YEARS + HOW TO INVEST YOUR
MONEY IN A BEAR MARKET

FREEMAN PUBLICATIONS

CONTENTS

20 FOR 20: THE 8-STEP BEGINNER'S GUIDE TO VALUE INVESTING

BEAR MARKET INVESTING STRATEGIES

HOW TO GET $182 WORTH OF INVESTMENT RESEARCH FOR FREE

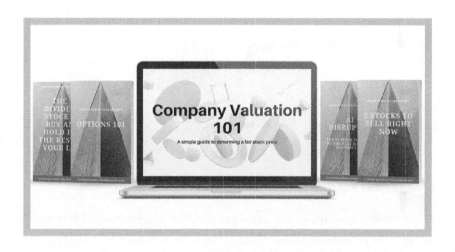

To get your bonuses go to
https://freemanpublications.com/bonus

Free bonus #1: Company Valuation 101 video course ($77 value)

In this 6 part video course you'll discover our process for accurately valuing a company. This will help you determine if a stock is overvalued, correctly valued or a bargain. Giving you an indicator whether to buy or not.

Free bonus #2: Guru Portfolios Analyzed ($37 value)

In these videos we analyze the stock portfolio's of Billionaire investors like Warren Buffett as well as top entrepreneurs like Bill Gates.

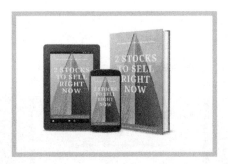

Free bonus #3: 2 Stocks to Sell Right Now ($17 value)

These 2 stocks more than any other are in danger of plummeting in the next 12 months. They're both popular with retail investors, and one is even in the top 5 most held stocks on Robinhood. Believe us, you don't want to be holding these going into 2021 and beyond.

Free bonus #4: AI Disruptor - The $4 Stock Poised to be the Next Big Thing in Computing ($17 value)

This under the radar company, which less than 1% of investors have heard of, is at the forefront of a breakthrough technology which will change our lives as we know them. Soon this technology will be in every smartphone, tablet and laptop on the planet.

Free bonus #5: Options 101 ($17 Value)

Options don't have to be risky. In fact, they were invented to *reduce* risk. It's no wonder that smart investors like Warren Buffett regularly use options to supplement their own long-term portfolio. In this quickstart guide we show you how options work, and why they're a tool to be utilized rather than feared.

Free bonus #6: The 1 Dividend Stock to Buy and Hold for the Rest of Your Life ($17 Value)

Dividends are the lifeblood of any income investor, and this stock is a cornerstone of any dividend strategy. A true dividend aristocrat with consistent payouts for over 50 years which you'll want to add to your portfolio for sure.

All of this 100% free, with no strings attached when you subscribe to our free investing emails. You don't need to enter any details except your email address.

To get your bonuses go to
https://freemanpublications.com/bonus

20 FOR 20: THE 8-STEP BEGINNER'S GUIDE TO VALUE INVESTING

THE 20 BEST STOCKS & ETFS TO BUY AND HOLD FOR THE NEXT 20 YEARS TO MAKE CONSISTENT PROFITS EVEN IN A BEAR MARKET

"I think it's a tragedy that the small investor has been convinced by the media that they don't have a chance. That the big institutions, with all their computers, all their degrees and all their money, have all the edges. And it just isn't true at all.

When people get brainwashed by the media, they act accordingly. They buy stocks for a week, then they buy options. They buy the Chile fund this week, and the Argentina fund the next week. Then they get results proportionate to that kind of investing, and that's very bothersome.

But if someone can sit back, and form their own opinion about a company or an industry, I think the public can do extremely well in the stock market on their own."

Peter Lynch, NYTimes Bestselling Author and one of the most successful investors in history. As manager of the The Magellan Fund he doubled the return of the S&P500.

STOCK INVESTING: A 30,000 FEET VIEW

What runs through your mind when someone mentions the stock market? Do you immediately think of a complicated machine that has the potential to bankrupt you? Alternatively, do you think of a casino where you can make millions?

Despite what you may hear from uneducated voices, the reality isn't close to either of these extremes. The stock market is a great place to build long-term wealth, but only if you make the right investment choices.

Between 1994 and 2013, the S&P 500, the index of the 500 largest public companies in the US, returned an average of 8.99% per year. But those who invested in individual stocks didn't fare as well. A study by Bernstein Advisors found that in the same time period, the average retail investor buying individual stocks made a return of just 2.1% per year. Which means during this 20 year period, the "man on the street" underperformed every single asset class, including cash (as 3-month treasury bills).

So why does this happen? Why do so many individuals make below-average returns?

Much of it involves education or lack of it. When people are first exposed to the idea of stock investing, it's often presented as an excellent opportunity to make quick money. This is why, for many investors, their first experience is a bad one.

They are enticed by a tip from a friend or family member. Or worse, they see a post on social media about a "once-in-a-lifetime buying opportunity" and don't want to miss out on potential profits. You may have had this exact experience in the past. If not, you likely know someone who has.

You may also have been lured by the prospect of making quick money by day trading stocks. Day trading is to investing, what visiting a casino is to starting your own business. Sure, you *could* win big at the casino, but you're very unlikely to, and over the long run, you'll go broke. But if you do your research and work hard, starting a business will make you way more money in the long run and way more reliably too.

The financial media doesn't do you any favors though. All of the reporting concerning the market is breathless. It's a land of extremes. Things are either going great, or they're falling apart without any hope in sight. Charts upon charts are displayed, and it seems as if every day brings news of some economic indicator causing turmoil in the markets, while the next day, everything is fine and dandy. One day it's the unemployment rate, another day it's the manufacturing output, the third day it's automotive sales and on and on it goes. There is never a middle ground. Instead, there are always intense reactions one way or another.

In the past 10 years, we've seen another force dominate the investing landscape, social media. Many new investors take to social media to get an understanding of where they should place their money. Not only is this the worst decision you could make (and we'll explain why later on in this book), it's a decision which often leaves people feeling burned, and deters them from making future investments.

With these combined factors, it seems incomprehensible how a regular investor could ever be successful in the market. This leads many to seek professional advice. However, this search comes with its own set of problems. A 2013 study by the Financial Planning Association found that 46% of financial planners did not even have a retirement plan of their own. These are people licensed to advise others on sound financial decisions, yet they can't even get their own house in order.

Additionally, the term financial planner or financial advisor is somewhat misleading. These are not impartial third parties. Many people are not aware that a financial planner is primarily a sales role. For example, many advisors often simply recommend whatever funds they are paid the most commission on. Like any profession, there are, of course, good advisors who truly have the best interests of their clients at heart, but to ignore the other side would be naïve.

So if mainstream media isn't helpful, and the professionals often have their own best interests at heart. Where do you start?

It is surprisingly hard to find basic information about investing. Much of this information is intentionally designed to be overwhelming so that you feel as if you *must* put your money in the hands of the so-called professionals we mentioned above.

Our goal with this book is simple. First, dispel the common myths you've been exposed to. Second, mute the noise around you and show you which timeless investing principles to adhere to. Third, help you develop your own repeatable and reliable process for analyzing which companies to buy and when to buy them.

Investing is not a get rich quick scheme. Our answer to the question "what's the best way to make $1 million in the stock market quickly" has always been "start with $2 million". There are rare occasions where you make fast returns. For example, our email subscribers who acted on our recommendation of Canadian royalty company Sandstorm Gold nabbed a 45% return in just 23 days. That being said, the majority of your profits will be maximized in 5-10 years, not 5-10 weeks.

Investing is not gambling. We've seen an alarming trend of new investors treating the market like a casino with high risk strategies like leveraged options trading, and we aim to reverse that trend.

This is not a book about technical analysis (or as we like to call it, technical astrology). We adhere to the principles of great investors like Warren Buffett, Peter Lynch, Carl Icahn, and Charlie Munger. People who have made consistent returns in the market over the long haul by focusing on companies, not charts or formulas.

In a world of instant gratification, we focus on the simple things. On identifying well-run businesses that serve a need to a significant market, have a competitive advantage, and are available at a fair price. We'll explain more about these principles further in Chapter 4 where we outline our selection process.

For now, we thank you for purchasing this book. As Warren Buffett would say, the best investment you can make is the investment in yourself, and by buying this book, you've done just that.

"THERE ARE 2 RULES OF SUCCESSFUL STOCK INVESTING:
RULE NO. 1: NEVER LOSE MONEY.
RULE NO. 2: NEVER FORGET RULE NO. 1."

- Warren Buffett

WHY INVEST IN STOCKS IN THE FIRST PLACE?

A question that is often at the forefront of people's minds is: Why should I even invest in the stock market? There seem to be so many other opportunities to make your money work for you, such as real estate, buying precious metals, and even cryptocurrency.

It turns out that the latest generation of adult Americans is the least invested one when it comes to the stock market (Martin, 2018). A survey conducted by CNBC indicated that only 23% of millennials preferred investing in the stock market when compared to other options.

The reasons for this are understandable. Since 1995, the financial markets have witnessed near-constant turmoil every five to ten years. First, there was the dotcom bubble, which wiped out many inexperienced investors. Then markets were thrown into chaos by 9/11. We then experienced a period of enormous growth that culminated with the housing crisis between 2007-2009. A few lean years were then followed by a massive bull run, which ended at the beginning of 2020. As of this writing, the markets are in a volatile period, thanks to the COVID-19 crisis.

Despite this perceived instability, the stock market is not something to be avoided. The numbers are simple. Over a 50 year period between 1966 and 2015, the S&P 500 returned an annual rate of 9.69%. Which means you would have made 102 times your initial investment after 50 years. If those same returns hold over the next 50 years, a modest investment of $2,000 today will be worth $204,000 in 2070. These numbers assume you don't make *any* additional investments during that time period. This is unrealistic, and with additional investments, your eventual return will be far higher.

In this book, we're going to show you how fluctuations and market dips are not things to be feared. In fact, the strategy we recommend will help you not only ride out those dips but even thrive when turmoil strikes the markets.

How can we do this? It's very simple. The reason many people fail at investing in the markets is that they think about them in fundamentally flawed ways.

Investing in stocks is simple. This doesn't mean it's easy. What we mean is that the current state of stock investing analysis makes it seem as if you need an advanced degree to be able to figure out what's going on.

We're here to tell you that the way the markets work is far more straightforward, and you don't need a high IQ, a specialized degree, or any secret code to 'unlock' them. The markets will provide you with profits as long as you're willing to do the work and can think about them correctly.

Where Investors Have Gone Wrong in the Past

Consider how the average retail investor behaves in the market when they first get started. This person has some cash on hand, they've heard that investing it is a good idea because just holding on to cash will make you a victim of inflation, and the days of getting a decent interest rate on a savings account are long gone. So their first step is to head over to a financial adviser for stock recommendations or, more commonly, post in a Facebook Group asking for tips on how to invest $500/$1,000/$10,000. This is their first mistake.

The investor sinks their money into a random assortment of companies, primarily based on tips from strangers or a carnival barker on TV, and then sits back, expecting vast sums of money in return. After all, to them, the market is like a casino. It seems like a game as well when they switch on Fox Business or CNBC to check on their newly held companies. They see red and green signs moving up or down, a horizontal bar at the bottom with symbols moving right-to-left, another bar below it that moves a little slower, pundits exhorting secret strategies and killer stocks to buy and so on.

After a while, their stocks either take a dip. Or they don't grow as fast as expected, and the investor becomes impatient. Their stock is down 20%, and they are not happy. So they decide to sell, because the guy on TV is now telling them to move into cash instead of stocks. They don't completely understand the logic behind this means but do it regardless. Soon the market begins to rise, and they rush to buy in again, only this time a higher price than what they previously sold at.

Throughout this routine, they successfully buy when prices are high and sell when they're low, which is the opposite of the most basic tenet of investing.

Some investors go even further and decide to try their hand at short-term moves like day trading. A few manage to do this successfully, but they are the extreme exception, not the rule. Any kind of financial trading has a significant survivorship bias. You only hear about the success stories. But for every success story, you aren't hearing about the 10 people who failed in the same endeavor. The fact of the matter is, depending on the source, 95-99% of day traders lose money in the long run, which is why in this book, we won't be discussing day trading, or any other short term financial strategy.

What to do Instead –Rational Process Investing

You're going to learn all about the correct thought process to adopt when it comes to the markets and how you need to analyze stocks. This book also contains 20 stocks that meet our criteria for buying and holding for the next 20 years. All of these stocks fulfill the needs of our Rational Process Investing system, and you're going to learn exactly why this is. For those of you tempted to just skip to that chapter, this is not a call to action to buy these stocks today, because you'll also need to understand what is and isn't a fair price to pay for a stock. We'll be explaining that as well later on in the book.

In addition to all of this, you're also going to learn about asset allocation and investment strategies. How you choose to invest your money has a direct bearing on the return you can expect to earn in the markets. A thorough evaluation of your risk tolerance is necessary, and we'll show you exactly to do this.

Our combined investment experience over the years has placed us in the best position to help both new and experienced investors make the best decisions possible. You don't need to overcomplicate stock investment. Follow some sound principles, master your emotions, and you'll make more money than you'll ever need in the markets.

By understanding the simple concepts listed here and you'll be ahead of 95% of new investors. Successful investing *does not* require you to have advanced degrees in math or statistics. In fact, there is little correlation between intelligence and successful investing. Even a genius like Sir Isaac Newton famously lost his entire Fortune (around $3m in today's money) in the South Sea Bubble of the 1700s. Newton was quoted as saying

"I could calculate the motions of the heavenly bodies, but not the madness of the people."

What you will need for success is some basic arithmetic, but more importantly: The ability to reason, the confidence to back your judgment, and the awareness to know when you are wrong.

First let's jump in and take a look at the very basics of successful, long-term stock market investing!

1

WHY THE LONG-TERM OUTLOOK?

W hat is the secret to successful investing? The answer will shock you. It is to do nothing. Well, not quite nothing, but our point is that to be successful, you need to limit your activity as much as possible when it comes to managing your investments. Tinkering with them and second-guessing yourself is what causes more losses than any market dips.

This chapter is going to walk you through the investing philosophy known as "buy and hold" investing. You'll learn why this is far superior to any other investing approach for new investors.

The Difference Between Speculation and Investment

Before understanding why buy and hold is such a powerful philosophy, we need to take a step back and understand the differences between investing and speculation. The first person who pondered this question was Benjamin Graham in his legendary book *The Intelligent Investor*. The book Warren Buffett frequently refers to as his "Bible."

According to Graham, investing or an investment operation was something based on we he called "intelligent principles." This ensured that it had a high probability of success. In contrast, speculation was something that was carried out using unsound principles and had a high chance of failure.

This definition sounds simple enough, but there are many caveats in here. What qualifies as intelligent, and what are unintelligent principles? In the context of the market, we can define an intelligent investment process as being one that takes the financial realities of the market into account.

The first reality to acknowledge about the market is that in the short term, no one can predict the direction of prices. This is because, in the short term, stock prices are fueled by emotion. Emotions which arise from the myriad of psychological biases that human beings have.

For example, you hear of everyone jumping into a hot new stock, and see the media telling you that this stock is a sure thing. You're likely going to think that this stock is great. This herd mentality or peer pressure is just one example of unconscious biases we carry. This behavior has been a factor since Graham's time (during the Great Depression) and is still present to this day.

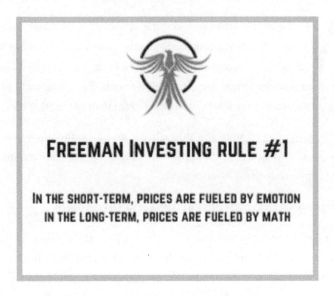

FREEMAN INVESTING RULE #1

IN THE SHORT-TERM, PRICES ARE FUELED BY EMOTION
IN THE LONG-TERM, PRICES ARE FUELED BY MATH

To further illustrate how flawed behavior affects the markets in the short term, let's discuss "Flash Crashes." A flash crash is a market crash (defined as any drop of 10% or more) that occurs over the span of a few minutes or even seconds. Flash crashes have become more common these days thanks to the advent of algorithmic trading, a method of automatic trading based on pre-determined variables.

Two "Flash crash" incidents occurred in the past decade that perfectly illustrate the short term drivers of the market, and the irrational nature of human behavior. The first occurred on August 24th 2015. The minute the markets opened, they immediately fell by 5% before gaining back most of their gains by the end of the day.

The Grandaddy of all flash crashes occurred on May 6th, 2010 when a single trade caused the entire market to lose 1,000 points (roughly 9% of its total value) and then rise right back up in under 15 minutes.

Many stocks reached unthinkably low prices. Accenture, the global consulting conglomerate, actually saw its stock touch zero before rising back up to $41.09. Similar massive movements occurred in the crash of 2015 as well. All of these movements led to much hand wringing in the media.

Complex reasons were put forward. The widely accepted reason for the 2015 crash was that traders were nervous after the end of the previous session which was on a Friday. The market had declined and they weren't sure what was going to happen over the weekend. The Chinese markets, which open before the American ones do, opened lower and hence this fueled a rush of selling in America as well.

Let's just take a step back from all of this madness. If the market was to be believed, a 54 billion dollar company at the time, such as Accenture, was temporarily deemed as being worth nothing because a bunch of Chinese traders happened to sell their stocks in China. Furthermore, the market then decided that the company was worth 54 billion dollars once again by the end of the day.

Does any of this sound logical? Let's say you own a piece of farmland that is consistently producing high-quality crops. Let's say some person comes up to you and declares that the price of this land is now worth zero. He goes away and then returns eight hours later and tells you that the property is now worth $1m million dollars. You'd rightly think that this person is a nut!

Yet when the stock market does the same thing, we invent intelligent-sounding drivel such as "traders were nervous over the weekend and Chinese selling triggered a wave of sell orders on the open." In the 90s it used to be the Arabs who used to trigger all kinds of havoc in the market (supposedly). These days, it's the Chinese.

There's a political lesson in there somewhere, but as far as intelligent investment goes, it's hard to see us learning anything of note. What we can learn is that the markets are *incredibly irrational* over the short term and that tailoring your portfolio to these moves will only result in your being exposed to this madness. So what is the best approach to adopt?

Short Term Trading Versus Long Term Investing

Short term trading involves all kinds of risks because of moves such as these. In essence, a trader is attempting to gauge how the market feels about the stock. Here's an experiment for you to conduct. Walk over to your partner and try to guess how they're feeling about something. You might be able to guess what is wrong some of the time, but not all the time.

Now walk over to a stranger and try to guess how they feel about something. You don't know this person, but your task is to guess anyway. How often do you think you'll succeed? Finally, try to imagine what some random person on the other side of the planet feels about Walmart's stock price. You don't know anything about this person or what their motivations are. All you know is that they have an opinion about the price of Walmart stock.

You'd come back saying that this is a hopeless task. How could you possibly know any of this? Well, this is what traders try to do every day. They seek to take advantage of short term price moves, and as you've already seen, these moves don't occur thanks to logic or business reality. They occur due to emotion. Often this can be as simple as a large financial institution placing a big sell order, so everyone else starts selling as well. This is the herd mentality in action, as we previously mentioned.

It stands to reason that if you wish to take advantage of these moves, you need to be able to predict the emotions other traders have concerning the stock. In real life, it is impossible to do this, but traders think that using indicators and angled lines on a chart will somehow solve the issue for them.

Does this sound like an intelligent thing to do? Welcome to the world of speculation! Speculation isn't restricted to merely trading. It is anything that is carried out in an unintelligent manner, and this encompasses many things. For example, you could be deluded in thinking that you know everything about a business opportunity. If you were to go ahead and place your money in it without doing your due diligence, this would be speculative and not an investment operation.

Given that stock market prices are driven by emotion in the short term and that we cannot predict emotions, it stands to reason that we need to take a longer-term view of the market. There is an excellent reason to do this. This is because emotions tend to exhaust themselves over the long run. As Benjamin Graham said, in the short term the market is a voting machine but in the long term, it's a weighing machine.

Think about your own life and set the markets aside for a second. How often have you seethed in anger for a few minutes, and then forgotten all about it a week, a month, or a year later? Do you remember if you lost your temper this time last year? We're not talking about situations where the emotion was justified thanks to life events. We're talking about those issues that seem petty in the long run. Your spouse or partner placed their shoes over yours and dirtied them, and you lost your temper. The dog decided to pee all over your shiny new carpet and so on. The delivery driver was 10 minutes late because he got lost. What would have happened if you had followed the lead of that emotion and made huge changes in your life? Would this have been the smart thing to do?

Of course not! Instead, you gave yourself time to calm down, and when you did, you forgot all about it and moved on. The same thing works in the market as well. On August 24th, 2015, the actions of Chinese traders were extremely crucial. Yesterday, the markets couldn't care less about what Chinese traders did. It's all emotional.

Over the long run in the market, the stock price of a company reflects its underlying earnings growth. Using the example of farmland that you own, the true value of the land is the crop yield it produces. It also depends on how profitable farming is as a business. Are you getting good prices for your crops? If so, the land is quite valuable if it produces high-quality crops. If not, it isn't as valuable.

The same applies to companies. One key element new investors miss is that there are real companies behind those little symbols you see on the screen. Buying shares is the same as owning a percentage of the company. These are businesses with suppliers, customers, competitors, and employees. All of these factors come together to generate profit and loss. The more profit they make, the more prosperous the company is, and this is reflected in the stock's price over the long term.

While you cannot predict human emotion, you can make intelligent decisions about a company's business prospects. You can evaluate their economic outlook and that of the business they're operating in. This process removes emotion and market sentiment from the equation and is the only way to make money in the long-term reliably.

Understanding the Costs of Investing

Now that you understand why having a long term view is essential, it's time to take a look at costs. Participating in the market is not free. You will need to pay your broker commissions when buying or selling stocks. This can be off-putting when you want to make an investment of $100, but you have to pay $10 in commissions to execute the trade. Fortunately, these days, this isn't a big deal because there are a ton of reputable brokers who offer very low and even zero commission accounts. We'll be talking about our personal favorite later on in this book.

While commissions are less of an issue than they used to be, taxes haven't changed. As it relates to the stock market, you will pay taxes on capital gains and dividends. Dividends are distributions from the company to you, and as such, they represent passive income. You don't have to pay anything other than the price of a share to earn a dividend. As such, paying taxes on them isn't too painful since they effectively reduce the cost of your investment to begin with. We'd like to add that companies are not obliged to pay dividends, and not all of them do.

Capital gains taxes operate differently. Capital gains are the profits you make when you sell your investment. This is the difference between the sale price and the purchase price of your investment. For example, if you buy 1 share of Disney at $100/share and then sell it once the price reaches $120, that $20 difference is your "capital gain". Taxes on capital gains will reduce your overall profit because capital gains do not happen to be free money like dividends are.

One area that can confuse new investors is when you pay capital gains tax. You only pay capital gains after you sell your investment. Therefore, the more you sell, the more are the taxes you pay. In turn, the more often you sell, the lower your overall gains are going to be.

Then there's the issue of long term versus short term capital gains taxes. The short term tax rate, which is levied on investments that lasted less than a year, is the same as your income tax rate. The long term rate falls between zero to 40% depending on your income tax bracket and which country you are paying your taxes.

Therefore, the longer you hold onto your investments, the less you pay in taxes. If you never sell your investments, you'll never pay capital gains taxes. In the real world, you will want to sell your investments at some point since this is the only way you'll get to enjoy the fruits of your investment unless you want to pass them onto your next of kin in your will. Our point is, it is smart to delay the decision to sell within the first year of owning a stock.

Another cost you need to take into account when investing is inflation. Inflation is a hidden cost, and many investors fail to take notice of this. The value of a dollar tomorrow is not the same as a dollar today. The best way to reduce the impact of inflation on your gains is to hold onto your investment for as long as possible so that it has the greatest chance to appreciate in value. We will explain more about how to take inflation into account in our chapter on calculating the true value of a business.

FREEMAN INVESTING RULE #2

REMEMBER TO ACCOUNT FOR INFLATION WHEN ANALYZING YOUR INVESTMENTS

It should come as no surprise to you that stocks rise at a far greater distance over the long run than they do in the short run. A good way to think about this is to ask yourself: Can you get more done in a minute or over a year? The answer is obvious. Hold onto your investments for as long as possible and give them a chance to make money.

By combining the above principles, it is clear that the most intelligent investment decision you can make is to buy and hold stocks for as long as possible. Leave the constant jumping in and out to the traders and other speculators. Resist everything that can potentially cause you to exit early or trade too much in a single stock.

This means you need to prepare well by researching your investments and then investing your money in the right way. Once this is done, you can minimize taxes and transaction costs by holding for long periods. The longer you hold onto your investments, the longer they have to potentially gain more, and this reduces the impact inflation has on your returns.

2

DEFINING YOUR INVESTING GOALS

A ll journeys need a goal. But just setting a goal is not enough. You'll need to plan how you'll get there. Our minds are like a GPS system in that unless you specify where your destination is, you run the risk of wasting time going down the wrong path.

This chapter is going to help you figure out the goals you should have and the mindset that is necessary for succeeding in the stock market.

Preparation

Successful investment planning begins much before you decide to invest in the stock market. Ensuring that you have a stable financial base before you invest in the market is essential since this will prevent you from making mistakes. For example, if you don't have the cash to pay your bills, you're going to be tempted to sell some of your investments before they have a chance to blossom fully.

Figuring out where your investment capital will come from is essential to the process. Let's take a look at the kind of money you should be investing in the market

Capital

At Freeman Publications, we adopt a long term approach. The rule of thumb we apply is that all money invested in the market should not be missed for at least 10 years.

To prepare a sound financial base for yourself, we recommend that none of the following should be invested in the markets:

1. Your rainy day fund – 3-6 months' worth of living expenses that you've saved up in case you or your partner lose your jobs. This money should not be invested under any circumstances. Your rainy day fund should be held in readily accessible cash.
2. Tuition payments - Money that is needed to pay bills or your child's tuition should not be invested in the markets.
3. Down payments - Even if you're planning on purchasing a home several years down the road, don't rely on the stock market to generate enough money for a down payment.

FREEMAN INVESTING RULE #3

ONLY INVEST MONEY THAT YOU DON'T NEED FOR THE NEXT DECADE.

The best way to begin investing in the market is via a tax free retirement account. Maximize your contributions to it, and if your employer offers a 401(k) with matching benefits, make full use of that as well. In short, do not rely on the market to make you money or to somehow generate money that you need to survive.

This may seem like a pessimistic outlook, but in reality, it works very well. By not having to rely on the market for money, you remove the feeling that you 'have' to make money. A lot of short term traders and speculators get caught up in this emotion and end up making fatal mistakes that lose them money.

Here is a typical "I have to make money" scenario. A person places a trade on a stock, expecting a quick bump in price. The trade doesn't go their way, so they exit their position for a 10% loss. Losing money is tough to deal with mentally, and in their frustration, they open another position in a different stock. This trade goes against them as well, and they exit that position for another 10% loss.

Now their frustration turns to anger. So they place a third trade, this time for a bigger position than they usually would, in an attempt to recoup the losses from both trades 1 and 2. They're telling themselves that because the last 2 trades went against them, this trade should go in their favor. Unfortunately for them, the market has no idea how their previous 1, 2, or 100 trades went, and the odds are no more in their favor than on trade number 1. This third trade goes against them as well, and they cash out for another 10% loss.

This isn't a book about trading, but from this example, it's easy to see how the irrational nature of human beings cause short-term thinkers to lose money. If we extrapolate this behavior pattern over a more extended period, you can see why over 95% of day traders fail.

But no matter if you're a short-term trader or long-term investor. The markets are highly emotional, and you *will* be caught up in their whirlwind at some point, no matter how rational you think you are. Therefore, it is best to minimize your chances of doing something emotional in the first place. This is so when the time does come; you won't be at an emotional extreme that will cause you to do something unintelligent.

The next step in your journey is to figure out your risk appetite.

Asset Classes and Risk

The concept of risk management is highly misunderstood in the markets. When you speak to an average financial advisor, they'll explain risk to you in two ways. The first is to use your age as a barometer for it. A common rule of thumb is to subtract your age from 100. Then use the resulting number as a measure of how much of your money should be invested in stocks.

For example, if you're 40 years old, they'll tell you to place 60% of your money in stocks and 40% in bonds. This is a nonsensical way to allocate money. The thought process behind this is that an older person needs to invest for income while a younger person should aim for price appreciation.

What happens is that every year, as you get older, you end up selling profitable stock investments and keep moving that money into new bond investments. The timeline for your bond investments keeps increasing while that of your stock investments keeps decreasing.

What if you find a profitable stock to invest in when you're 60 years old but have already allocated 40% of your money to stocks? Should you simply let this opportunity slip? This makes no sense. The real determinant of whether a person needs to invest for income or capital gains is their financial situation, not their age. 60 year olds tend to have assets on hand, and if they have a secure income, why should they invest in bonds and fixed income?

The second manner in which risk is explained to investors is to use asset classes. You're told that small-cap stocks (the shares of companies under $1 billion in size) are risky, and large cap ones are less risky. Bonds are less risky than stocks and options. This is an equally nonsensical manner of classifying risk.

The asset class of a stock does not indicate its risk. Let's use an example. Let's say you were Jeff Bezos back in 1995. You have had a good career in finance and have money saved up. You get the idea to start this company, let's call it Amazon, and you have a clear vision of where you want it to go. You trust your abilities and know that you have the wherewithal to succeed.

However, your financial adviser tells you that starting Amazon (and by proxy, investing your money in it) is extremely risky. Mr. Bezos is 31 years old and should invest 69% of his money in stocks, with 60% of them in large cap stocks, 5% in mid caps and the rest in small caps. Amazon is a startup and is none of those. Let's say Bezos loses his mind momentarily and decides to follow this advice.

Given that he's worth approximately 124 billion dollars today, largely thanks to his ownership stake in Amazon, it's safe to say that this would have been a hall of fame worthy mistake to make.

FREEMAN INVESTING RULE #4

RISK IS DEFINED NOT BY THE ASSET CLASS OF YOUR INVESTMENT, BUT BY YOUR EXPERTISE IN EVALUATING IT

The same factors apply when analyzing small-cap companies (defined as a company with a market capitalization of less than $2 Billion) versus large-cap companies. The commonly held belief is that small-cap companies are riskier than large-cap companies. This might be true on a macro level but is not correct on an individual level. If you know a small-cap company inside and out, then it is a far better company to invest in than a large cap like ExxonMobil or Goldman Sachs, where even the CEOs likely don't have a full clue as to where the company's money is going.

If you're unsure as to the extent of your expertise, it's best to outsource it to capable managers who know what they're doing. A financial adviser or your broker is not a capable manager. Instead, investing in index funds and ETFs or mutual funds is the way to go. Index funds and ETFs follow broad based indices in the market. By purchasing a single share of these funds, you can gain exposure to all of the underlying stocks in the fund and get to have your money managed by a professional money manager for low costs.

In addition to asset allocation, you need to evaluate your personal risk tolerance. Let's take a look at some of the factors that will help you define your risk tolerance.

Risk Factor #1 - Time

How much time do you wish to devote to the markets? The more time you can devote to analyzing companies and figuring out how they do business, the more risk you will be able to bear since you'll be able to spend more time mitigating it. This doesn't mean you need to be glued to the markets 24/7 like most traders are. For long-term investors, this behavior is counterproductive.

However, you will need to spend more time monitoring the companies you invest in if you wish to absorb more risk. You will need to spend more time finding quality companies to invest in, and you will need to spend time thinking about how to exit your investments correctly.

If you wish to make your investments passive, then you cannot have too much of your portfolio in single companies and will need to diversify your portfolio so that the risk is spread out. We'll be explaining more about proper diversification in chapter 5.

Factor #2 - Your Expertise

Everyone is good at evaluating some form of business. You might not think of yourself as being an expert or even a business person, but there are businesses out there that are extremely simple to figure out. There are an equal number of companies that are complicated.

If you wish to invest in a complicated business, you'll need to spend more time evaluating it. You might find that even after spending a lot of time, the business makes no sense to you, and you're unable to figure out its prospects. Therefore it's far better to choose simple companies to invest in, especially when you first start out. You're going to have a better grasp of their economics, and you'll make better decisions as a result.

Just because a business is simple, does not mean it can't make great returns. For example, in 2014, while trendy tech companies like Facebook, Netflix and GoPro dominated the financial news cycle, the best performing stock on the S&P 500 was Southwest Airlines, which grew more than 110% in a single year.

Additionally, you probably have far more experience in your own company's sector than the average Wall Street analyst. It's a good idea to begin with companies in that sector.

Even if you don't have much experience in a sector, you are still a *consumer* of products. For example, let's say you're a coffee drinker, and you visit Starbucks every morning before work. If that location is always busy, it's a good indicator, if it's always empty, then it tells you the opposite story.

Let us be clear; understanding a company or using a company's products is not the *only* reason to invest in a company. It is crucial to make this distinction because many new investors use this as their entire analysis. But it is a great place to start your research.

To give you a real life example our how being a consumer is a great place to begin your research. One of our best investments over the past few years has been McDonald's. Our research process started when one of our team commented that they'd traveled to 30 different countries, and had never seen a McDonald's location that wasn't busy.

Factor #3 – Emotional Risk Tolerance

Let's say you've invested a sum of money in the market. You promptly see that the stock has declined by 30%. What do you do? What are your emotions at that moment going to be like? Will you have the confidence and discipline to act rationally despite this huge dip?

People don't take the time to ask themselves if they're willing to lose more than half of their investment on paper before it ever makes them a single cent before investing. Instead, everyone dreams of stock prices soaring and doubling their money in a matter of months.

This can happen and does happen in the markets quite a lot. However, you cannot expect constant rises without experiencing dips. How much of a dip are you willing to stomach? Your investment in a single stock is far more likely to see a serious dip than the entire market will.

If the entire market, or an index fund that tracks the market, dips by a lot, you can rest assured that it will bounce back unless something truly catastrophic happens. It is unlikely that all of these companies are going to disappear overnight and for the markets to remain at zero forever. However, a single business can go bankrupt overnight.

Therefore, evaluate how much of a loss on paper you're willing to stomach and adjust your investments accordingly. If you're only willing to accept a 10-15% loss on paper in your investment, then sticking to index funds and ETFs is your best choice. If you're going to invest in individual stocks, be prepared to stomach a loss of at least 30% on paper. On paper is the operative phrase here, because you don't realize a loss until you sell your stock.

FREEMAN INVESTING RULE #5

YOU MUST BE ABLE TO MENTALLY SEPARATE PAPER LOSSES FROM REAL LOSSES.

Initial Investment Amounts

We typically advise people to invest at least $5,000 in the markets when starting out. This means $5,000 in total investments, not $5,000 per company.

This is because to capture meaningful gains; your investment amount needs to be somewhat significant. Turning a $100 investment into $1 million is an unrealistic scenario. Turning $1,000 into $1 million is unlikely, but still achievable. Turning $10,000 into $1 million is completely possible with the right company. With smart investments, turning $100,000 into $1 million is expected. Those numbers might sound unrealistic, but you have to remember the power of compound interest. With a 9.69% rate of a return (the market average) it takes 26 years for $100,000 to turn into $1 million. With a 15% rate of return, it only takes 17 years. With a 20% rate of return, it only takes 13 years.

The way to get compounding to work for you is to invest a large sum of money and then have it grow rapidly. Let's look at this via an example. Let's say there are two investors A and B. A invests $1,000 in the market and B invests $5,000. Both of them earn modest 7% gains over the course of 30 years. What is the value of their portfolios at the end of the 30 year period?

A's portfolio has grown to $7,612 while B's portfolio has grown to $38,061. The amount by which B's portfolio has grown is $33,061 which is far more than the paltry $6,612 that A has witnessed. This is why it is important to capture the power of compounding by investing a larger amount of money.

However, this doesn't mean that you should hoard your money until it reaches $1 million and only invest then. You need to give it time to grow as well. This is why we recommend a minimum amount of $5,000. From the above example, you can see that even this modest amount grows to quite a significant sum over 30 years.

If you don't have $5,000 but are determined to make a start, then go ahead. Providing you do proper research, investing in stocks is nearly always a superior option to just holding cash. If you only have a small amount to invest, it's essential to choose the right investing platform, because you don't want massive commissions to eat away at your potential profits.

How to Place Orders

If you already have a brokerage account, then you can go straight to chapter 3. However, if you do not, we've included a short guide for opening your first brokerage account.

With the rise in comparison websites, it can be overwhelming to choose an investing platform. We'll simplify the process for you. For new investors, there are 3 major factors which matter most when selecting a platform to use.

1. The commission structure (how much you have to pay each time you buy or sell a stock)
2. What financial instruments you can buy (stocks/bonds/mutual funds/ETFs)
3. How user-friendly the platform is

Based on the factors above, for new investors in the United States, we recommend the Robinhood platform. The most significant selling point of Robinhood is that it is commission-free for buying and selling common stocks. Zero commission is important because if you *are* only investing small amounts, fixed commissions on each buy or sell order can put a significant dent into your potential profits.

You can read our complete guide to setting up a Robinhood account by using the link below.

https://freemanpublications.com/how-to-buy-stocks-online

More experienced investors will likely favor other platforms like E*Trade, TD Ameritrade or Charles Schwab. Each of them have their pros and cons, so we advise you to do your research and pick the one best suited to your situation.

For those readers outside the US, a simple Google search for "Best investing platform in [your country]" will let you compare your options.

3

THE 7 BENEFITS OF LONG TERM INVESTING

There are a number of benefits of following the buy and hold strategy, and this chapter is going to go in-depth and explain what these are. You've already learned about a few of these in the first chapter. You'll now gain a better understanding of them.

Tax Advantages

We've already mentioned the tax portion of your investment consideration. By investing for longer periods, you'll significantly lower your capital gains tax bill. Currently, here's how taxes on long term capital gains (gains on investments held for more than 1 year) are assessed in the United States.

- 0% capital gains:
- Single filers earning up to $40,000
- Married joint filers earning up to $80,000
- Heads of Households earning up to $53,600
- Married separate filers earning up to $40,000
- 15% capital gains:
- Single filers earning from $40,001 to $441,450
- Married joint filers earning from $80,001 to $496,600
- Heads of Households earning from $53,601 to 469.050

- Married separate filers earning from $40,0001 to $248,300
- 20% capital gains:
- Single filers earning above $441,451
- Married joint filers earning above $496,601
- Heads of Households earning above $469,051
- Married separate filers earning above $248,301

As mentioned earlier, short term tax rates are assessed on the basis of your current income levels. This means you'll always be paying higher taxes on your short term investments than on your long term holdings.

The true impact of paying short term capital gains taxes can be felt in terms of compounding. You've already seen from the previous chapter that a $10,000 investment that grows at 7% every year matures to $76,122 at the end of 30 years. Let's say you pay 15% taxes on this amount. Your final after-tax investment is worth $64,703.

Let's say you invested $10,000 every year in a one-year investment and that this investment gained 7% as well. Since this is a one-year investment, you'll sell it and pay a tax rate of 25% on the gains before reinvesting the after-tax amount the following year. How much does this investment mature to after 30 years?

It grows to $46,415. This is a difference of $18,288. In other words, if you had avoided withdrawing your money and paying higher taxes on it at the end of every year, you could have earned close to 40% more money. That's a pretty significant difference! Short term taxes have effectively cost you 40% over a 30 year period.

More Emotional Discipline

We always counsel readers to invest their money with the mindset that they will not need it for a ten year period at the very least. This doesn't mean that you need to hold onto your investment for that long, but it helps put the importance of your investment in perspective.

If you knew prior to making an investment that you will need to hold onto this stock for ten years, you're far more likely to do your homework and follow rational principles. Think of it as buying a piece of furniture or renting an apartment for the next 10 years. Would you simply rush in and move without taking a good look at the place? Would you neglect to carry out due diligence? Unlikely.

Another reason why buy and hold works very well is that, contrary to popular perception, most investors do a decent enough job of figuring out which stocks they want to buy. It is the selling that they find tough. You need to sell your investment in order to realize gains and once your stock has amassed a good amount of unrealized gains, your challenge begins.

Let's say your investment has risen by 25% over a year, which is a phenomenal return. The following year, the market begins to decline, and your investment is now displaying an unrealized gain of 10%. Your brain immediately thinks that you've lost 15% gains when in reality, all of this is on paper. You haven't actually lost anything.

The financial media often reports of market declines as 'wiping out' a certain amount of money. They also make statements such as 'investors lost $1 trillion dollars.' These are nonsensical statements. You will lose or make money only when you sell your investment. Buy and hold removes the pressure of figuring out when to sell since you need to hold onto it for as long as possible.

We'll address the issue of selling shortly.

Passive Income

We've already mentioned the existence of dividends as it relates to stock investment. Dividends highlight why the traditional approach of risk, in terms of income investment in bonds versus capital investment in stocks, is flawed. You can invest in stocks and still earn a good income. Dividends make this possible.

A stock dividend also allows you to earn income on your investment, regardless of whether the stock price is going up or down.

Dividend yields on stocks generally hover between two to five percent. Of course, it is possible to earn higher yields but you need to take certain factors into account.

A stock's dividend yield is calculated by dividing the dividend payment amount by the stock's price. The higher the payment is, the higher the yield is. However, the price plays a role as well. A declining stock price can also push yields higher, so it's not as if chasing yields is the best way to spot great dividend-paying stocks.

It's a bit like earning rent on a property you've bought. The best part is that unlike the rental investment, you're not going to have to work to maintain your investment. You don't need to chase tenants for payments; you don't need to conduct regular maintenance, you don't need to advertise for tenants and so on. You simply invest your money, and you get paid a dividend.

Finding this level of passivity in any investment outside the stock market is impossible. What's more, the longer you hold onto your investment, the more income you earn until your effective cost of investment decreases. For example, if you've paid $200 for a stock and are receiving two percent yields annually, you're earning $4 as income on your investment. Once you receive the first payment, you've earned a realized gain of $4, and therefore your effective cost is now $196.

The longer you hold, the lesser the effective price is, and you'll increase the odds of you making a profit.

Entry Price Doesn't Matter (as much)

Short term traders worry a lot about getting the exact prices they want on entry. This is because if you're going to buy at $95 and sell at $96, entering at $95.50 will make a huge difference. You'll reduce your potential gains by 50%.

When investing over the long term, though, your exact entry price doesn't matter. After all, your investment horizon is at least 10 years long. A dollar here or there over 10 years' time will not matter if you invest in a great company with long-term prospects.

In other words, if you identify a company that is primed to move upwards, it is going to move by quite a big distance over 10 years' time. What will it matter if you entered at $95.50 instead of $95 in such a scenario?

It's Less Stressful

Buying and holding is far, far easier than trying to trade your money in an active manner. We've already mentioned the futility of trying time the market. Or trying to predict the emotions present in the market. With buy and hold, you identify a stock that you like, do your homework on it, buy it, and that's it, you're done.

You receive huge tax advantages, manage to remove yourself out of your own way and free up your time to find even more great stocks to invest in. By removing the headache of trying to figure out when to exit, you'll also sleep better. Take it from us!

No Need to Chase Unicorns

A unicorn is that magical stock that increases its value 100 or 1000 times over in a short period of time. This sort of thing is that many venture capital investors chase, and it is a tough thing to do. Most of the time, venture capital investments fail due to the extremely high risk involved. We see a similar venture capital mindset with people who choose to only invest in penny stocks.

With buy and hold, you'll remove the need to chase these extraordinary gains because your mindset will shift.

You'll realize a good investment that earns 10-12% every year, even if it is before taxes, has serious power when it comes to building wealth. Over the long term, this sort of investment is what really makes money, as opposed to finding that magical stock that increases 100 or 1,000 fold in a short period of time.

The best way to find these unicorns is to practice a long term holding strategy. This way, you give your investments enough runway to actually grow instead of expecting them to increase by this amount over the course of five or 10 years.

FREEMAN INVESTING RULE #6

LONG-TERM INVESTING HAS MULTIPLE ADVANTAGES OVER SHORT-TERM TRADING

You Can Practice Proper Diversification

Diversification is another term that gets misconstrued by new investors. The reason for diversifying is that it helps reduce volatility and risk in your portfolio.

For example, if you had your entire portfolio in Apple stock, and there was a sudden supply chain issue which meant the company couldn't manufacture any iPhones for 2 years, then you would be in trouble.

But if Apple were one of the many companies you owned, the drop in Apple stock price would not have as big of an effect on your overall returns.

Now the problem we see with short term investors is that their diversification strategy falls into the category of "Diworsification," a term coined by Peter Lynch is his 1989 classic *One Up on Wall Street*

Before we cover proper diversification, we will outline the 2 most common "Diworsification" strategies new investors have.

Diworsification problem #1: New investors often overexpose themselves to a single industry, which increases their risk without maximizing the upside. We see this frequently with trendy sectors (like marijuana) or people looking for perceived bargains during market downturns (like airlines). They load up their portfolio with every large and mid-cap company in the sector, hoping for a quick buck, but are left holding the bag when the entire industry hits a downturn or doesn't recover as expected.

FREEMAN INVESTING RULE #7

JUST BECAUSE YOU OWN A LOT OF DIFFERENT COMPANIES DOES NOT MEAN YOU ARE DIVERSIFIED.

Diworsification problem #2: New investors get so caught up with the idea of owning stocks that they think *everything* is worth buying. They easily justify this decision by telling themselves that with each additional company they own, they are becoming more diversified. Before they know it, they own more than a hundred different companies with tiny positions in each one. Unless you're doing this full time, there is no way you can keep up with the inner financial workings of 100+ companies in a variety of sectors.

Diversification is not proportional. By that, we mean each new company you own does not provide an equal amount of diversification. In their book *Modern Portfolio Theory and Investment Analysis*, Edwin Elton and Martin Gruber showed that by owning 20 stocks, your portfolio risk was reduced by an average of 29.2%, when compared to just owning 1. But by owning 1000 stocks, your risk was only reduced by a further 0.8% when compared to owning 20.

There is no magic number for how many stocks you should own, but the consensus for the individual investor is between 10 and 30. We chose 20 companies to profile in this book because we believe 20 to be a good number of companies for an individual investor to hold at once. It's enough to have exposure to a broad range of industries (which can be further supplemented with mutual funds and sector or index-tracking ETFs), but a manageable number meaning you can keep track of each company's performance.

"IF YOU KNOW WHAT YOU WANT AND WHY YOU
WANT IT AND WHEN YOU WANT IT, YOU'LL GENERALLY PAY A
LOT LESS FOR IT THAN YOU
WILL IF YOU BUY SOMETHING THAT SOMEBODY ELSE
PERSUADES YOU TO BUY"

- Gerald Loeb

4

RATIONAL PROCESS INVESTING

We've mentioned thus far that you need to do your homework on the stocks you plan on investing in. How exactly are you supposed to do this? What are some of the things you need to look for when analyzing a company and its business? This chapter is going to introduce you to our process of analyzing a stock's prospects.

The Warren Buffett Test

The Warren Buffett test isn't a single criterion. The aim here is to follow the simple principles that Buffett talks about when he mentions his investment criteria. A regular statement he has often made is that he looks for companies that are run by great management teams.

This means that he values integrity and honesty in them, aside from competence. Adherence to expanding the company's bottom line and giving shareholders the highest possible return for their investment needs to be their top priority (LaRoche, 2019). While he does aim to buy entire businesses, he's perfectly happy to own a percentage of a good business as well.

This is because a good business is one of the best assets a person can own. A company that is regularly expanding its bottom-line earnings and is growing them at a certain rate like clockwork is hard to find. Therefore, selling it doesn't make sense. Your aim should be the same.

These kinds of companies do not sell for cheap, though. The market is aware of how good they are, and as a result, you're unlikely to find the stock selling for a 60% discount from its value. Buffett instead focuses on finding great companies and paying a fair price for them instead of finding average companies at great prices.

The average company will have to be sold at some point since its earnings are unlikely to grow forever (which is what makes it average after all). This means Buffett needs to find better investments and keep searching constantly. By buying a great business, he gets to work once and earn profits forever. This doesn't mean he never sells. It's just that his mindset upon entry is to ask whether he wants to hold onto the business forever.

By doing this, he automatically screens for great companies, not mediocre ones.

Understand the Business

We talked about briefly in chapter 3 regarding buying stocks in business you the products of. This is a great starting point for your research, but you need to *truly* understand the business before you invest in it.

If you decide to buy Walmart stock, make sure you understand the ins and outs of Walmart's business. Can you explain what Walmart does in 30 words or less? Alternatively, could you explain your rationale to a 10 year-old so that she would understand? If not, you probably don't understand it well enough.

For example, you might think you know all about a movie streaming company's operations (like Netflix) simply because you have a Netflix account. But if you don't know basic numbers like how many new subscribers they are adding per quarter, or what percentage of their revenue they need to reinvest into content creation, then you shouldn't buy shares until you do know these numbers. The good news is, they're easier to find than you think.

We've not saying Netflix is a good or bad investment at this time. But our point is that many Netflix investors don't understand how the company works, and more importantly, where it plans to make its money in the next 5-10 years.

It's also important to make distinctions between the surface level business the company is in, and their bottom line profits. For example, McDonald's might be a "fast food company," but the real money is made in its real estate business and franchise model. The fast food business is just a catalyst for this. While ensuring that food gets made quickly and on time is a priority, this is not what really drives the company's profits. McDonald's owns the real estate on which all its restaurants are built. The company then turns around and leases them to its franchisees and charges them rent that is well above market price. They can do this because the McDonald's brand is so strong, meaning franchisees are willing to pay a premium on rent. One estimate placed rental costs at 22% of gross profits per year from a franchisee's perspective (Daszkowski, 2019). This gives the company a significant cushion to weather tough business conditions.

If sales do decline, the company still owns all of its locations, and it doesn't have to worry about not paying rent. It can repurpose its locations with ease and create new revenue streams. This is a significant advantage in the fast food business.

Another example of a business that is in seemingly another line of business is Starbucks. On the surface, the company is a coffee chain, but really, it's in the third space business. What Starbucks is selling is not coffee, instead, it's a place you can spend time that isn't your home or office. It is the place where people meet one another for informal meetings, to catch up, go on dates. It is a convenient place to work from as well given the rising number of remote workers. Sure, the coffee prices are high and this is something that detractors point out over and over. However, people still frequent the chain, and it clearly is not a detriment to the business. Many Starbucks naysayers will laugh at the idea of paying $5 for a cup of coffee, but if their customer base thought this way, they would have gone bankrupt in the 1980s.

Differentiating between sector and company

A common problem with new investors is they buy into the hype of shiny new industries. In the past few years, we've seen Marijuana, CBD, sports betting, biotech, 5G, and other "hot sectors" have their days in the sun and become the 'cool' industries to jump into. It's not uncommon to meet a new investor with 60% of their portfolio or more in one of these sectors.

In the image on the next page, you'll see a visual representation of how most investors think about new industries. They only take 1st order consequences into account. These are often already accounted for in a company's share price. But if you can identify the 2nd and 3rd order consequences of any decision, then you will be able to find undervalued companies with huge potential.

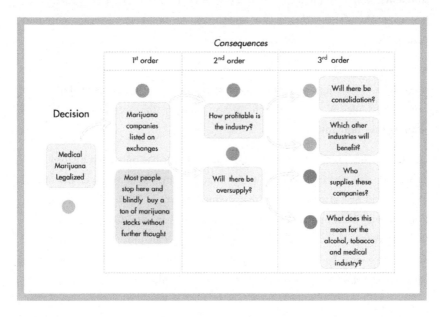

It's essential to make a distinction between sector growth and company growth. Just because 5G will be a big sector in the next 5-10 years, does not mean *every company* with 5G exposure will be a good investment.

A growing sector is a good place to start your research, but it's not a good place to end it.

Like we've said previously, for many average investors, the best place for them to start is the sector or industry they work in. Even if the 5G or Marijuana industries appear sexier than the industry you work in, you probably don't understand them nearly as well.

CEO/Founder Syndrome

Many companies that have their founders still in place as the CEO tend to be safer investments because founders understand their businesses a lot better than outside CEOs do.

The example of technology companies is a good case in point. Almost all of them are run by their founders and all of them operate in extremely competitive environments. While Apple has been an exception, the fate of Microsoft is an excellent example of how the lack of a founder at the helm leaves a company vulnerable in a changing and dynamic industry.

Even Apple would not have grown to its current size without the leadership of Steve Jobs. The company's fate in the years when he was ousted (before his return) provides a good example of the dangers of externally hired CEOs running the company.

On the flip side, is there a point where the founder has outstayed his welcome. At the time of writing, there is a legitimate debate about whether the fate of Tesla would be better if Elon Musk stepped down as CEO. We saw a similar trend when WeWork was completing their IPO in late 2019. CEO and Co-Founder Adam Neumann was forced to resign after inappropriate behavior and an ongoing legal battle where he trademarked the word "We" and forced the company to repurchase it from him for a cool $5.9 million.

Intangible Assets

Also known as "what you won't find on the balance sheet". A company has two types of assets: Tangible and intangible. A building or a factory is a tangible asset, as are the goods that the company produces. Intangible assets are a bit trickier to nail down. For example, Coca-Cola has one of the biggest intangible assets in the world: Its trademark.

The phrase "Coca-Cola" is recognizable all around the world. If we were to pour Coca-Cola into another bottle and call it "Freeman Cola," would you drink it? Even if it tastes the same as Coca-Cola, you'll be unlikely to switch your preference to the new drink. This is the power of an intangible asset.

Ferrari is another company that has a similar pull. Swap the badge on a Ferrari with anything else, and people will suddenly want to pay far less for it, even if it is in the right shade of scarlet. The best companies have some form of intangible assets that work for them. This could be a brand name, a patent, or a process that gives them a competitive advantage in the marketplace.

Management quality is also a key intangible asset. For example, Apple under Steve Jobs had one of the biggest intangible assets that could not be quantified on their financial statement. Their asset was Jobs himself. Disney is another example of a company that has significant intangible assets in the form of intellectual property.

Management Quality

It isn't easy to evaluate the quality of management. Most shareholders look at the stock price and then reverse engineer whether management is any good. This is a bit like looking at the quality of windows in a house and trying to figure out whether it's a good investment. There's a lot more to it than just that!

One of the biggest qualities you need to look for in management is its ability to adapt. For example, Kodak was one of the biggest companies in the photography space thanks to its development of the film. When the digital revolution came, it doubled down on film and is now just an afterthought.

The development of the smartphone, in turn, left many digital camera producing companies in the dust. Some pivoted successfully to making high-end cameras for professionals (Canon, GoPro) while others never quite made the leap (Vivitar). It often comes down to honesty.

Honesty in communications is one half of this. How willing is management to disclose the business conditions to shareholders in their reports? Are they willing to admit faults and mistakes? Do they frankly discuss the upcoming headwinds for the business? Another part of honesty is management's ability to stop themselves from drinking their own Kool-Aid.

The Management's Discussion and Analysis (MD&A) section of the company's financial reports provides a good read on how honest management is. Reading prior reports and looking at how management evaluated the business environment at the time is a good way to get a handle on how they tend to communicate and view conditions. An excellent example of this was Jeff Bezos' letters to shareholders when Amazon was still a fledging company. Bezos constantly reiterated his vision for the business and did not focus on minutia like whether they hit a Wall Street analyst's earnings estimates. This is the kind of long-term thinking you want to see from management.

We saw a similar situation with Mark Zuckerberg's actions around 2012. Zuck does get a lot of hate but an undeniable fact is that he knows his business inside and out. Following the release of the iPhone and mobile computing, Facebook remained buried in the desktop era and risked obsolescence. He didn't mince words when he announced that Facebook needed to switch to mobile from desktop because the company was facing extinction (Wagner, 2019).

His foray into getting a Facebook phone manufactured failed, but his other efforts paid off, and Facebook is now firmly established as a giant.

On the flip side, we have examples of CEOs believing their own hype. While it wasn't a public company, the saga of Theranos' Elizabeth Holmes is instructive. While she has a considerable list of faults, almost all of her conduct stems from the fact that she was unable to be honest with herself about what the company could deliver in a reasonable timeline.

Sales and Marketing

These divisions of the company are the lifeblood of the organizations. Not all of us might like salespeople, but their efforts go a long way towards ensuring the company makes a profit. The organization of a company's marketing efforts provides good insight into how careful the management is when it comes to deciding on the company's future.

Consider the fact that Facebook still runs ads for itself, and Google still publishes direct mail pamphlets to get businesses to advertise with them. These efforts show that the management is not complacent despite occupying a premier position in their industries.

Coca-Cola is another example of this. They have one of the strongest intangible assets in the world and yet, they feel the need to advertise themselves. Looking at the turnover and quality of managers in charge of sales and marketing is a good way to gauge how much the company values this part of the business.

One important element of this principle is knowing *which* numbers matter the most to a company's bottom line. For example, many Software-as-a-Service businesses have a tremendous amount of free users (who cost the business money in server fees). Still, they have a difficult time converting these free users into paying customers.

So when reading a company's annual or quarterly report, focus on figures such as the number of **paying** customers or average customer purchase value. Rather than relying on misleading numbers like "total users" or "monthly average users." These are often used by unprofitable companies to make their prospects look more attractive than they are.

Another essential element of this principle is that a company's income is not reliant on a single factor. For example, if a semiconductor manufacturer relies on a contract with Apple for 80% of its revenue, then Apple ending that contract would plunge the economics of that business into disarray. This is exactly what happened with the UK firm Imagination Technologies. It had a contract with Apple to provide graphics processors for the iPhone. This single contract accounted for 45 percent of the company's total revenue. After Apple ended the agreement, the stock took a huge hit and was down 71% from its peak.

As we explained in the previous chapter as to why diversification is important as an investor, the same applies to the businesses you invest in. Don't buy businesses that are overexposed to a single economic factor.

Long Term Focus

You're investing for the long term and therefore you want to invest in companies that align with that focus. It isn't easy running a public corporation. There's constant media pressure and analyst's opinions that shift the focus from long term health to short term profits.

A typical scenario that often occurs with companies is this. The CEO decides to allocate capital towards a project that will ensure long term competitiveness. Doing this requires significant cash, and they increase the company's short term debt burden. This has the effects of reducing earnings during that quarter.

Wall Street immediately reacts and begins questioning their motives. Will the long term project really work? Will the company be able to sustain the short term earnings projections? Earnings projections are figments of analysts' imaginations that they expect companies to adhere to. If the company doesn't meet this standard, a wave of selling begins, and the stock price gets depressed.

This, in turn, enrages shareholders who begin to think that the analysts were right after all. A good manager knows how to manage both sides of the equation. Short term projections need to be hit, and long term projects need to be prioritized as well.

Bill Gates was a good example of this back when he ran Microsoft in the 1990s. The company always magically hit analysts' projections and still managed to drive competitors like Apple out of the market at that time. It isn't an easy job, but that's why the CEO gets paid what they do. Someone obsessed with short term prospects and worried about the damage it will cause their reputation is unlikely to produce long term growth at the company.

Economic Moat

This is a term Warren Buffett uses frequently when speaking of what he looks for in businesses to invest in. Internally, when one of our team brings up a new company to research, our first question is often, "where's the moat?".

An economic moat is some condition that gives a company a significant competitive advantage. It could be anything from size, to trademarks and patents, or a business process.

For example, Amazon's size offers it a considerable economic moat. The company offers customers bargain-basement level prices, and it's able to do this thanks to its sheer size. Its average cost per unit is far lower than what a smaller retailer can offer, and thus, Amazon can afford to earn a small percentage of profit, but it sells so much of it that the amount of profit it earns is high.

Coca-Cola has a strong economic moat through its brand name. Everyone recognizes it and everyone buys it because of that. Interestingly, both Amazon and Coca-Cola are owned by Berkshire Hathaway, Buffett's investment vehicle.

Another factor that can create a moat is a large number of users. For example, Google and Facebook are popular thanks to the large number of users they have. This is an example of a moat caused by the network effect. This happens when companies build a significant userbase, which provides a better customer experience, which then leads to an even higher userbase.

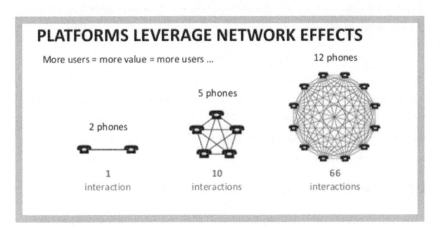

Facebook is the perfect example of this. There comes a tipping point in many people's lives where not being on Facebook is more detrimental to their quality of life than being on it. Take for example a woman in her early 60s. For a long time, she considered herself technophobic and avoided social media as a result. However, she has just become a grandmother for the first time, and her daughter has explained that the best way to get pictures of her new grandson is to use Facebook. She then realizes many of her friends are on the platform as well, so she encourages her other friends who don't yet use the platform, to sign-up. All of this creates a better user experience for the people on the platform and fuels more growth. We see similar examples in the workspace communication space with companies like Slack and Zoom.

Customer acquisition processes can also create a moat. There is no end to what exactly can create an economic moat. All that matters is that the company has one.

One trap new investors full into is mistaking pioneering for a moat. What we mean is this: people assume that being first gives a company a significant competitive advantage. This really isn't true. Does anyone remember Altavista or Orkut? You likely have no idea what those names are. Altavista was a popular search engine that existed before Yahoo search did (remember when Yahoo, not Google was the search king?) As for Orkut, this might shock you, but Google was one of the first companies to build a social media platform and it was years ahead of Facebook. However, the site was shut down in 2014 after it lost market share to other platforms.

You might point to Amazon as a counter-example of this, but even Jeff Bezos' company was not a pioneer. Book Stacks Unlimited came a full three years before Amazon's original avatar of an online bookseller. Our point is that pioneers are the ones that deal with all the obstacles and inefficiencies only for the newcomers to take advantage of the processes that have been built. This results in them growing faster and eventually obliterating the pioneer.

Weathering Storms

How robust is a company's business model? Can it withstand a stress test? Stress tests are scenarios where analysts project profitability numbers based on the assumption of adverse conditions. For example, a hotel chain is unlikely to survive an 80% vacancy rate for too long before things get ugly. Airlines are also notorious for their inability to handle the slightest disruption to their business conditions.

For every business, a standard stress test is a reduction in sales. The higher the business's ability to withstand this stress, the safer your investment will be. Another example of a stress test is multiple Acts of God in quick succession for the insurance industry.

This is why recessions destroy companies who are built solely on debt, whereas companies who maintain healthy cash reserves (like Berkshire Hathaway) can ride the wave through to the other side.

Freeman Investing rule #8

When analyzing a business, remember to take into account the potential downside risk.

"WHEN MOST INVESTORS, INCLUDING THE PROS, ALL AGREE ON SOMETHING, THEY'RE USUALLY WRONG."

- *Carl Icahn*

5

WHAT DOESN'T MATTER WHEN ANALYZING STOCKS

There are many misconceptions about what matters when researching companies to invest in. In this chapter, you're going to learn about some of the most popular ones. A lot of this advice is peddled in the mainstream and you might be surprised to hear that some of them are incorrect.

Keep an open mind throughout this chapter and evaluate the arguments we make for yourself.

Dividends

Dividends are a good thing to have in stocks, and we do not deny that. However, there is a lot of investing literature out there that has elevated dividends to a God-like status. Dividend investors claim that the presence of a dividend alone justifies investment because it signifies that the stock has a ton of advantages within it.

Chief among these is the argument that dividends ensure that management will not act recklessly since they know that they have to pay the dividend. This makes them take fewer risks and thereby guarantee a safe and steady income stream. Let's start with this claim and look at some of the purported advantages to see whether they make sense.

Dividends Ensure Stability

The presence of a dividend does ensure stability but only to a point. The fact is that managers routinely maintain dividend payments for fear of adverse effects on the stock price. Some investors believe this is a good thing and that it scares management into doing the right thing.

This kind of thinking happens because investors are unable to evaluate the quality of a company's management effectively.

FREEMAN INVESTING RULE #9

THE PRESENCE OF A DIVIDEND IS NOT AN ADEQUATE SUBSTITUTE FOR A THOROUGH EVALUATION OF THE QUALITY OF MANAGEMENT.

Poor management is perfectly capable of paying a dividend and still running a company into the ground.

Let's say poor management takes over a company and carries out some less than favorable projects. Revenues decline, but management knows that as long as they can maintain the dividend, stock prices will remain steady. This is because many investors favor dividends far too much.

However, since revenues are declining, the dividend comes to represent a greater portion of the company's earnings. As this proportion (called payout ratio) increases, there's less money available to allocate to projects that will ensure the company's competitiveness is maintained.

In short, the dividend causes management to stop looking at the future and start focusing on the present instead. This is the exact opposite of what proper management does. Notice that the presence of the dividend cuts both ways. In the presence of good management, it is a good thing, but it can turn into a disadvantage when poor management is in charge.

Therefore, the dividend by itself means nothing. Using it as a barometer to measure stability is incorrect. A business is a multi-faceted entity, and reducing the question of stability to a single factor is wrong. Don't misunderstand this point to mean that poor management will always pay out a greater proportion of earnings than good management.

It all comes down to the nature of the business. Some businesses don't require much reinvestment, and therefore, a 90% payout ratio might make sense. This is the case with Real Estate Investment Trusts (REITs). Some businesses require significant reinvestment and in such cases, paying even 10% is a considerable feat and is an indicator of excellent management.

Another argument posits that stable companies in stable industries pay dividends. This is true to an extent. However, it ignores the fact that an unstable sector does not necessarily mean that the companies in it are bad investments. If you had a chance to invest in Google back in 2004, would you take that chance today? What about Amazon in 2001 or Facebook in 2013?

None of these companies pay a dividend, and they probably never will. This doesn't mean they're bad investments or that they're unstable. As an example, Berkshire Hathaway has never paid a dividend since Warren Buffett bought it in 1964. He purchased the company for $11.50 per share. The current stock price is $282,600 per share. It's safe to say his investors are quite happy with his performance.

Dividends Represent Shareholder-Friendly Managers

The term "shareholder friendly" has been turned and twisted to mean a lot of different things. These days the very presence of a dividend gives management an automatic "shareholder friendly" label. From the scenario presented in the previous example of the poor management maintaining the dividend, is this really a shareholder-friendly thing to do?

Surely, the better thing to do would be to suspend the dividend and absorb the short term blowback. As long as the long term investment plays out, who cares what the stock price will do in the short term. Shareholders who value the business and understand the long term consequences of the decision will find this a lot friendlier than the ones that insist on investing on the basis of a few media tropes.

Dividends Over Capital Gains

A particularly problematic attitude that accompanies dividend investing is that dividends matter more than the capital gains a stock provides. Here's the thing that many dividend lovers miss: Capital gains will always be a more substantial portion of your investment return than dividend payments will be. The average dividend payment represents between one to two percent of the stock's price.

A rise of even 3% per year in the stock price means that capital gains outstrip dividend gains. Where do capital gains come from in the long term? From earnings, of course. This is also where dividends come from, or stable ones at the very least. The lesson here is that you need to pay attention to the earnings prospects of the stock and not just its dividends.

Trendy Companies

This is a common pitfall that many investors walk right into. They read the news and feel that they have to be a part of the industry of the future. Alternatively, they feel that some company has been in the news quite a lot recently and therefore, it must be a good investment.

A good example of this is Tesla. This company has been in the news right since its birth. They developed the first electric sports car, are headed by a billionaire who is more of a messiah than a businessman and it's in the electric vehicle space which means that it fits right in with the overall conversation about climate change.

Elon Musk is covered in the same way rockstars are, and his quotes and thoughts are repeated with breathless excitement. Musk is a very passionate man, and he knows a lot about building successful companies. However, does any of this make Tesla a good business to invest in?

The company makes sleek looking cars, but it hasn't earned a cent of profit as yet. In 2019, the company lost close to $862 million (Tesla, 2020). This was a good year, comparatively speaking.

To be fair, the company did post a steady increase in profits and sales to close out the year. However, none of this addresses the fact that there is probably a good reason traditional car manufacturers haven't entered the electric vehicle field as yet. It's prohibitively expensive.

Does it really make sense to believe that the likes of Mercedes, Porsche or Honda, all of whom have grassroots motorsport testing programs along with Formula One hybrid engine development experience, do not have the expertise that Tesla has? Honda developed an alternative fuel source car back in 2006!

Many companies manage to attract shareholders by being media darlings. A great example of this is Enron. The energy firm was once the golden child of Wall Street, and named "America's Most Innovative Company" for 6 years straight. In 2001, Enron declared the largest bankruptcy in history, after it was revealed that systematic accounting fraud had plagued the company for years. In just 18 months, the share price went from $90 to zero.

FREEMAN INVESTING RULE #10

DON'T INVEST IN THE HYPE. EXAMINE THE UNDERLYING BUSINESS AND INDUSTRY PROSPECTS INSTEAD.

Consensus Opinion

There is no shortage of opinions when it comes to stock analysis. We're not talking about the casual gossip that occurs between you and those around you. Professionals indulge in gossip-mongering as well. The difference is that they get paid to do it.

Wall Street analyst opinions hold great sway over the short term movement of the stock's price. A sell rating or a downgrade (which is when an analyst becomes less bullish on a company's prospects) can cause the price to move down in a hurry while a strong recommendation can create hype that pushes its price up equally quickly. This happens because there are large numbers of people who hang onto these analyst ratings as a crutch and use them as a substitute for conducting stock analysis themselves.

However, examining the relationship between analysts, the trading desk of an investment bank, and the companies they analyze is instructive. A good case that highlights this relationship is that of Amazon back in 1997. This was the year that Amazon filed its IPO.

Filing an IPO is not an easy task thanks to the large number of regulatory hurdles that exchanges and the authorities impose. Companies have to hire an investment bank to ensure the process is carried out smoothly. Often, investment banks prepare years in advance in anticipation of a possible IPO. It was no different with Amazon.

The company was a darling of Wall Street thanks to Jeff Bezos' efforts and analysts regularly touted its strong balance sheet and earnings prospects. The primary driver behind such reports was the fact that the number of users on the internet was set to explode, and this put Amazon in prime position to capture their shopping activity.

There was just one problem. The company wasn't making any money. Amazon famously pushed everything back into its businesses to achieve size, and for many years, its free cash flow was dangerously low. None of this mattered to analysts, however. Asking whether Amazon was capable of riding out such low levels of cash with constant venture capital injections was a reasonable thing to do.

Yet, no one did this. A big reason for this was that Wall Street was actively courting Amazon in anticipation of its IPO. Morgan Stanley was the firm that ultimately won the contract, in no small part due to its analyst Mary Meeker's glowing reports of the company. Meeker denied that the business she generated for Morgan Stanley had anything to do with her ratings (Schwartz, 2000).

In contrast, the lone analyst that questioned Amazon's business policy found himself pushed aside by his firm Lehman Brothers. IPOs are especially profitable for investment banks since they earn money in two ways: The first is via fees, and the second is through trading profits.

The stock that is initially sold to the public comes directly from the promoter or investment bank. Naturally, the aim here is to sell it for as much as possible since this results in the highest amount of profit. Given that analyst opinions count for so much, it stands to reason that the analysts at the bank would talk up the stock.

However, Wall Street insists that a so-called "Chinese wall" exists between the analyst and trading departments. The track record and ethics of this industry is a matter of public record. The reader can form their judgment about such claims quite easily.

The point here isn't about whether analysts were right or wrong. In this case, Meeker was right about Amazon in the long run. However, it certainly wasn't due to the reasons she cited in her original glowing reports. Amazon almost went bankrupt during the dot com crash around the turn of the millennium.

The thing for you to note instead is that analysts' opinions and the consensus of the market isn't worth the paper it's printed on. There are many conflicts of interest inherent in the process, and the story of Amazon's IPO and the role analysts played in it is instructive. Amazon fixed its issues, and despite this, the company was unloved in the mid 2000s. This was a case of analysts being wrong once again by holding onto outdated opinions.

While Amazon is an example of how things eventually worked out and how problems were brushed under the carpet, the credit crisis of 2007-2008 is an example of when all these issues were laid bare. In that case, it wasn't just analysts' opinions that were the issue, but the same system was at work.

Analysts at ratings agencies rated complex derivatives as being investment worthy primarily because Wall Street banks would not approach them for business unless such ratings were provided. This caused sophisticated investors to invest in them, and the result was a complete meltdown (Lewis, 2011).

So, the next time you hear the chat on TV or social media saying that stock X is due for a rise or that stock Y is due for a fall, take it with a truckload of salt. There are other factors at play here. Acting based on hearsay is an example of groupthink. You're better off following the simple analytical framework that we've already highlighted.

Market Sentiment

Closely related to groupthink is the phenomenon of market sentiment. Is the market going up or down? Popularly peddled financial wisdom often states that you should not try to time the market. But how the markets are covered causes investors to try to do this exact thing.

Who cares what market sentiment is at the moment? Remember that in the short term, prices are driven by emotions and not logic. By focusing on investing for the long term, you're going to place yourself in the best position to ignore all the chatter that will cause you to sell low and buy high.

A great piece of advice on this comes from legendary investor Peter Lynch. We should note that this quote is from 1994, but you can reliably substitute newspapers for online news or social media.

"If you own auto stocks, then you shouldn't be reading the financial part of the newspaper. Instead, read the section of your local paper about automobiles. See how they talk about new car models, which ones have good reviews and which ones stink. That is what you should be reading. You shouldn't be checking stock prices 4 times a day. Checking stock prices first thing in the morning is not useful. You shouldn't be dealing with the minutia of "what's the market doing today". Instead focus on "what is this company going to be doing 2 years, 3 years, 5 years from now."

Numbers in isolation

There is not a single number on a balance sheet or financial statement which tells a company's entire story. For example, Price to Earnings ratio (PE) is often touted as a good indicator of fair value of a company. But PE differs drastically between sectors. For example, healthcare services has an average PE ratio of 42, which is almost 3x the average of the entire market. So if you only decided to only invest in companies with a PE of 20 or less, you'd miss on great companies in the healthcare services sector.

The same goes for something like earnings growth. If a company is up 20% in the past year, that could be incredible. Or it could be worrying if all their competitors are growing at 100% during the same time period.

With any financial numbers, you need context. This is why it's essential to analyze a company's competitors during your research phase.

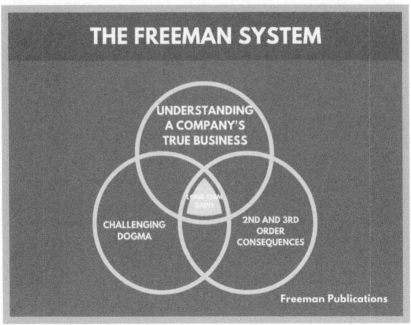

"THERE IS ONLY ONE BOSS. THE CUSTOMER. AND HE CAN FIRE EVERYBODY IN THE COMPANY FROM THE CHAIRMAN ON DOWN, SIMPLY BY SPENDING HIS MONEY SOMEWHERE ELSE."

- Sam Walton

6

THE 20 BEST COMPANIES TO BUY AND HOLD FOR THE NEXT 20 YEARS

Taking all of the principles we've discussed thus far in mind, here are 20 great companies that meet our criteria. We consider all of them to be great options to buy and hold for the next 20 years. You will have heard of some of these names, while others might be unfamiliar to you. Due to the nature of analyst reports, you will also read mixed reviews of every single company mentioned here. Keep in mind the principles discussed in the previous two chapters when reading about these companies.

Disney

Market cap - $188.67 billion

52 week high/low - 153.41/79.07

Disney is one of the companies most affected by the COVID-19 crisis. Its parks have been shut, and direct to consumer sales have dropped significantly. In fact, Disneyland has even been dubbed 'the emptiest place on earth' thanks to the shutdown after the virus pandemic.

There's no denying that Disney faces rough weather over the next 12-18 months. This is primarily because the effects of the virus will spread far and wide. It is gradually becoming clear that the longer it takes to find a cure for it, the worse the economic outlook.

As of this writing, Disney stock has plummeted t0 around $101 from highs of $140 in February. That's a drop of over 25% in less than two months. Market sentiment is bearish. So, why do we think Disney is a great stock to own for the next 20 years?

Parks

While the short term future for Disney's parks and direct to consumer retail businesses is pretty bad, there's no denying that the brand and its intellectual property has a highly sustainable moat. Put it this way: If your child was given a choice of visiting either Disneyland or going to Pete's Fun Park, which one do you think they'd be likely to choose?

Disney has been associated with fun and cartoons for such a long time now that it automatically invokes feelings of childhood when a person hears about it. Despite this strong moat, the company has continuously worked to make the experience at its parks even more enjoyable.

The launch of the PlayDisney Park app turns even longer wait times in lines into a fun experience. This indicates the innovative nature in which the management of the company attacks its weak points. People don't like waiting in long lines. While the PlayDisney Park app may not remove this weakness entirely, it does go a long way towards reducing its negative effects.

Another critical development to watch out for is this: The company has purchased 26 acres of land in Orlando that lie adjacent to the Magic Kingdom, which is one of the oldest Disney parks in the world (Saibil, 2020). This is not the only purchase the company has made. In fact, it happens to be the smallest purchase. Overall, the company has bought close to 5,000 acres of land in an attempt to improve the experience at its parks and resorts. Reinvestment of such scale indicates that management is quite confident of the cash position of the company and are looking to extend their competitive advantage.

Disney+

Disney is a lot more than just its parks, even if this is the first association people make. The company is a media conglomerate with its hands in almost everything you can think of. We'll get to the extent to which Disney dominates the media world shortly. For now, the most significant development has been the launch of Disney+, the company's streaming service.

Disney has been seemingly late to the streaming game and on the surface of it, competing against the likes of Netflix and Amazon Prime Video seems like a tough job. However, the company has successfully avoided trying to be a pioneer. Instead choosing to wait for its rivals to work out any kinks in the process.

The success of Disney+ shortly after its launch proves that the strategy has paid off. As of this writing, Disney+ has over 28 million subscribers in the United States alone. In comparison, Netflix has 60 million subscribers despite having been around for more than a decade now.

Given that Disney+ has just launched, this number is only going to grow in size. It isn't just the domestic market that the company has managed to penetrate. With sensible acquisitions of streaming services in emerging markets, the company has managed to gain an outsized footprint in these markets.

A good example of this was the purchase of the Indian streaming app Hotstar. India has one of the highest penetration and usage rates of mobile data in the world. It also happens to have some of the cheapest data plans in the world, and the price is the primary evaluation tool before signing up for any service.

Netflix and Amazon found this out pretty early, and both companies have not made any significant headway in this regard. Netflix currently has just 2 million subscribers in India (Gupta, 2020). In contrast, Disney+, launched via Hotstar, had over 8 million subscribers on day one.

Licensing

A significant chunk of Disney's business comes from the licensing rights it owns for a number of movie franchises and other content. All those Marvel movies that occupied our imagination for over a decade? Disney owned all of them. The

Star Wars franchise? Owned by Disney. The company is more than just Mickey Mouse.

The extent of Disney's domination of the entertainment industry is highlighted by the fact that the company owns even smaller animated studios. Pixar is a name that is associated with high-quality animated films and Disney owns the studio outright.

In short, almost all content that is distributed to children is owned by Disney, and this creates a steady and gargantuan revenue stream in form of royalty payments. Imagine writing a book that continues to sell for 100 years, and you simply get to pocket the royalties forever. Now, multiply that by a few billion. That's what Disney is sitting on. That's without taking into account the lifetime customer value of these children as they grow into adulthood and have children of their own. Such is the power of an intangible asset such as nostalgia.

Acquisitions

Disney's most robust quality over time has been the pragmatic nature of its acquisitions. The company has never been shy about acquiring competing businesses and then allow those businesses to have a free hand while under the Disney umbrella. Pixar is a great example of this.

Pixar was originally an upstart competitor that disrupted the traditional Disney animated movie formula. While Disney's movies were epics loaded with songs and all sorts of heavy-handed dialogue (think The Lion King), Pixar's movies were light and still managed to pack a punch to the gut of every adult who watched them.

Conventional wisdom would have dictated that Disney use its significant resources to crush the upstart. However, Disney made the pragmatic choice of simply buying Pixar out and giving it full freedom to whatever it wanted, even if it competed against Disney's non-Pixar animated movies.

A similar example was Disney's acquisition of television networks ABC and ESPN. A first, it seemed that Disney was playing far outside of its field of competence. However, the strategy is quite clear now. Despite there being no link between cartoons and sports, Disney now occupies significant market share in the media sphere, and this almost guarantees the success of its ventures in the entertainment field.

As such, the company is a snowball rolling downhill when it comes to the media and entertainment business. It sustains itself and will continue to do so in the future. This is because its subsidiaries have substantial moats of their own to support themselves.

Issues

These are extraordinary times as you can imagine, and there are significant challenges for Disney to face. The first is the significant loss of income from the park and merchandising business. In 2019, as per Disney's annual report, the company earned over $6.7 billion from these avenues.

In addition to this, it also earned over $2.6 billion from studio revenues. Both of these income streams will be massively affected, thanks to the shutdown. The company does have $12 billion in cash reserves. This ought to be enough to tide the company over any short term crisis, however, replacing close to $9 billion in earnings is going to be pretty tough.

However, Disney is hardly the only company facing such a crisis. Pretty much every single business in the world has to weather the storm. Disney has the luxury of leaning on its media network businesses, which ought to see a rise in earnings as time goes on. As of 2019, this division earned $7.5 billion and was the profit leader for the company.

The short term is uncertain for Disney just as it is for the rest of the world. If we were to bank on human societies figuring out solutions to the current crisis, there is no doubt that Disney is better positioned to bounce back once the tough times pass.

Sandstorm Gold

Market cap - $1.01 billion

52 week high/low - 7.90/3.32

Sandstrom Gold is a company not many investors have heard of. It's probably the least well-known company on our list. The company is based out of Canada, and it represents a great way to invest in gold and mining opportunities. The business model of this company is known as gold streaming, and here's how it works.

In the precious metals world, the practice of streaming refers to a company providing financing to a miner or driller. In exchange, the financing company receives the commodity that is being excavated. This practice has long been present in the oil drilling sector, where drillers face huge capital costs and an uncertain, fluctuating market for their goods.

They can spend a lot of money drilling for oil only to find that the market price for oil is low, and this leaves them with a massive hole in their pockets. Drilling for oil takes time and this causes a considerable amount of risk for drillers. This is where the streamer comes in.

The streamer pays the driller cash, and in return, the driller promises to sell the commodity to the streamer for a fixed price. This price is usually a percentage below whatever market value is present at the time.

This makes a lot of sense for the driller since they receive an immediate cash injection. From the streamer's perspective, they're receiving an asset that they can immediately sell back to the market for a profit. They'll need to wait until the resource is available, of course but they don't bare any of the costs of running a mine. A streamer can technically run their business out of their basement.

Gold streamers implement this business model in gold mining, and Sandstorm is one of the standout companies in this regard. The company was founded by Nolan Watson and David Avram in 2008, right when everything else was falling to pieces. 2009 saw the company ink its first two streaming deals.

Streaming deals take a while to start producing because the miner needs time to extract gold. To cover costs in the short term and to also provide financing for these deals, streamers borrow money from banks. However, due to the lack of cash flow from the mining assets, the company needs to find a way to pay interest on these bank loans. The result is that streamers issue equity or issue debt and bypass banks, to begin with.

There is a risk for shareholders that their shares will be diluted over time thanks to the issue of equity. Thus far, Sandstorm's management has exercised great prudence and has managed its debt to equity mix admirably.

The stock was listed on the NYSE in 2012 and has carried out significant acquisitions since then. As of current writing, the company owns 191 different royalty streams and has a free cash flow of $225 million from 23 different gold mines.

Advantages

So why should you invest in Sandstorm Gold? The more pertinent question to ask is, why should you be investing in gold streaming to begin with? Only once this question has been answered should we even consider Sandstorm as an investment. The first reason to invest in gold streaming is the business model itself.

Streaming companies are essentially a bank as far as miners are concerned. Traditionally, miners had to approach banks for short term loans and place their assets as collateral. This isn't the case when it comes to sourcing financing from streamers. The streamer is a business partner in the deal since they are also exposed to the output from the mine.

This provides miners with a fair source of financing that doesn't strain their balance sheets too much. After all, a miner's financial position is risky, to begin with. Adding interest-based debt is hardly a sensible move. This means that the streaming business model will always be in demand. It has a strong moat, and a miner needing cash injections will always be on the lookout for a good streaming deal.

It isn't easy to become a streamer. While you might think that anyone with oodles of cash can rock up and finance a mine, the reality of the business is quite different. To evaluate the potential of a mine, management needs to have significant experience in the field. They need to have experts on board who can reasonably assess the predicted output of the mine.

Only once this is done can any kind of financing terms be agreed upon. At this point, further experience is needed because there are various ways in which the deal can go wrong. For starters, the streamer needs to have a good idea of future commodity prices. They'll be receiving the commodity in the future, so current prices don't matter.

Next, they need to assess the capabilities of the miner. While the mine may be fit to produce gold, does the miner have enough resources to make this possible? Will the investment be enough, or will the miner need more? These are not easy questions to answer.

Our point is that the business has significant hurdles to jump over, and the economics of it is built for a small number of companies to dominate as long as they have management expertise. The quality of management is the most important thing since there are no traditional assets that the business owns.

However, this is a good thing because the lack of traditional assets means that overhead expenses are low, and as a result, free cash flow levels are high. There are no significant capital expenditures necessary, and this reduces the strain on the company's financials. The only risk to mitigate is the waiting period between providing financing and receiving royalty payments.

As we mentioned earlier, streaming companies need to find ways to raise cash.They do this by either seeking financing from banks themselves or by issuing debt and stock. There are many ways to go wrong here and experience is what counts. This means that a company that has survived and thrived in this business for long is in a much better position to earn a profit and lower their risk than a new company. Experience really does pay off when it comes to streaming.

Thus, when looking for a company to invest in, it pays to evaluate management experience as well as the cash flow qualities of a company. In this regard, Sandstorm checks all boxes.

First, the deals it structures are intelligently done. The company structures what are called NSR deals. NSR stands for net smelter royalties. This means that Sandstorm provides financing based on the output of the mine and not on the viability of mining operations. There is a big distinction between the two. NSR royalties are paid on the basis of the output that comes directly from the ground. This what Sandstorm earns. The miner, on the other hand earns a profit only after they sell the gold to Sandstorm and subtract their own mining costs from this revenue.

In other words, Sandstorm is effectively buying shares in the mine's deposits and isn't concerned with the fortunes of the miner or the miner's operation costs.

It completely cuts Sandstorm's risk in terms of mining operations and ties it directly to the output of the mine. Since this is something that the company can evaluate well, it is playing within its field of knowledge.

Shareholder dilution is a primary concern for any investor and Sandstorm management is on top of this as well. The company has repurchased close to 10 million shares between 2018 to February 2020. With plans to repurchase even more shares given the depressed state of the market.

This shows both confidence in the company's performance as well as a considerable reduction in dilution from an investor's perspective. Given the current industry outlook, Sandstorm Gold is well set to dominate its niche for a long time.

Gold streamers have historically proved to be better investments than traditional gold itself. Gold is often used as a hedge within investor portfolios. If the value of the U.S Dollar decreases, then gold usually witnesses an upswing thanks to the correlation that exists between the two. Gold is viewed as a safe haven in tough times, and this is what causes the upswing in gold prices when the dollar declines in value.

Despite this, gold is a risky investment. Some supply and demand forces apply to it, but it is a tricky thing to predict. Between 2008 t0 2018, gold prices rose only by 45%. You'd have thought that gold mining companies would have been able to make money thanks to this, but in fact, their stocks were **down** 38% in this 10 year period.

In contrast, gold streamers' stocks rose by an astronomical 189% during this time. A significant reason for this is all of the factors that we outlined previously. A built-in profit margin and low overheads turbocharge investment returns, and this is reflected in the rise in stock prices.

Walmart

Market cap - $344.97 billion

52 week high/low - 128.08/96.79

Walmart is one of the mainstays of the American retail space. Industry experts have always worried about the ability of the company to overcome challenges, but the fact is that the company is still standing. More importantly, it has survived the gargantuan challenge that Amazon poses.

Amazon has succeeded in wiping out almost every retailer in America and continues to do so around the world, wherever it decides to enter. The fact is that not only has Walmart survived Amazon and the digital revolution, but it has also barely felt the impact of it. This is because it has a significant moat.

You might think that the brand name is what sustains it, but the real moat that Walmart has significant economies of scale. Its sheer size allows for it to take more substantial risks and reduce the economic impact of taking such risks. This, in turn, enables the company to achieve huge consumer satisfaction levels.

Recession-Proof

The advantage that Walmart's moat gives it is that it is practically recession-proof. This was one of the few companies that actually managed to thrive during the economic crisis of the previous decade. Think about it: When times are tough, the first place you think about when it comes to grocery shopping is Walmart.

The current crisis will most likely lead to a recession. With more than 33 million unemployed in the US, the economic impact of COVID-19 is being felt far and wide. While Walmart's physical stores might be closed, its online delivery system is in full swing. We'll address this shortly. As of now, keep in mind that stores cannot remain closed forever.

Despite the challenges the COVID-19 virus brings, at some point, people are going to have to go back outside and buy groceries. When they do, they're going to have less money on average than before, and the first place they'll head to is Walmart. The store stocks virtually everything you can think of, and if saving money is the top priority, this is the place to head to.

Perhaps the biggest strength of Walmart is that 56% of its sales come directly from groceries and food sales. As you can imagine, the demand for this is unlikely to dampen anytime soon. The market prices of Walmart reflect this. While 2020 has been massively bearish for stocks as a whole, with the S&P 500 declining by 30%, Walmart stock declined by just 3.8% overall.

Not only is the company robust in tough times, but its stock also holds up pretty well, too.

Management Philosophy

Sam Walton was one of the first people to make economies of scale a business policy actively. What we mean by this is that while other retailers at the time focused on stocking goods and serving local customers, Walton realized the power of a chain store model where sheer size could allow him to dictate prices to his suppliers and thereby drive costs down.

This allowed him to open several small stores at first and essentially encircle his competitors. When it comes to shopping items such as groceries, consumers are incredibly price-conscious for the most part. Achieving economies of scale allowed Walton to address his consumers' biggest need directly.

Consider that Walton managed to go from running a single store in Arkansas to running a billion-dollar company within his lifetime, and you'll see the power of his business model.

One of Walton's greatest innovations was to locate his stores in small towns at first instead of large cities. Conventional wisdom at the time was to locate big stores in big cities and smaller ones in small towns, thanks to smaller populations. Walton's large stores managed to dominate not just a single town but the entire area around it. What's more, the presence of Walmart discouraged anyone else from entering and thereby reduced competition.

Another innovation he pioneered was to insist on fast logistics. He did this by locating Walmart supply centers at less than an hour's drive away from his stores and insisted on Walmart's fleet of trucks supplying the stores to ensure speedy delivery of goods. This way, Walmart was assured of its prime position in the market.

This policy continues to this day. If anything, Walmart's practices have only become stronger since the founder's death. Warren Buffett is just one of many notable investors who made mention of this in 2006. Walton's legacy lives on in his book, *Sam Walton: Made in America,* which continues to be one of the best business books ever written.

The principles that Sam Walton instilled in his company created a massive advantage for them, and it continues to power the corporation to this day.

E-commerce

Walmart has always been thought of as being late to the e-commerce game. However, in our opinion, this was simply the firm doubling down on its already strong business model and expanding only when it made sense. The majority of Walmart's sales come from small towns to this day, and consumers in those markets do not traditionally purchase goods online.

This behavior is changing, and Walmart has responded brilliantly to it. As of this writing, online ordering and kerbside pickup is available in 60% of its stores. With this number projected to increase to 90% by the end of 2021. Despite this seemingly late entry into e-commerce, Walmart is still alive, while the majority of its competition is dying with e-commerce companies facing a raft of bankruptcies.

Most telling is the behavior of the giant that killed the competition: Amazon. Consider the fact that Amazon operates a very similar business model to Walmart but does it in the online space. It makes sense for Amazon to enter the low-cost grocery and essentials market.

Yet Amazon resists doing so. The company instead chose to buy premium grocer Whole Foods instead of trying to compete with Walmart in the budget grocery space. The fact that Amazon shied away from a direct confrontation is pretty telling. It communicates to investors that Walmart, despite all the gripes about the company being stuck in the past, is firmly entrenched in the hearts and minds of its customer base.

Walmart has expanded significantly abroad and has made repeated forays into the market that suits its business model the best: India. The government of India had to pass laws guarding the interests of small shopkeepers once news broke that Walmart was considering Indian investment. While it was a setback to the company, this event once again shows how pretty much no one wants to compete against this behemoth.

As of now, Walmart is operating in the country as a wholesaler. However, its biggest move there has been to acquire a portion of Amazon's Indian rival Flipkart for $16 billion. The move initially didn't make sense, but there are clearly echoes of its earlier investment in Chinese company JD.com in the Flipkart deal.

In China, Walmart operates online stores for small retailers as well as some of its competitors, such as British grocery chain Asda. In bigger cities, Walmart also runs hybrid online and offline retail stores where customers can scan and go. Clearly, Walmart's move into the developing world is putting it ahead of the curve of many of its competitors.

The company is willing to go to any market as long as the terms of the deal are right. This could be in India or Vietnam. It doesn't matter. Its strong balance sheet and hoards of cash ensure that Walmart will always remain in a strong position for the future.

Brand Value

The economies of scale that Walmart has pushed its brand value to stratospheric heights. This is a unique occurrence when it comes to chain stores. Every chain store retailer struggles against the brands it sells in terms of name recognition. For example, people know what Nordstrom is, but why would they go to Nordstrom in a mall that has Gucci and Versace stores as well?

However, this is not the case with Walmart. Consider this scenario: Let's say there's a brand of cheap cereal that is available for the same price at Luke's Groceries and Walmart. Where will people go? Most likely Walmart. Even if the cereal company decides to sell exclusively to Luke's Groceries, people will still flock to Walmart because that's where you get all kinds of cheap stuff.

By choosing not to sell their product in Walmart, the cereal company is effectively removing itself out of its customers' reach. It's saying that it isn't a budget brand anymore. In other words, it would be suicide for them to do this. This illustrates the moat that the Walmart brand has.

A similar phenomenon exists with its big-box retail outlet, Sam's Club too.

All in all, the stock is not one of those high flying or sexy stocks that you can boast about owning. However, when it comes down to it, Walmart has all the qualities you look for in a good company and a stock that you want to hold onto for the rest of your life.

McDonald's

Market cap - $136.94 billion

52 week high/low - 221.93/124.23

McDonald's might not be your preferred option when it comes to eating out, but this doesn't mean it's a bad investment. In fact, it might be one of the best investments you can find right now. First off is its track record. The reason McDonald's has always performed well is due to its robust business model. We highlighted this in an example previously and will delve into it shortly in more detail.

The company has an enviable track record when it comes to providing shareholders with value. McDonald's is a dividend aristocrat. This moniker is bestowed upon companies that have consistently made and increased dividend payments every year for the past 25 years. This is not an easy achievement, and it further indicates McDonald's' ability to weather crises.

Then there's the appeal of the fast-food chain. Generally speaking, in recessions or downturns, fast food chains tend to perform well since they're a source of cheap and quick food. Sit-down restaurants tend to struggle in contrast.

What's more, McDonald's has also invested significant sums into reducing costs even further by investing in AI and technology when it comes to the ordering process. There's no denying that the COVID-19 prompted lockdowns have heavily hit the restaurant industry. People are staying and eating at home more than ever. Therefore, it is worth analyzing how McDonald's is positioned regarding the immediate crisis as well as the repercussions of it that will occur down the road.

Current Impact

Let's begin by taking a look at how badly operations have been hit due to lockdowns and closures of locations. In this regard, McDonald's has suffered, but it hasn't been as bad as you might initially think. This is because of three major factors that it has going for it. The first is the way the business is structured.

McDonald's is in the real estate business as much as it is in the restaurant business. The company owns all of its locations and leases them out to franchisees for a high markup. This means that the company is guaranteed cash flow every month to a much higher degree than its competition.

As of current writing, as much as 85% of its outlets are franchisee operated. This means that the large majority of its locations are regular cash producers and the risk of the shutdown is primarily outsourced to the franchisees. While the company has announced plans to work with franchisees, the failure of a single franchisee simply means that there's someone else to occupy the place. After all, the location itself isn't in jeopardy. While there will be a short term cash hit, this has little relevance to the long term viability of the business.

Another advantage of this business model is that the company operates its restaurants at far lower costs than its competitors do. After all, it doesn't bear any expense when it comes to utility bills or any other rental expense. The franchisee takes the costs throughout. In return, McDonald's lends them the weight of their brand name and a large cut of revenues.

The second advantage is that the emphasis on fast food has allowed McDonald's to build drive-thru outlets as well as implement a range of AI-powered ordering systems in its stores. For example, in specific locations in China, there is no need for a customer to interact with a human being. They simply walk up and place their order at a terminal and receive their food.

Drive-thrus are witnessing a huge leap forward thanks to self-isolation measures, and until a vaccine is found for the virus, this state of things is likely to remain. In 2019, McDonald's reported that 65% of its sales in the U.S came from drive-thrus. This number is only going to increase. This means that the closure of seating areas are unlikely to have too much of a negative impact on earnings.

Another great move the company had previously taken was to partner with food delivery firms. Critics pointed out that McDonald's didn't have a dedicated partner, but, to be honest, this just reflects the fact that there isn't a single company that has been able to dominate the niche. McDonald's's decision to partner with different firms is simply the company diversifying its risk across partners.

As of now, there are no predictions that can possibly quantify exact numbers from the effect this move has had. However, these factors make it likely that the negative impact of the virus will be blunted quite a bit when it comes to McDonald's.

Recession Impact

The economic impact of the virus is already being felt in the U.S. Unemployment numbers now top 33 million, and many businesses show no signs of immediate recovery. All of this points to the fact that there will be a recession. A bad one. So, how is McDonald's poised to perform during these times? For starters, being a cheap fast food restaurant is going to work in its favor in the majority of the world. People are unlikely to stop eating McDonald's just because times are rough. If anything, the opposite is the case.

Looking at the company's performance in prior recessions is instructive. In the crisis of 2008, the company managed to increase its revenues every year from 2007 until 2011. The same happened once the dotcom bubble burst around 2000. McDonald's increased its revenues like clockwork from 1999 until 2001.

An important point to note is that earnings growth rates didn't match sales growth during these periods. This indicates that the company reduced its margins, but given the economic conditions, this is an understandable move. All of this points to the fact that McDonald's is well poised to handle the upcoming economic recession, should it ever occur.

Financial Strength

This is where things get a little risky with McDonald's. At the end of 2019, thanks to major investments in technology and other assets, the company's cash position was low. As soon as the lockdowns started hitting, this low cash position became an even bigger concern thanks to the decrease in revenues.

This prompted the company to withdraw its $1 billion credit facility. A credit facility is like an overdraft account that companies can borrow from. However, the fact remains that it has $34 billion in debt on its balance sheet, with $6 billion coming due in 2023. This payment might prove to be problematic for management.

There are no easy solutions for its debt problem, despite experts noting that it fully expects McDonald's to pull through this time. However, companies the size of McDonald's have greater power to renegotiate payment terms and kick the can down the road until a moment when revenues stabilize. This is likely to with the 2023 payment.

This year is going to be a tough one for McDonald's as it will be for the rest of the world. How well the business model manages to support McDonald's remains to be seen. There's no doubt that it will ensure that McDonald's navigates these times with more certainty than its peers.

Another important factor to consider when it comes to McDonald's is its dividend's status. Any suspension of a dividend will result in it losing the aristocrat label, and this will result in a downward plunge in stock prices.

As of this writing, the company has suspended its stock buyback program. This is probably in order to save cash for the dividend payment and to increase it by marginal amounts. Generally speaking, the company has weathered crises in the past, and as such, one can expect it to pull through, even though the short term picture is uncertain.

Bottom Line

The company's biggest issue happens to be its high levels of debt which has placed it in a tricky situation right before an unforeseeable crisis. Despite this, it is well placed to handle tough times. Even if the worst does happen and earnings plummet, the company is still a real estate giant that owns all of its properties.

It is not going to lose locations just because it cannot pay the rent. It is free to find different ways to boost revenues, and the increased cash flow will enable it to survive on shoestring margins. Think of it this way: As long as it pays all of its creditors, does the existence of a profit matter all that much? We're not saying that the company will deliberately run a loss.

The point is that even the worst-case scenario is not going to result in as much pain as some of its competitors will feel during the next few years. All of this makes McDonald's a safe haven stock that is most likely going to be around and thrive for a very long time.

Markel

Market cap - $13.86 billion

52 week high/low - 1347.64/710.52

Typing Markel into Google usually results in the search engine asking you if you meant to type 'marvel' instead. This is a pretty apt way to describe what Markel is all about. It is one of the biggest companies on the planet no one knows, and this is a very good thing. Markel has been dubbed 'the baby Berkshire' due to the similarity between the way it is structured.

Markel is an insurance giant, and it began its life as a specialty insurance company for long haul truckers and jitney buses in the 1930s. Specialty insurance is an excellent field for many companies to carve a moat in because the number of customers that require such insurance is low, and any company that can successfully underwrite policies tends to be quite successful.

The insurance business itself is an immensely profitable one, and it is one that a lot of professional investors seek to get into. The famed founder of Stansberry Research, Porter Stansberry, once quipped that insurance was the one business that he would teach his children. Despite this, the average investor doesn't truly understand the power of the business. In order to fully understand the potential of Markel, we need to first examine how the insurance industry works and why it is so desirable.

An insurance company writes policy and receives premium payments like clockwork in return for promising to pay a sum in case things go wrong. The sum that needs to be paid is usually far more than the premium that is charged. The insurer's job is to figure out how much risk they're running on the policy and accordingly price their premiums. However, they can't price them too high because their competitors might undercut them.

If a policy expires and the company has to never payout, this creates what is called an underwriting profit for the company. An underwriting profit is a unicorn for insurance companies since they're notoriously difficult to come by. It's tough to predict risk after all, and at some point, the insurer has to pay out the amount for which the policy is insured.

This is why most insurance companies don't even try to earn an underwriting profit. Instead, they aim to breakeven or even run a loss in order to simply capture market share and keep the cash flow levels high. Now, there is usually some period of time between receiving premium payments and having to pay out the insured sum.

For example, you make health insurance payments every month, but it's not as if you're going to claim benefits every single month. You'll most likely claim them at some point down the road. During this time, the insurance company gets to keep your cash without any obligation to return it. This money is called float.

If the company manages to secure an underwriting profit, it creates a free float. In essence, a free-float is simply free money. Insurance companies that don't generate a free float can still earn a profit. They do this by investing the float into the market. In short, they act as fund managers and aim to generate returns with all the cash that they have lying around.

Many insurance companies rely on generating profits with the float they have instead of underwriting. The best companies such as Berkshire Hathaway and Markel tend to produce both investment returns as well as underwriting profits. This creates a free-float that effectively leverages their investments.

Think of it in this way. Let's say you buy stock A for $100 and it pays you $25 in cash dividends. You reinvest this $25 into another stock B that pays you $10 in cash. You reinvest $10 into C that pays you $2 and so on until you're invested in a number of stocks. However, your original investment amount is still $100. You've turned $100 into an investment into at least four stocks that have spawned even more investments.

Float creates leverage as well, but since this isn't free money, the overall returns are hampered a bit. The company needs to pay this amount back at some point since their customers will make claims on their policies. In essence, the float a company carries is a short term loan to the insurer, and a free float is a loan that never has to be paid back.

Markel is one of those insurers that understands the power of cash flow and practices this with its own investments.

Quality of Investments

Markel's portfolio over the years has reflected management's philosophy that businesses that generate a high degree of cash flow are the best ones to invest in. In fact, management is so confident in their ability to pick investments that they don't pay dividends, which is unusual amongst insurers.

Typically, the free cash flow that an insurer generates is returned to the shareholders since the company cannot find adequate uses for it. However, Markel has successfully used its free-float and cash flow to increase its holdings in its portfolio and deliver even greater returns to its shareholders.

Shareholder Base

When speaking of Markel, special mention must be made of the quality of the shareholder base that the company has. The company seems to have a high number of shareholders who are focused on capturing long term gains through their investment and, as such, are willing to stomach a few negative quarters or two.

I say quarters and not years here because the average public company faces intense scrutiny after a few quarters of losses. Wall Street gangs up on them and this forces management to place short term results above long term growth as we explained previously.

This is not the case at Markel since there aren't any agitators present. As such, the company is run like a private company. Where the business aims are aligned with the long term growth of the company.

Niche

Property and casualty insurance remains the primary driver of the business, and these are great niches for Markel to operate in. This is because the company faces little competition and it has a great deal of pricing power. This is a direct result of excellent customer service and competitive pricing that keeps competitors out as well as ensures a moat for the company.

Reinsurance

It's not all great news with Markel, and there are some risks you need to be aware of. All of these risks typically center around the reinsurance business. Reinsurance is insurance for insurance companies. For example, if insurance company A decides that it has some pretty risky contracts on its books, it approaches a reinsurer to insure those contracts.

As you can imagine, reinsurance is a pretty risky business. The biggest risk here is the fact that all of the situations that the company has to insure are so-called long-tail situations. A long-tail refers to the fact that payouts can occur many years into the future, and when they do, they tend to be substantial.

Thus, a reinsurer can carry a huge amount of risk on their books without ever knowing the true cost of the policy until the time comes, if it ever does, to pay. Typically, reinsurance policies are sought for extreme events such as a global pandemic like the one we're living through right now.

How does one estimate the odds of a disease spreading like wildfire? Furthermore, how does one even begin to calculate the economic impact of such pandemics? It depends on the disease of course. How can anyone predict what kind of a disease might occur next? These are impossible questions to answer.

Reinsurance company underwriters thus need to be masters of risk management, and they need some luck on their side as well. For the most part, reinsurers generate high levels of free float, but when they do find themselves in a position of having to pay, they end up draining their cash reserves and going into the red. The levels of losses they typically sustain cannot be compensated by the returns they receive from the free float.

Even the esteemed Berkshire Hathaway has been burned at the reinsurance game a few times, and Markel is no exception. Insurance companies use a metric called the combined ratio to calculate their profit and loss levels. This is calculated by dividing the total expenses and losses incurred by the premiums earned.

The smaller the number is, the greater the profit is. Markel's combined ratio for 2019 was a healthy 93%. This means that expenses were 93% of premiums earned which means they earned a good amount of free float. However, this clouds the fact that the company's reinsurance division posted a ratio of 120%.

It was property and casualty that brought that number down to 93%. You might wonder why a company would even consider entering the reinsurance game if it's so risky. Well, it has to do with the rewards on offer. It's a bit like asking why would you borrow money to buy a home. The value of the asset and security makes up for it.

The prospect of the value of the home decreasing is just a risk you have to take. It's the same with the reinsurance business. Having said all of this about Markel's reinsurance business, it must be noted that the managers of the company have wisely minimized the effect of it on their overall portfolio.

If a 120% combined ratio in reinsurance still results in 93% overall combined ratio, then this is a risk that the company can justifiably take.

Smart management and a carefully engineered moat make Markel is a fantastic company for the long term and a great addition to any portfolio.

Starbucks

Market cap - $86.71 billion

52 week high/low - 99.72/50.02

Starbucks has been an interesting case study to evaluate how companies will perform during these tough times. This is because the two biggest markets for Starbucks happen to be the US and China. Given the global situation, Starbucks was one of the first major companies to get hit with store closures and self-isolation measures.

Given that the Chinese situation is ahead of the rest of the world at the moment, in terms of recovery, the initial for Starbucks made for interesting reading. First off, the company announced that while sales dropped disastrously during the first quarter of 2020, there was a growth in-store visits as lockdown curbs eased.

The picture isn't all that great, but it does prove that the business model of Starbucks is still very much viable. The company might be in the coffee shop business on the surface but its real appeal lies in the fact that it is a great third space for people to meet. Whether it is to meet for a date or a business meeting or even sit and work, Starbucks is an obvious choice for most people.

The company is coming up on its 50th anniversary next year and in 2019, it opened 1,439 new stores worldwide. As the year ended, the company reported an increase in same-store sales to the tune of three percent. Then the virus hit and things took a turn for the worse. The biggest gripe about Starbucks, from people who don't understand the business, is the fact that it has always been a bit too luxurious a brand to appeal to people during a recession.

The price of a single cup of Starbucks coffee has always been on the higher side. Paying $5 for a single cup does sound ridiculous when compared to its competition but people pay this amount for much more than just the coffee. The ordering experience and ambiance are what people *really* pay for.

There are a number of factors that ensure that Starbucks is well placed to handle the tough times ahead.

Brand Loyalty

As we just mentioned, people who drink Starbucks coffee usually drink only Starbucks coffee. The addition of food options to the menu in recent years and the general ambiance of their locations means that customers tend to return to the location more often than not.

Starbucks is one of those rare companies that rewards its customers back once they're shown loyalty. The rewards program is one of the most generous and is a drawing point for many new customers. Apart from having the ability to order ahead of time, rewards program customers also receive free refills of hot coffee or tea in-store.

Customers in higher tiers receive free snacks and food as well, and this guarantees that they'll always be back to visit. All in all, the company has brand loyalty figured out really well, and this will keep it in good standing through tough times. On the surface of it, closure of shop locations will hurt sales. However, once lockdown curbs ease, people will be keen on socializing once more.

Given the negative impact on their wallets, spending $5 for a cup of coffee and chatting at a Starbucks is a pretty cheap way to socialize. The coffee might be expensive, but the purpose of a customer's visit isn't to just have a cup of coffee.

Prior Experience

Much like with McDonald's, it's instructive to take a look at how Starbucks managed to handle the previous recessions. Here, there isn't as much of a track record we have to play with. The previous recession coincided with the business model of Starbucks circling the drain as well. The company was in trouble headed into the recession and the crisis only made things worse.

The return of Howard Schultz, the founder, as CEO helped get things back on track. Starbucks embarked on an unprecedented program of winning back its customers' trust. It began with a series of surveys and questions that the company asked its customers concerning the customer experience.

The response was tremendous and the company carried out many of the recommendations that its customers wanted. It remained one of the few instances when a large public corporation gave its customers free rein when it comes to suggesting improvements and directing the course of the company. All of this helped Starbucks exit the crisis in much better shape than how it entered it.

Will the same experience help the company this time around? The exact steps it took last time might not apply during these times because the nature of the crisis is different. During 2008, customers were dissatisfied while this time around, this doesn't appear to be the case.

What will stand the company in good stead is that its focus on customer loyalty has paid off massively, and this has led to a strong brand presence. This is a very good thing when it comes to handling tough times. While there's no way to predict how the company will handle the recession, its focus on its customers does put it in a good place.

Diversification

While the brick and mortar locations remain Starbucks' primary earners, the company has been diversifying to create additional revenue streams. One of the side effects of brand loyalty and recognition that was born from the previous crisis is that it enabled the company to sell its brand of coffee in supermarkets.

This brought in a decent chunk of cash, and while this isn't nearly enough to sustain the company all by itself, it does dampen the negative impact quite a bit. In addition to this, Starbucks has partnered with several delivery companies and has been expanding its drive-thru and mobile ordering platforms.

All of these platforms will see increased consumer interaction as buying habits chance post this crisis.

All in all, despite having many factors working against it, Starbucks is a company that is poised to break out once the lockdowns end, and people begin to adjust to the new economic and social reality that the virus will bring about. The short term might be painful for investors, but the long term does promise stable growth.

Crown Castle International

Market cap - $68.41 billion

52 week high/low - 168.75/114.18

Crown Castle is a relatively unknown stock thanks to the fact that it happens to be a real estate investment trust or a REIT. These companies don't have to pay corporate taxes but are obligated to return 90% of their profits to their shareholders in return. Typically REITs invest in real estate assets and make money by managing those properties.

REITs have become increasingly popular over the past five years. Crown Castle is a specialized REIT that doesn't invest in the usual residences or commercial spaces that are associated with these instruments.

Instead, Crown Castle is a cell phone tower REIT. As the name suggests, the company owns a number of cell phone towers around the country and also manages miles of fiber optic cables that enable communication. In short, this company is a service provider to one of the fastest-growing phenomenon in the world currently: The internet of things.

This phrase is used to signify the increasing degree to which everything in our lives is connected to one another. Each day witnesses new smart devices being launched and the day isn't far off when our vehicles will be able to communicate with our devices at home and exchange data. Wearable tech such as the Fitbit and other smartwatches have witnessed huge increases in demand during this decade and this will only continue to grow. The IoT economy is projected to reach up to $11 Trillion by 2025.

All of these devices need one thing in common: A network. To be precise, they need a network that can handle the increasing number of connections and data being exchanged. This data will need to be transmitted faster and with more efficiency than current networks can handle. Communications protocols aren't far behind at the moment.

4G networks were a huge step forward in terms of reducing latency (the delay between sending data and receiving it), but they cannot handle the rate at which connections are increasing. 5G communication networks are already being set up and the world needs the faster speeds that 5G promises.

While more research is needed, the fact is that existing communication towers and infrastructure are capable of handling 5G's demands. With the number of people connected to the internet only set to increase, communications businesses are a great bet for the future.

This is where cell phone tower REITs come in. These companies earn income by leasing towers to operators and earn a steady income for the lease period. On average, the lease period lasts for five years. In addition to this, these companies also lease their fiber-optic communications facilities to network providers for a fee.

All in all, the future is bright for the industry. The question is, why is Crown Castle the best bet of the lot?

REIT Structure

The first cell phone tower company to convert itself into a REIT was American Tower. This is the best known company of its kind, and since 2011, which is when it became a REIT, the company's stock has returned well in excess of 300% (DiLallo, 2019).

Crown Castle turned itself into a REIT in 2014 and since then has returned 140% for its shareholders. While AMT is the more prominent company, Crown Castle happens to have far better growth prospects. What's more, since it's a REIT, it is legally obligated to pay out 90% of its income to its shareholders. This means that its dividend yield is higher than the average dividend-paying stock.

As of current writing, the yield on Crown Castle is 3.05%, which is double the size of American Tower's yield. This makes the company an income earner as well as a capital gains machine.

Infrastructure

Currently, almost all of Crown Castle's infrastructure is located in the United States which means it has a stable business environment to work in and doesn't need to worry about international laws and licensing. This is in contrast to American Tower, which operates internationally.

A third cell tower REIT, SBA Communications is also operating internationally thanks to saturation in the American market. This is good news for Crown Castle since its existing infrastructure is unlikely to be disrupted anytime soon.

The company, as of December 2019, has 40,000 towers and 80,000 miles of fiber networks. The business is simple to understand. There are just two divisions: Towers and cable. Operating costs are low and are usually front-loaded when networks and towers need to be installed and brought online.

These costs are typically lowered by adding more tenants to existing infrastructure and thereby reducing unit costs. The addition of more tenants usually boosts operating cash flows quite a bit because costs are low, to begin with, and they dramatically reduce once this happens.

40% of gross income from the towers segment is derived from the land that the company owns. As for the remaining 60%, the average remaining life on the land leases are 35 years long. The largest cell phone companies in America account for 75% of revenues, and there isn't any danger of default with regards to payments. As of now, the towers division is the primary earner with 67% of income derived from it.

As of 2019, the company has invested money into developing its fiber business and they expect income to rise in forthcoming years. Given the demand that 5G is going to place on fiber networks, this seems like a reasonable assumption to make.

Cash Flow Growth

Crown Castle is one of those companies that is poised to make huge growth. As of this writing, the company is about half the size of its competitors but owns a wide variety of great assets across the United States. According to the company's latest annual report, 71% of Crown Castle's towers and fiber networks are present in major business areas around the country.

Given the increase in demand that 5G will bring and the high quality of its assets, investors can expect high levels of cash flow from the company. As such, cash flow has grown at a faster pace thus far when compared to its competitors. A lot of this has to do with the smaller size, and investors cannot expect the same growth rates as the company gets bigger.

However, there is a significant runway for the stock to grow. And the economics of its business seems to be lining up well in this regard.

Risks

No investment is without risk, and Crown Castle has inadvertently stumbled upon a huge risk thanks to the current political climate. 5G finds itself at the heart of the US-China trade war because of the potential it has to unlock greater levels of data transfer. As such, China is considered to be the leader in developing 5G technology, and one firm is the leader when it comes to developing electronic equipment that suits 5G.

This company is Huawei, which found itself being accused of being a spy front for the Chinese government. Right now, Huawei is banned from conducting business in America, and American companies cannot supply or use any of their products. However, this is not the case worldwide.

European governments, in particular have had no qualms about installing Huawei equipment and have resisted American attempts to move away from the company's products. It doesn't help that there isn't a single American company that has the capabilities to develop these products.

The Trump administration, and the Chinese government, view 5G as being the key to global dominance. Given China's massive investments in this technology, it could conceivably dominate the market, and this will result in every technology company using Chinese products to transfer data and conduct business. This is where allegations of spying come from (Rydon, 2020).

While the specifics of the trade war are immaterial here, what investors should keep in mind is that there are likely to be second-order effects on cell tower REITs such as Crown Castle. At this point, we can't predict what these effects will be, but unforeseen circumstances might impact their business.

Right now, the major American carriers have stated that they do not use or plan to use Huawei or Chinese products in their 5G infrastructure. Given that 5G has barely been rolled out as yet, this claim will be tested in the coming years. Will Crown need to upgrade its infrastructure? Will it need to invest more in installing fiber networks? There is a significant risk here to cash flow growth.

This is not to say that the company is going to make a loss due to these risks. After all, 5G demands pretty much the same infrastructure as 4G does. You can think of both networks via an analogy: 4G is a collegiate swimmer while 5G is Micheal Phelps at his prime. The latter is a lot faster, but ultimately, both of them swim in the same pool. Crown Castle is the pool in this case.

A bigger risk to the company than the trade war is the fact that 70% of its revenues come from the major carriers. Any consolidation of these networks is going to reduce its earnings. In fact, T-Mobile and Sprint agreed to merge in 2018 and are in the process of completing the merger. While the impact on Crown's revenues won't be as large, there will be some decrease as overlapping networks get eliminated.

Companies such as Crown tend to grow via acquisition for the most part and disruption to revenues might impact this. While the company has enough cash to fuel growth, it might find that acquisition is not the most practical thing for it to do. Given that there are no other ways for it to grow, this puts it in a sticky situation.

We say that there are no other ways to grow because practically speaking, it takes time to buy land and to erect a tower manually. While a company spends a few months doing this, a competitor can go out and buy another company and instantly add a few 100 towers to its portfolio.

Despite these risks, the quality of Crown Castle's management and its track record proves that the company can weather these storms. The growth in cash flow and the upcoming demand for 5G is certain to fuel overall growth, and Crown is in pole position to lead the way in this sector.

Amazon

Market cap - $1.19 trillion

52 week high/low - 2475.95/1626.03

From a company very few have heard of, we move onto a company that even your technophobic grandma has heard of. Amazon is everywhere these days, and that is not an understatement. It has become the second company to reach the one trillion-dollar market valuation mark and joined Apple at this spot.

Amazon started off as an online bookseller but has since taken that business model and has replicated it over and over. It begins by raising a war chest through financing. In its earlier days, it did this by venture capital funding. Once this was done, it slashed prices to such an extreme that the competition was forced to quit or risk bankruptcy.

Having gained close to complete market share, the company then consolidates and adds other products to its offerings and generates more lines of cash flow. In its early days, Amazon was all about cash flow and not earnings. In fact, it took Amazon a long time to post a profit, and the business model was questioned widely at the time. The logic was simple. As long as Amazon could fund its expansion with other people's money (venture capital or equity and loans at low-interest rates), and it could pay its expenses, profits didn't matter.

Profits would eventually come when the company reached a specific size where customers would automatically turn to it. This model has repeated over and over again with every single business Amazon enters. The second major business the company entered was IT infrastructure with Amazon Web Services or AWS.

AWS offers cloud-based data centers and a number of large companies such as Zoom and Slack use it as part of their daily business needs. As Amazon expanded into more product segments, the same formula was applied over and over, and gradually, the older business segments began turning a profit.

Today, as the company continues to expand, it doesn't need to raise additional cash because its existing lines of business provide it with all the cash flow it needs. It has even helped Jeff Bezos fund personal investments such as buying the Washington Post newspaper and founding a space rocket company.

Product Lines

Amazon these days has a wide and varied product line. The most prominent one is Prime membership, and this is effectively a loyalty program. Prime membership gives its customers access to discounted rates and offers on a number of products and also includes Prime TV access which is Amazon's streaming service.

The company has stayed true to its roots in book retailing and has a vast library of eBooks and paperbacks. Amazon's self-publishing platform incentivizes self-publishers to churn out hundreds of thousands of ebooks every year, and with the acquisition of Audible, Amazon has diversified its book offerings. All of these platforms represent a source of recurring revenues for Amazon.

Amazon's technological forays include developing the Echo home device with its assistant Alexa. This helps amazon collect all kinds of data about consumer behavior that helps tailor product recommendations on the platform.

In addition to this, Amazon has expanded into the grocery business by buying Whole Foods and developing its own pay and go stores. To help support these stores, Amazon has developed a patented Just Walk Out or JWO technology that is still in its early stages of maturity.

As of now, the only customers for this tech are Amazon's own stores, but in the future, it isn't inconceivable to see it spread to smaller and medium-sized retailers everywhere.

Financials

In its early days, Amazon's financials were under constant scrutiny and justifiably so. Bezos' strategy of minimizing earnings at the expense of cash flow was risky, but it paid off. The margin of error was small, but to his credit, he pulled it off, and Amazon is now well within safe territory.

The firm has a good amount of cash, and given the events of the crisis, it should only see increased activity on its website. Amazon is already the biggest shopping search engine on the planet, and this number is only going to grow. What's more, its free cash flow (which is the cash left over after all operating expenses and investments are deducted) has also steadily increased since 2017, which indicates that a number of its internal investments are nearing maturity.

This means the company can expect an earnings boost in the upcoming decade. The sheer extent of the number of products it offers as well as the multiple businesses it is involved in making sure that Amazon is going to find it close to impossible to fail.

Impact of COVID-19

Amazon has not been spared from the impact that the virus has had on the world. The primary casualty has been the delivery services that are offered with Prime membership. Typically, members receive their orders the very next day. However, with the crisis unfolding, Prime orders are being delayed by up to a month.

Amazon has made it clear that they are prioritizing the shipping of essential items above all else. This is probably what has led to alarming sounding numbers like that, but there is no doubt negative impact at the moment. Given its sheer size, one would expect Amazon to recover in short order.

Given the changing behavior of consumers that once can expect in these times, the development of JWO is great news for the company. While its competitors, such as Walmart and Target are unlikely to implement it thanks to data sharing concerns, Amazon is likely going to find several businesses interested in the software. It helps minimize human contact and removes the need for workers to be in harm's way.

The other line of business that is likely maturing at just the right time is digital advertising. As Amazon's platform has grown, it's advertising services have famously lagged. For the longest time, Amazon's marketing services AMS was the most unsophisticated platform when compared to Facebook or Google's platforms.

This has changed rapidly over the past two years, with digital revenues now significant enough to warrant a mention on the quarterly earnings call. As more shoppers turn to Amazon, targeted advertising offers a great way to boost earnings, and here, Amazon is primed to take advantage.

Management

Amazon's success is often ascribed to its CEO Bezos and this is largely true. His management style has been described as prickly and lacking in any sort of empathy. However, his results speak for themselves, and to his credit, Bezos has never been involved in any scandal or dishonest business practice during his career.

Bezos' vision is what ultimately drives Amazon and forms the biggest reason to invest in the company. Much like how Steve Jobs was Apple's biggest economic moat while he was alive, Bezos has created a similar situation for himself and his company.

While he isn't the most forthcoming with his vision, it is safe to say that he has built enough of a track record to justify investing in Amazon. Warren Buffett seems to think so as well with his recent investment in the company. Despite his dubious record when it comes to managing his own employees' wishes, there is no denying that Bezos places customer satisfaction at the top of his list and is willing to go to any extent to satisfy their concerns.

In fact, Bezos has managed to create a truly unique economic moat for his company, and it is one that few other CEOs have succeeded at creating.

Diversified Moat

Given that Amazon straddles so many different lines of business, it is staggering to think of how varied and diversified its moat is. The first and most apparent moat it has is its economies of scale. Amazon is so large and their pockets are so deep that they can afford to drive prices as low as possible and still make a profit.

This is impossible to match, and perhaps Walmart is the only other company on the planet that can do this in the consumer goods segment. However, Amazon does this with every product on its platform. A side effect of this is that it manages to generate large user numbers.

With a large number of users comes data, and this is at the heart of how Amazon does business. The mountains of data that Amazon has, be it from customer behavior on its platform or through digital ads or through AWS, Amazon gets to use this as a free float of sorts to deliver an even better experience. In short, it receives perfect customer feedback all the time, and thanks to user volumes, its competition cannot even hope to match it.

Lastly, there is the one that the Bezos himself creates. As we just mentioned, he presents a great reason to invest in Amazon all by himself. These three moats combined create a pretty unique opportunity for a company in this day and age. Even Google doesn't have the diversity of data that Amazon has.

All in all, Amazon is a no brainer investment for the future and is one that will only grow from here.

The Trade Desk

Market cap - $9.74 billion

52 week high/low - 323.78/136

Here we have yet another billion-dollar company that some experts call "the next Netflix." The Trade Desk (TTD) operates in the B2B advertising space, and as such, its business model is likely going to intimidate a few investors. However, the model itself is simpler to understand that it seems on the surface.

TTD is what is called a "buy-side advertising enabler." This means that if you work for an ad agency and are looking to buy advertising space across different forms of media, you can log in to TTD's platform and instantly purchase slots. In the past, given the dominance of television networks, ad buyers used to negotiate with the networks directly.

These days, there are many more ad platforms, and thus, there is a need for a single consolidated platform that allows buyers to buy space and thereby plan their budgets more effectively. The old process used to take time, and this is another benefit of a platform like the one TTD provides.

There are many platforms that do what TTD does; however, the business models are fragmented. What this means is, there is much variation between how these platforms do what they do. TTD positions itself as a platform that is solely focused on the buy-side and does not favor any sell-side network. This helps it avoid any conflict of interest.

After all, favoring a particular seller might result in a poor experience for the buyer and even worse, cost them money. The ad industry has traditionally been a buyer's market thanks to the increasing number of sellers. After all, the number of TV networks grows every day and these days; streaming platforms sell space on their networks as well.

Thus, TTD has positioned itself as a trustworthy name in the industry, and this gives it a significant moat in the minds of buyers. The company divides its operations between two categories, informally speaking. The first is what it calls 'linear TV'. This refers to selling ad space on television channels.

Despite the increasingly bleak prospects that cable TV faces, the fact remains that audience numbers are still high. However, it is a highly inefficient market since advertisers cannot collect data or measure the success of their campaigns to a large extent. After all, how can you measure whether someone saw your ad and decided to buy your product if they saw it on TV?

The second line of business is what TTD calls connected TV or CTV. CTV refers to digital advertising platforms outside of Google and Facebook, which are heavyweights in the industry and handle their buy-side all by themselves. What we mean by this is that both companies allow ad buyers to create their accounts and manage everything themselves after analyzing the mountains of data provided to them.

TTD sells ad space on platforms that are outside of these two tech giants. For example, ad space on Hulu is sold through TTD. A number of other streaming services advertise their space on TTD's platform as well. It is in the CTV space that the company stands to make explosive growth.

Analytics

The modern ad world is vastly different from what it was just a decade ago. Back then, ad agencies mostly focused on the creative side of things and used disciplines such as psychology to drive their ad campaigns. These days, advertising is a matter of data crunching.

Pretty much everything can be tracked and interpreted, and as a result, human psychology can now be quantified. A good example of this is how advertisers run A/B split tests where they test different versions of ad copy to measure what works best. The ad executives don't need to guess what will work anymore; they can measure it.

This has led to increasing demand for data from buying platforms. TTD shines in this regard since it is a fully customizable and open platform. This means users are free to add whatever module they wish and can customize tracking metrics. In contrast, even platforms such as Google and Facebook aren't open or customizable. You're stuck with whatever metrics they provide, and that's it.

The customizable nature of TTD has allowed it to stay ahead of its competition, which provides similar facilities to varying degrees. Add this analytical ability to the growing relevance of CTV advertising, and it becomes obvious that TTD is well-positioned to take over a still-nascent market that is growing exponentially. The CEO of TTD, Jeff Green, had this to say recently about the nature of the ad buying industry (Zafar, 2020):

"...the TV ecosystem today, we think of as a little bit of a ticking time bomb...in traditional TV...the users are going away, the number of people watching is declining, but the cost of providing the service has been going up. And the price of the ads has been going up, even though fewer people are watching...so that's making it...less effective on a per-dollar basis than it has been."

This proves that the company is headed in the right direction by ramping up its focus on analytics and customization.

Another aspect of buying patterns that the ad industry is witnessing is the growing need for automation. This is commonly referred to as programmatic ad buying. Programmatic buying is an algorithm-driven process where advertisers can input their desired criteria, and the algorithm goes ahead and bids and buys whatever space is available. This creates greater efficiency in the process since the algorithm can assess which space offers the greatest cost to benefit ratio.

The increased use of analytics in the ad industry has led to buyers becoming ever more cost-conscious, and programmatic ad buying is at the forefront of their needs. A data-driven platform, such as the one TTD provides is necessary for advertisers to tweak their automated ad buys and create greater efficiency in their bidding process.

International Presence

A neglected fact of digital advertising is that many countries in the world are lagging behind the technologically mature markets in terms of infrastructure available and analytics spend. This presents huge opportunities for companies such as TTD to expand their reach.

Having access to data in more sophisticated markets will allow buyers in less developed ones to place more intelligent buys. Think of it this way: If you've ever tried to advertise on Facebook, you will have noticed that the cost of acquiring an American customer is far greater than acquiring one in Denmark.

This is because there is far less competition in the Danish market, and as a result, you receive more bang for your buck. If you cut your teeth in the American market, dominating the Danish space will be easier. This is pretty much what TTD allows advertisers to do by providing them with relevant data measuring capabilities.

In particular, the company plans on expanding in China and Indonesia, where it believes massive growth potential exists. This is something that no other competitor has managed to pull off and TTD's growing presence in the traditionally sealed off Chinese advertising market is cause for optimism for investors.

Client Concentration

TTDs clients are spread out across the board and no single client represents more than 10% of revenues. Two clients currently represent more than 10% of total billings, and this number is down from three in 2018. What's more, the company has a client retention rate of 95% over three years from 2017. This is a great sign since the more diversified a company's client base is, the less it depends on one customer to generate revenues.

Risks

There are a few risks that investors must make a note of when it comes to TTD. The business is a highly technical one, and as such, all tech-driven businesses are open to disruption. TTD is no different in this regard. It is operating in a space that is still immature (programmatic buying), and this market will evolve in ways that management cannot always predict.

The other thing to keep in mind is that TTD is a relatively immature company compared to the other recommendations in this list. It is operating in a highly competitive market, and any loss of technological ability will result in it losing its moat extremely quickly.

Then there's the fact that some of TTD's competitors such as Google's marketing platform and Verizon Media have better resources than them and could decide to enter the space and introduce more innovation at a rapid pace, which TTD cannot handle. Alternatively, it also means that TTD could be the target of an acquisition. This is not a negative, to be clear. Acquiring TTD would be a smart move on the part of a large competitor at this point, and shareholders will likely see significant gains if this happens to pass.

As such, keeping these risks in mind is prudent, and none of them dampen the case for investment in TTD. The stock is set to skyrocket and is a growth stock in every sense of the term.

Keysight Technologies

Market cap - $17.34 billion

52 week high/low - 110.00/71.03

Keysight is one of those companies that is integral to almost every single company out there. This is because it is a manufacturer and supplier of 5G chips. It also makes software that is used in every industry from aerospace, auto manufacturing to defense. The primary investment thesis of investing in Keysight is the same as the lesson that was learned back during the gold rush.

The gold rush inspired tons of people to move out West to seek their fortune in desperate little mining towns in the middle of nowhere. The odds of the prospectors being successful was low thanks to the large competition that faced them. Enough movies have been made about what these men went through.

What is not mentioned, is that there were people who became extremely rich off the gold rush. It wasn't the prospectors but the saloons and prospecting equipment sellers. In other words, during the gold rush, the only people who became rich were the ones who sold shovels and booze. This thesis of investing has been reliable throughout the course of history and is the basis for our 2nd and 3rd order consequences cornerstone.

Instead of investing in a hot niche that is crowded with competition, it's far better to invest in companies that are suppliers to the hot niche. The supplier is sure to benefit from the huge demand that will flow to them thanks to the number of companies in that niche.

A good example of this thesis are companies such as Keysight and Intel. These companies don't manufacture the finished products but make products that are integral to those finished goods. Every electronic item out there needs a chip. While Intel focuses on producing chips for computers and smartphones, Keysight focuses on chips for industrial purposes.

This is what has led the company to establish a broad customer base, and this is unlikely to change. The niche that Keysight operates in has high barriers to entry thanks to its being a hugely technical field. Furthermore, the established nature of Keysight's business means that competition is unlikely to win over too many of Keysight's clientele.

The company began life as a subsidiary of Hewlett Packard and was spun off in 2012. Thus, while its life as a public company is short, its expertise stretches a long way back. This is what has enabled it to grow spectacularly since its formation, and it has avoided the usual hiccups that new companies face.

Keysight's business is grouped into three different categories. The first is the communication solutions group and this group serves the aerospace, dense, and government industries. One of the key drivers of growth here is the rise of 5G, as well as the growing complexity of semiconductor devices as automation grows. The group's products find their way into products that are used for communication, satellites, radar, and surveillance systems. This group raked in $715 million in profits during the previous year.

The second division is the electronic industrial solutions group, and the profits for this group come in at $294 million. The group's focus is on consumer technology, and in this regard, the group designs software and testing solutions. This software has a major role to play in the validation, optimization, installation, and manufacturing of consumer products.

Manufacturers of computers, computer peripherals, consumer electronics, OEM products, medical equipment are the group's primary customers. Given the broader breadth, this group typically sells more units and is less specialized than the communications group.

Lastly, we have Keysight's Ixia solutions group that is responsible for $29 million in profits. This group focuses on testing the security of virtual networks and their associated components and applications. This means the group is involved in producing software to secure a company's hardware, software and other services. The group's primary income is derived from installation and warranty contracts.

Growth

It's easy to forget that Keysight is still a growing company despite its size. A lot of its existing business stems from when the company was a division within HP, and the company has begun implementing its own sales channels effectively. The results of this have been phenomenal.

The last three quarters of 2019 witnessed huge growth and all quarters resulted in the company earning far in excess of analyst estimates. As a result, share prices have become a bit inflated but they still remain a bargain over the course of the long term.

As of this writing, 78 of the Fortune 100 companies are clients of Keysight. The business the company is going to source from them is only going to grow thanks to the ever-increasing demand on processor chips that the internet of things is going to require.

The upcoming decade is going to witness the birth of self-driving cars and increasingly smart devices. All of this will only accelerate demand, and Keysight is well-positioned to handle all of this. The research firm Gartner estimates that by 2022, the average American home will contain 22 smart devices.

The defense industry is also another sector that is going to witness increased demand for Keysight's products. The massive human toll of warfare has led to a push to create robots that have greater involvement in combat, and these will need sophisticated technological inputs.

Overall, Keysight is in a great position to serve all of these increased demands.

Software

Despite the firm's focus on hardware, it is the Ixia solutions group where the most investment is taking place. This is because as time moves forward, implementing software as a solution (SaaS) revenue streams will become of primary importance. After all, hardware needs to be installed only once, but the software requires regular maintenance and upgrades.

At some point, Keysight will be called upon to maintain the hardware it installs, and this is why the shift in investment to SaaS is a good sign. The best part of this business model is the relatively high margins it generates. All of this is an excellent sign for the company moving forward.

Customer Base

The customer base of Keysight is varied, and the best part of this is that not a single company accounts for more than five percent of the overall business. This means that the company is not overly exposed to natural disasters such as the COVID-19 crisis. Evidence of this can be seen in the performance of the stock. Which has held up far better than its peers thus far.

This being said, some risks are present for Keysight. The highly technical nature of the business means that significant cash needs to be spent on R&D. As we mentioned earlier, America is behind China when it comes to the adoption and development of 5G technology.

The defense sector will especially place a huge demand on Keysight for these products, and if they don't happen to be up to scratch, the prospect of losing a key customer looms. It also opens the door for an upstart competitor to enter the market. Despite this risk, the pedigree of management, as well as their track record, indicates that the company should be able to handle this well.

The recession that will most probably follow the viral outbreak should pose no threat to the company. It has a strong balance sheet and is secure in terms of cash and financing options. Continued investment into research and development is the key to growth and executives seem to understand this basic fact pretty well. The switch to SaaS and software-centric business models also indicate that they are on top of the changing economics of the industry.

Chinese Exposure

Given the technologically sensitive nature of their business, Keysight has almost no Chinese exposure. It does source a few parts from that country, but all in all, the lockdowns have had no effect on Keysight's business.

Competition from Chinese OEMs is what threatens Keysight's domination in overseas markets where buyers are not as keen to buy American. The challenge here will be for the company to maintain its dominance in the face of an increasingly aggressive Chinese supply in the 5G and related technological space.

There are mitigating factors here, though. While the consumer-facing business lines will be impacted by the threat of Chinese products, the governmental business operations, and other high tech operations are unlikely to be affected for now. It remains to be seen how Chinese firms such as Huawei pivot from manufacturing low-level consumer-centric 5G goods to more complex hardware solutions.

For now, though, Keysight is ahead of its competitors and is a great investment. It has stable management that has a clear succession plan in place and has a history of stable earnings growth. Its customer base is extremely varied, and Keysight produces the one thing that all of them need no matter what. This ensures a steady demand.

All in all, the company is well poised to grow its profits well beyond the next decade.

Coca-Cola

Market cap - $210.38 billion

52 week high/low - 60.13/36.27

Coca-Cola needs no introduction. Everyone has heard of it, and everyone has drunk the beverage at some point in their lives. The company has been a financial giant of America with an increasing dividend for 57 years in a row. This makes it a dividend aristocrat with astonishing ease.

The company itself has always been viewed as a steady earner in times of distress and has always rewarded long term investors. Coca-Cola stock has never been an exciting headline grabber, but its real returns come from its steady dividend as well as the fact that it tends to outperform markets during downtrends, even if it lags during uptrends.

A huge seal of approval as far as the investment worthiness of the company is the fact that Coca-Cola remains one of Berkshire Hathaway's largest holdings, with Cherry Coca-Cola being the chairman's beverage of choice. This endorsement notwithstanding, Coca-Cola has been facing some headwinds in the past decade.

The world keeps changing, and consumer preferences change along with it. It began with firearms and tobacco companies being attacked in the mainstream and having vigorous campaigns mounted against them. We're not here to judge the moral relevance of these campaigns but are merely tracing a trend factually. Advertising bans soon arrived, and these days, while tobacco companies are profitable and steady earners, they have lost the ability to grow explosively.

The same trend is catching on when it comes to the fast food and soft drinks sector. Companies that own their assets, such as McDonald's, are good bets when it comes to the ability to thrive during such times. With soft drinks, the challenges are different. There are no real estate assets the company can own. After all, no one goes to a sit-down restaurant just to drink Coca-Cola.

Instead, the focus ought to be on reducing overhead expenses and diversifying away from a single product line. While health consciousness will reduce the demand for Coca-Cola over the upcoming years like never before, this doesn't mean that the company has to sell bottles of Coca-Cola to remain profitable.

Coca-Cola has taken several steps in this regard, and these form the primary reason as to why it is a great investment.

Reduced Overhead

Coca-Cola is one of the best-structured businesses on the planet. While people think of it as a soft drinks company, the fact is that in business terms, Coca-Cola is a beverage distributor. It has always separated its distribution business from its direct to consumer bottling business.

The company owned a number of bottling plants around the world and in the United States, but the revenues from bottling were separate from the revenues earned via syrup distribution. This decision was a far-sighted one and is paying off now. Given the headwinds Coca-Cola faces, it has begun divesting its bottling plants and is increasingly shifting towards becoming a syrup distributor.

This reduces overhead massively since bottling plants are factories that require massive capital investment and maintenance. A syrup distributor, on the other hand, has to simply manufacture the mix and sell it to the bottlers. The infrastructure required to make syrup is far smaller than what it takes to bottle the finished product.

For starters, bottles aren't needed. The syrup is transferred in refrigerated trucks and is stored in plastic bags within cardboard boxes. All of this reduces overhead massively. Which indicates that Coca-Cola has read the signs and is restructuring its business to meet the challenge.

Its operating margin now stands at 29% as a result; this is unheard of for a company of its size.

Diversification

Coca-Cola has long favored diversifying beyond its Coca-Cola syrup product offering. The company owns a number of brands around the world that have significant market share in their own right. Here is a list of brands the Coca-Cola owns:

- Sprite (soft drink)
- Fanta (soft drink)
- Schweppes (soda water)
- Appletiser (sparkling juice)
- Dasani (mineral water)
- Powerade (sports drink)
- SmartWater (mineral water)
- Vitaminwater (sports drink)
- ZICO (sports drink)
- Minute Maid (juice)
- innocent (juice)
- Simply (juice)
- fairlife (dairy)
- AdeS (assorted beverages)
- Costa Coffee (coffee chain)
- Georgia Coffee (coffee chain)

This isn't the full list, but as you can see, there are a number of brands in here that are heavyweights in their own right. All of this means that Coca-Cola as a company, still has a lot of demand beyond sugary drinks.

Growth

Tagging a company of this size with the 'growth' label might seem ridiculous, but the fact is that Coca-Cola has a long way to grow at the moment. Brands within the Coca-Cola family such as Diet Coca-Cola, Coca-Cola Zero, and Coca-Cola Vanilla and so on have a smaller footprint than the primary product.

Investors often confuse the American market as being representative for the rest of the world, but this is not the case. Internationally, classic Coca-Cola is still the bestseller, but the company has only begun to market and push the other lines of Coca-Cola. For example, five years ago it was close to impossible to find Diet Coca-Cola in India, but now, the country consumes the drink in massive quantities.

Add to this the fact that there are other product lines that the company can push. For example, Dasani water isn't widely available outside America at the moment, but the company is actively pushing the product, and there is massive potential for sales to increase.

Moat

When it comes to Coca-Cola it is impossible to ignore the sheer size of its moat. The name 'Coca-Cola' is widely recognized to the extent that it is used to talk about other types of products as well. Everyone and their grandma has consumed the product, and the color and font of the Coca-Cola script are widely recognized.

Then there's the longevity that the company has displayed. It has been around forever and has weathered six recessions in the United States alone. It has expanded into countries that have come to associate Coca-Cola with America and stand as a symbol of refreshment and a lot more around the world.

It is fashionable to make statements that imply that a giant is about to fall but, to be honest, such statements tend to be false for the most part. It takes a lot of work for a mainstay of the American economy to fall apart, and as of now, this day seems very far away for Coca-Cola. As of this writing, there are less than five countries around the world where Coca-Cola isn't the top selling soft drink.

Risks

As with everything, there are risks to investing in Coca-Cola. The company has been investing in creating further product lines and diversifying its product portfolio. It has expanded into snacks as well. All of this is a clear sign that it is witnessing a decrease in demand for the core product.

This might seem like bad news, it is, to a certain extent, but it can be mitigated with good diversification. It remains to be seen how well the management carries this out. It is a significant challenge the company faces. Replacing income that will be reduced from the Coca-Cola lines is a stiff task.

Due to these developments, the company's balance sheet has become more leveraged. Currently, the debt to equity ratio stands at 0.71. Debt stands for the sum of all the loans and liabilities the company has. Equity is the capital it has in the form of shareholder value and represents the amount of a company shareholders own. This is despite divesting a large number of its bottling plants. In comparison, the debt to equity in 2010 stood at 0.1.

What's more, Coca-Cola is increasing the level of debt it will carry by issuing bonds worth $5 billion with maturities ranging from 7, 10, 20, and 30 years respectively. This will increase the burden of interest expense it has to carry. Currently, interest expense is 2.7% of revenues, which is still manageable, given the fact that Coca-Cola doesn't carry too many capital heavy assets.

The case for Coca-Cola mostly comes down to this: The expertise of management and their ability to diversify and evolve the core business. There is no denying that demand for the core Coca-Cola products will be lower 30 years from now. However, Coca-Cola has already diversified to such an extent that it isn't solely dependent on the core drink line as it was 20 years ago.

As such, this means that the company has been anticipating a slowdown in demand for a long time. Which explains the re-structuring of the company to meet these changing conditions well in advance. Then there's the fact that almost none of its product lines are likely to witness a drop in demand no matter how tough the economic outlook gets. Be it a recession or a boom, soft drink consumption will remain steady, and as the biggest bully in the space, Coca-Cola is unlikely to go anywhere but up.

Zoom Communications

Market cap - $40.41 billion

52 week high/low - 181.50/59.94

This company has become one of the coronavirus darlings and is one of the few companies that have benefited from the pandemic. If you weren't acquainted with the software before, you sure are now. However, popularity alone doesn't make for a great investment thesis. A good example of this are marijuana stocks that have been the rage since legalization. A large number of those stocks are now exploring new lows.

Zoom has long been a great investment. Since its IPO in 2019, where it debuted at $61 per share, the company has managed to grow despite a tough market. Tough in this context describes the conditions that were facing cloud computing companies. Many stocks in this sector saw selloffs of over 30%. However, Zoom managed to rise above its IPO price which was impressive.

The company has also been one of those rare Silicon Valley unicorns that managed to make money before going public. As of 2019, the company's total revenue grew to $622.7 million, which represents an 88% increase from 2018.

However if you note the market cap number listed above, you will notice that the valuation of the company is ludicrously high, based on current numbers. There's no denying that Zoom fits the qualities of a stock that you should ignore if you were to follow our previously listed principles. It is a media darling at the moment. Which means everyone is piling into it because they've heard the name, and have experienced the platform to an increasing degree thanks to the pandemic.

This has led to Zoom selling at a ridiculous 50x multiple to sales and an even more ridiculous valuation when it comes to the earnings ratio. A lot of sensible investors will be scared away by these multiples and they would be justified in doing so. So, why are we recommending Zoom as an investment?

For starters, there's the product itself. The software was popular even before the pandemic thanks to its sleek interface and ease of use. Now that active users have grown to 12.92 million on a monthly basis, the software is all set to become even more popular. A large part of Zoom's rapid growth in its user base has to do with its product-market fit.

Tech analysts often use this term to describe the 'X factor' that a particular stock or company has. They use this to explain why a product achieves virality. As such, no one knows what this really means, and it's one of those terms that are a catch-all for inexplicable behavior. Much like how market selloff in the 90s and in the previous decade was due to Arabs selling stuff, "product market fit" is a catch-all term for viral phenomena.

One of the key reasons for Zoom's growth that we can easily discern is that it does not need any account-based dependency across platforms. This means you could be working on MS Outlook and still use it. Other collaboration software such as Skype and Google Hangouts are either clunky or require authentication from multiple accounts before logging in.

This played a key role in the early adoption of Zoom. Most importantly, growth was driven from the ground up. Meaning, it wasn't imposed on workers by management. Instead, it was lower-level employees who insisted that management use the software. All of this bodes well for long term user retention. With telecommuting on the rise and set to become the norm over the next decade, Zoom is right where it wants to be.

Future Prospects

As we mentioned earlier, the earnings multiples on Zoom stocks are nonsensical. The company is selling close to 260X projected earnings, which is extremely high even for a darling tech stock. Compare this with a multiple of 130X for Shopify and Slack, and you'll see how overvalued Zoom currently is.

Despite this, Zoom has excellent long term growth prospects. The market size of communications as a service has been estimated to be $43 billion (Mckenna, 2020). Zoom's position as a leader in this space and its current valuation means that there is a long way to go.

What's more, Zoom is in the process of releasing a new feature called Zoom Phone which is VoIP calling without the need for video. As of current writing, 16% of the total workforce in the United States telecommutes. This was before the virus hit, and it doesn't include American workers traveling overseas or the large gig economy that exists in the form of freelancers and consultants.

All of these numbers are set not just to increase, but explode. What's more, this doesn't take into account the international market where Zoom has witnessed huge growth. From 2018-2020, Zoom sourced 17-20% of its total revenues from EMEA regions as well as Asia-Pacific countries.

Another great quality that Zoom has consistently displayed is its ability to convert free users into paid customers. A lot of SaaS companies rely on the Freemium model of business. The Freemium model means they offer basic features on a free basis but more advanced features for a fee. A high conversion rate indicates that the premium features add significant value, and this is a great sign for sustainable growth. Many SaaS companies fall victim to free users driving up operating costs, and not being able to offset set that with the required number of paid users. Zoom does not have these issues.

Problems

Despite all of the positives that we've highlighted, the fact remains that Zoom is still an extremely young company, and there are many risks it faces. Despite the growth in users during this time, it still faces the challenge of having to retain those users. Tech apps are extremely prone to having their users flee to some other platform at the drop of a hat.

Remember when Skype was all the rage? It existed back when apps were still called programs! You would reason that backing from a huge company such as Microsoft would do it a world of good, but this hasn't really been the case. The software is often mentioned as an also-ran at this point.

Zoom is susceptible to these risks as well, so user growth alone won't cut it. The primary feature that drew people to the app was the ease of use and the ability to work across platforms. While the consumer usage is what is making headlines of late, it is the business usage that drives the business. How Zoom handles the surge of users remains to be seen.

As of now, the signs are promising. Zoom recently made news when it was sued by a developer out in California, claiming that the company had shared his data without his consent. Soon, news websites were flooded with headlines stating that Zoom was unreliable and that it wasn't end-to-end encrypted. A lot of this was hysteria, so it's worth delving deeper into this and understanding what really happened.

First, let's deal with the case that brought all of this to light. The developer's claim was primarily that the company had shared his data without proper notice. Zoom responded in a blog post by saying that the issue had occurred due to them installing a Facebook software development kit, which allowed users to login using their Facebook Id.

As a result, Facebook collected information about the users logging in and stored it on its platform. As such, it was Facebook that was at fault, and Zoom's mistake was not to know that this was possible, which is sloppy. However, the company owned up to this mistake in a blog post and stated the following (Yuan, 2020):

'We originally implemented the "Login with Facebook" feature using the Facebook SDK for iOS (Software Development Kit) in order to provide our users with another convenient way to access our platform. However, we were made aware on Wednesday, March 25, 2020, that the Facebook SDK was collecting device information unnecessary for us to provide our services. The information collected by the Facebook SDK did not include information and activities related to meetings such as attendees, names, notes, etc., but rather included information about devices such as the mobile OS type and version, the device time zone, device OS, device model and carrier, screen size, processor cores, and disk space'

Following this, further investigations were conducted, and this is when the lack of end to end encryption came to light. Initial reporting suggested that Zoom had marketed their software as having this level of encryption, but it looked like they had lied. This is untrue.

The issue lay with the way the encryption keys were being stored. The data itself is fully encrypted, and it is impossible for Zoom or anyone else to access. However, the keys that unlock the data were being stored by Zoom in its own cloud. The reason it was doing so was this: Zoom was originally designed for business use.

Business users typically place additional security measures across their networks prior to logging in and this ensures that encryption keys are stored on their own servers. The sudden rise in consumer usage meant that Zoom had to begin storing keys on its own cloud since there was nowhere else for them to store it. The sudden and massive rise in user numbers is what caused the issue, and there wasn't malice on the company's part.

The CEO of Zoom, Eric Yuan described it in a blog post. He stated that the product was designed to be used by large corporate users who carry out their own separate security checks on their networks. As a result, Zoom didn't need to carry a lot of protocols that are required for daily consumer use.

The rapid and unprecedented growth of the user base didn't leave the company with enough time to build these features, and as a result, Zoom was caught off guard.

All in all, the company had issues and dealt with everything in a transparent manner and didn't lie to its users or cover up its efforts, like how Facebook and Google have done in the past. This is a sign of competent management that understands the current climate surrounding data privacy and takes it seriously.

As far as management indicators go, these are pretty strong ones. This didn't stop the negative headlines from rolling in. Media darling Elon Musk banned Zoom usage across Tesla while in what was effectively a candid admission of an inferior product, direct rival Google banned the usage of Zoom as well. The implication here is that Google's own employees preferred Zoom to Hangouts.

All in all, Zoom is not without risk, but the ability of management to weather this crisis and display transparency is something that bodes well for its future. We would like to see Zoom trade at lower prices, and you'll learn why after using our company valuation tool in the next chapter.

Teladoc Health

Market cap - $11.25 billion

52 week high/low - 176.40/48.57

With everything becoming digital these days, it stands to reason that healthcare would follow in these footsteps as well. The global telehealth market is projected to reach a size of $55.6 billion by 2025, and Teladoc is at the forefront of this revolution. In-person visitation has lagged behind the rest of the healthcare segment thus far in terms of digital applications.

After all, it is tough to diagnose someone without seeing them in person. The outbreak of COVID-19 has changed this space completely. With increased risks associated with in-person contact, video conferencing ability, and e-consultations are on the rise. While you might be tempted to think that this is just a virus related fad, the numbers say otherwise.

Teladoc has witnessed huge growth over the past decade. In fact, in the field of telehealth services the company is far ahead of giants of the space such as Humana and UnitedHealth Group. It also happens to be the only telehealth service provider that trades publicly, which puts it far ahead of its competition.

Furthermore, the viral outbreak had opened people's eyes as to how effective virtual doctor visits can be. An initial analysis suggests that this behavior will continue in the future as people become more secure with this form of doctor consultation. Overall, telehealth and telemedicine is a "mega trend" that is bound to become even more popular over the coming decades, and Teladoc is right at the forefront of it.

The company currently covers treatment for a variety of medical issues. As of 2019, Teladoc provides virtual consultation services for over 450 medical subspecialties. These also cover mental health services through its subsidiary BetterHelp.

Within the United States, the company has over 36.7 million unique users (up 61% YoY) who are paid members and 19.3 million users (up 104% YoY) who pay one-time visit fees on the platform. Thanks to the acquisition of Advance Medical Healthcare Management Services, the company now provides services in 130 countries and in 30 languages 24 hours a day.

Acquisitions are the primary mode of growth for Teladoc. In addition to patient-facing services, the company also invests in developing enterprise platforms for hospitals and physicians to bring them on board its network. Nine out of 10 insurance providers are supported on the platform, and this has ensured broad appeal.

B2B

Teladoc currently provides B2B healthcare solutions to over 12,000 businesses across America, with 40% of these businesses being Fortune 500 companies. The company has also partnered with CVS pharmacy to position itself as the virtual healthcare service provider of choice. In addition to this, Teladoc works with 50 major American health insurers and over 70 international health insurers and finance firms.

The CVS partnership, titled MinuteClinic expanded from 18 to 26 states last year. The revenue model is pretty simple. Clients pay a monthly subscription fee, and there are no hidden fees within this.

The real driver of growth in the B2B segment has been the adoption of multiple services by clients already on the platform. Teladoc states that 40% of existing clients subscribe to two or more services within its network with BetterHelp witnessing the largest growth.

Technical Abilities

A significant advantage that Teladoc has is that it can collect usage data and analytics about the users and physicians on its platform. The company has strict data protection policies, so patients do not need to worry about medical histories being leaked. The analytics that the company collects are primarily designed to develop better engagement with existing users as well as to drive growth by signing up new users.

These analytics are what fuel the company's marketing strategy, and thus far, all campaigns have been a success with new user signups increasing at a record pace. The company's platform itself has been designed, so that introduction of new services is seamless.

This happens due to deep investment in infrastructure that allows Teladoc not only to provide a robust platform but also allows for real-time eligibility checking and integration with insurance companies.

Research

There are many roadblocks that telehealth companies need to navigate as of this writing. First off, many of the treatments for complex or severe conditions cannot be prescribed without an in-person visit. This is understandable and is something that telehealth providers will not overcome anytime soon.

A bigger hurdle that can be overcome is the ability of doctors to prescribe treatments virtually. To this effect, Teladoc has partnered with Thomas Jefferson University to offer a fellowship aimed at training doctors in virtual care. The company has also teamed up with the University of Southern California to research antibiotic prescription in virtual healthcare.

These efforts prove that Teladoc takes its commitment to its business seriously. They have been in business for over 10 years and have been steadily expanding in a growing industry. While it has been gaining attention thanks to the COVID-19 outbreak, the company is more than just a short term fad.

There is a lot going to Teladoc. It is a relatively mature company operating in a fast-growing field. It has ample cash reserves and doesn't have many competitors in sight. The fact that it is far ahead of the curve of its much bigger rivals in the space means that if its upward curve continues, it should be a prime takeover candidate which will ensure investors receive some pretty sizable gains.

Lululemon Athletica

Market cap - $25.94 billion

52 week high/low - 266.20/128.85

Another trend that has been growing is holistic fitness. While the previous decade saw the expansion of gyms and fitness clubs, this decade has seen the growth of fitness routines such as calisthenics and yoga.

The thing with such routines is that they're a lifestyle as well as a training regimen. They inspire extreme loyalty amongst those who practice them, and this royalty extends to any brands that serve this space. One of the biggest companies that inspire such cult-like loyalty is Lululemon Athletica.

From the outside looking in, Lululemon sells a bunch of overpriced clothes along with mats and other accessories that seem to make no sense. For instance, one of its products happens to be a yoga mat that is priced at $88 and headbands for women that are priced at $40. These prices don't make much sense to the outsider, but to someone who lives the lifestyle, they're perfectly fine. It's the same phenomenon as with Starbucks' prices. Lululemon Inspires extremely high levels of loyalty, and purchasing its products is a bit like buying your way into a club of fellow lifestyle seekers.

The majority of the brand's customers are women. Which makes sense since, in North America, the majority of yoga and alternative fitness practitioners happen to be women. Lululemon's apparel and accessories are hot sellers but they also stand up to scrutiny in terms of quality. Unlike apparel from other fitness brands, the clothes are not produced in sweatshops in third world countries, and this is often something that appeals to shoppers.

Scarcity and Growth

One of the things that Lululemon has going for it is the fact that for a brand that inspires so much loyalty, the number of physical outlets it has is laughably low. The brand had just 38 physical stores around the world till the end of 2018 and by the end of 2019, had opened an additional 51 stores.

Obviously, in hindsight, this seems like a bad investment, and no doubt it will hurt during the short term. Given that yoga studios and fitness centers of all kinds have closed, the brand is likely to witness a few tough quarters this year. However, a lot depends on when isolation protocols will ease. If we witness restrictions ease before the holiday season this year, sales could increase and power profits.

However, all of that is conjecture. As of now, we can conclude that the low number of physical outlets contributes to creating low overhead costs as well as creates a scarcity effect. The fact that its stores are located mostly in trendy cities only adds to its allure. All in all, Lululemon does a great job of marketing its life-style-based message instead of pushing itself as just an apparel manufacturer.

This allows it to differentiate itself from the other giants in the space such as Nike, Adidas, and Puma.

Niche

The company is based out of Canada but counts the United States as its biggest market. Over 90% of its customers are based in the US. A good way to think of its appeal is to liken it to Starbucks. It is a place that offers luxury at affordable prices, even if it isn't the cheapest.

Its customers recognize all of this and see it as an indispensable part of their life-style. Then there's the fact the company was perhaps the first fitness apparel maker that dedicated itself to creating clothes for women. The founder of Lululemon, Chip Wilson, (we'll deal with him in more detail shortly) mentions the practice of 'shrink it and pink it' that was relevant in the fitness apparel industry at the time (Lieber, 2018)

This refers to shrinking the size of men's fitness apparel and coloring it pink, thereby creating women's apparel. Women noticed this needless to say and had to resort to wearing dance leggings that were simply not made for exercise routines such as Yoga. Wilson's solutions to redesign apparel created a splash, and this is what helped develop the cult-like obsession that its customers have.

There is a roaring second market for used Lululemon clothing. Luxury brands such as Chanel and Gucci often witness huge interest in used goods of theirs but Lululemon is the only athletic apparel manufacturer that draws such interest. Scarcity is at the heart of this once again. It begins with the way each style is introduced into the market.

Garments are given names that signify their uniqueness as well as their color. Next, the company gives purchasers just 14 days to return goods they're unhappy with. This is a far stricter return policy than what most retailers practice, and it does leave them with unhappy customers. However, it creates supply for the secondary market.

Lastly, Lululemon produces fixed quantities of its styles and never replenishes stocks. This means that if you own a pair of leggings, you're one of the few people in the world that do. The scarcity model is even enforced geographically. Styles that are released in say, Tokyo, are not released in New York.

This has led to blogs and communities being set up that follow Lululemon's style releases with a fervor that is usually reserved for fashion week luxury brands. Lululemon is well aware of these practices and has gone so far as to deny service to suspected resellers. During certain periods, it bars people from buying more than a certain number of items of clothing to stop them from reselling it at a higher markup (Lieber, 2015).

Events the company holds, such as the Sea Breeze Half Marathon, tend to witness huge sales of items that immediately pop up on eBay and other reseller sites. While the company discourages these practices, from an investor's perspective, all of this screams economic moat.

Diversification

Lululemon has long since recognized its brand power and has invested in a tech startup named Mirror. This company aims to develop smart mirrors that can be used to provide fitness instruction along with further recommendations. It's not hard to see how this could help Lululemon expand its product offerings.

While its retail outlets are small in number, Lululemon's website is a huge driver of sales, as are its special events that are regular fan fests. While physical stores will naturally be closed right now, the high level of loyalty, the brand inspires will only boost online sales and will help it diversify its revenue streams well into the future.

Management

This is going to be perhaps the most soap-operatic portion of this book. While the founder of Lululemon, Chip Wilson, is rightly credited as being one of the retail industry's visionaries. The company he created refuses even to acknowledge him on their 'about us' page. A major reason for this is the drama that Wilson created while he was in charge of the company.

Never one to hold back on his views, he said he created Lululemon primarily to help women "make their butts look better" and one of his self-confessed metrics for this was the number of compliments men would give women without realizing exactly why the woman's butt looked better than before (Lieber, 2018).

One of his more famous policies was to hire employees who were family-oriented and wanted to have children in the future. He even went as far as to dub kids as being "nature's orgasm." None of this pleased shareholders, but there's no denying it did create an aura of rebellion around the company and helped it achieve a cult-like following.

Speaking of cults, Wilson is also credited with developing the self-help employee training program that all recruits go through when they join the company. The details are far too bizarre to recount here, and you can refer to the sources at the end of this book for a full account.

Despite all of his faults, Wilson also ended up designing perhaps what is one of the best protocols for on-floor sales techniques. Lululemon's salespeople are instructed to adhere to a very specific sales manner. If the customer stares at a product for six seconds (yes, it's timed), the salesperson (called an "educator") has to deliver an enthusiastic speech about how wonderful the product is. At this point, if the customer doesn't have further questions, the salesperson walks away.

They return when the customer stares at another product for six seconds and the same routine begins all over again. This sounds strange, to say the least, but it has resulted in Lululemon achieving per square foot sales numbers on par with Tiffany's and Apple, both of whom sell vastly more expensive products.

Wilson is long gone from the company, having been ousted acrimoniously in 2013, and the management that is in place now is far better suited to run a large public corporation. While Wilson was best suited for the company's buccaneering days, Lululemon is a giant now and isn't really an underdog. As such, his presence would only destabilize the brand's position.

Financial Position

It isn't all just cults and spandex when it comes to Lululemon. The company has an astonishing $1 billion in cash and has close to zero debt. This is pretty remarkable for a retailer that has just opened 51 new stores. As a result, the management does not foresee the need to have to borrow money via debt offerings or equity financing.

What's more, the company has been buying back its stock throughout 2019 and will probably continue to do so, provided sales don't fall off a cliff completely in 2020. Despite the headwinds facing the company and the female-centric sales material, men's apparel saw a jump of 34% along with the operating margin increasing as well. Based on current numbers, projected growth and unique marketplace positioning, the company is in a good financial position to deal with the current crisis and is well set for the future.

Baidu

Market cap - $34.02 billion

52 week high/low - 186.22/82.00

As we've already outlined before, China has made the leap over the past decade from a growing economy to emerge as a truly dominant world power. The country seems to be shedding the last few characteristics of a 'growing economy' and is now a fully grown one, even if the immediate effects of this are not being felt.

One of the major reasons for this is the nature of the government, and the way it controls the spread of information. Transparency is extremely low in China, and investors are wary, correctly so, of investing in any Chinese company. While the likes of Alibaba prove that fully private enterprises can flourish, the fact is that it is far easier to grow in China when you have strong government ties.

Political leanings aside, this means that any investment in China is better off if it is done in a company that has good ties to the government and is in a critical area of growth. Chinese government is focusing its efforts on developing its technology. The country is seeking to move away from its image as a manufacturer of cheap toys and goods. Instead moving into the high tech space.

The rise of Huawei, a firm that was founded by a former high ranking Chinese soldier, in the 5G space is proof of this. All tech stocks receive patronage from the government, and Baidu is one of the beneficiaries of this. The company is virtually unheard of outside of China but within the country and in parts of SE Asia, it trounces Google completely.

Baidu is one of the largest search engines on the planet thanks to the volume of its users. Google is officially banned in China thanks to censorship issues, and this gives Baidu a near monopoly over the Chinese internet. As of current writing, the platform has over 700 million users. The staggering aspect is that this number represents just half of the Chinese population.

With internet coverage set to grow in China and with the government effectively favoring Baidu's monopoly over the internet and flow of information, the company is almost certainly going to witness an increase in the number of users over the next few decades.

Revenue Model

The business is a replica of Google, and as such Baidu's revenue model is the same. It relies on pay per click (PPC) advertising, and as the largest ad platform in China, its earnings have been rising steadily over the past decade. Recently, PPC revenue dropped thanks to increasing controls of ad standards, but once the dust settles and as advertisers adjust to the new standards, revenues should be back where they were.

Like Google, Baidu has long since moved away from its search engine roots and has become a full-fledged tech company. It is the only company in the world that has received a license to operate self-driving vehicles and currently operates a bus successfully within its campus.

It has also invested heavily in driverless cars, and over the next decade, these are expected to rollout. News is predictably bullish as it is with every Chinese news source, but there are signs that these news items are genuine. While these lines of business are not profitable or even collecting revenue at the moment, they do hold huge promise for the future.

In addition to the vehicles themselves, Baidu has also developed an open-source software named Apollo that can be used to program driverless cars. The business model here is the same as what Google did with the Android phone operating system, and the hope is that as more companies enter the space, Baidu can become the software provider of choice instead of getting into costly hardware investments.

As Google has YouTube, so does Baidu have iQiyi. Here, Baidu faces some pretty stiff competition. The first competitor is Tencent video, which is backed by the giant Tencent, and the second is Youku Tudou, which is owned by Alibaba. These three companies are present in the same space and engage in one form of state-sanctioned competition or another.

It appears that for now, Baidu is not favored in this race with Alibaba leading the way. One reason for this is that its platform is actually an amalgam of two earlier video platforms that were developed late in the previous decade. As a result, the company received an early boost in terms of the user base. However, Baidu's dominance of the search engine world does mean that it can compete with these other platforms even if it cannot dominate.

Ad revenue from the video-sharing platform is lower than PPC ads in search. This has as much to do with Baidu's lack of penetration as it has to do with how unsuitable video platforms are for the PPC model. After all, even YouTube barely makes any money and its ads aren't the most efficient.

iQiyi is much more than just a YouTube clone though. In fact, all of the Chinese video platforms can be seen as a combination of Netflix and YouTube. iQiyi is often dubbed the Netflix of China but this is simply because it's an easy way to explain what the platform is all about. It's a bit more than that as we've just described. It is also an online gaming platform that is a bit like Steam and Twitch where players can subscribe to play games as well as share their in game heroics across the network.

One of the fields that Baidu is spending a lot of money on is AI. Chinese firms have a massive head start on the rest of the world in terms of AI thanks to the surveillance that the government engages in. This gives them access to far more data than is available in other societies. Moral quandaries aside, Baidu is no different in this respect.

It has developed a voice assistant (think Alexa) called DuerOS which seamlessly works on smartphones and other smart devices. It is witnessing huge growth. While the company isn't clear on the user growth, one way of measuring this is via the growth in users of the app. This number grew by 21% over 2019 with previous years recording growth as well.

In addition to this, the number of voice queries on DuerOS grew fivefold to 4.2 billion queries per month. Currently, DuerOS is available on Baidu produced Xiaodu devices which span from speakers to smart displays. In the B2B space, Baidu has an AWS clone in Baidu Cloud which offers server space and IT infrastructure services to enterprises.

The company has a few diversified revenue streams but is still heavily reliant on the effectiveness of its PPC ads. In this regard, it is similar to Google, but like Google, the plan is to ramp up earnings from other areas of the business as technology continues to mature.

Performance

A major knock against Baidu is that its stock performance has been abysmal over 2019 and this was before the virus hit. However, this is just a reflection of the emotion driven selloff that afflicted its sector.

A big reason for the terrible performance was that all Chinese tech stocks were overvalued to begin with. The increasing growth and prominence of China as a technological hub prompted many investors to move into Chinese companies and tech were recipients of this money.

As a result, valuation levels grew to absurd levels. Consider that the stock is now selling at a 14x earnings multiple. For comparison's sake, Google is selling at 24x. This shows how grossly undervalued Baidu currently is and how the impact of the virus has been mispriced.

While it is true that a recession will impact Baidu's earnings, just how bad will the impact be on its core business? With physical stores shutting down, businesses will be forced to turn online. This leaves Baidu as the only viable outlet for advertising, and it already dominates 80% of the sector.

Thus, the domination is likely going to be extended moving forward. Over the short term, the company is addressing its cash needs by issuing debt to the tune of $1 billion in short term notes. This should see it tide over any recession concerns.

The Chinese government has been moving swiftly to contain the impact of the virus within the country. All of this means that the Chinese economy is likely to bounce back faster than the rest of the world, and as a result, Baidu's prospects will behave the same way. All in all, Baidu might be a bit more opaque than other Western companies, but this doesn't mean that it is incapable of growing its earnings.

The economics of its industry look good. Additionally, the political importance of the company in terms of information flow, Baidu is well set for the future.

Zuora

Market cap - $1.09 billion

52 week high/low - 23.04/6.21

Zuora (pronounced zoo-aura) is yet another stock that has taken a pounding over the past year. On the surface, all news surrounding this company is bad. It hasn't been able to turn a profit as yet, despite going public in 2018 and being founded back in 2007. Its business is in the B2B space which means that a lot of information surrounding it is loaded with technical jargon that is all but incomprehensible to the average investor.

The company was initially founded by two engineers K.V Rao and Cheng Zhou, who worked at WebEx at the time. Rao is the one who had the idea to build a platform that could handle SaaS billing models. These days, the SaaS billing system is everywhere, and from a consumer's perspective, it's pretty easy to handle.

You simply click a button that says subscribe and pay a monthly fee for the software service. However, from a technical standpoint, SaaS is a headache of gargantuan proportions. In 2007, most companies relied on billing their customers once for the product and delivering it. SaaS posed technical challenges to the very architecture of their databases.

Think of it like this: You've built a large mansion only to find that instead of building a single large house, there is greater demand for a number of smaller apartments. You can either tear down the mansion or modify the place to create some sort of a complex, but this isn't going to really do the trick.

Even if you do tear down the place and look to build smaller apartments on the land, who's going to design it for you? Remember that in this analogy, no one has ever built apartments (SaaS databases) before. Therefore, companies were forced to modify their existing databases, and this led to a number of things breaking.

This is what prompted Rao to brainstorm a solution along with Zhou, and they arrived at an initial solution. However, they lacked marketing skills and, as a result, could not convince venture capitalists to back them. This is where the current CEO Tien Tzuo came into the picture.

Tzuo was a big believer in the efficacy of subscription-based models, and as a senior executive at Salesforce, he was well aware of the challenges. Tzuo polished the original ideas and his contacts in the industry managed to land the funding needed, and thus Zuora was born.

While the original founders have since exited amicably, Tzuo continues to function as the chairman and CEO. He's seen as an evangelist for the subscription business model, and has even written a bestselling book on the topic. Zuora currently develops and manages custom solutions to handle subscription payments for their clients.

The problem is that, much like with the evangelist of electric cars, Tzuo's company doesn't make any money. Over the past year, Zuora's stock has dropped by 51%, which is a pretty epic fall for a company so many people expected great things from. So, what's really happening here, and why is Zuora still a great investment?

Business Economics

There's no denying that the subscription-based payment model is here to stay. Zuora happens to be suffering from the pioneer syndrome we previously mentioned. Being the first to the space, the company has had to deal with problems and unforeseeable circumstances every step of the way.

The fact that company revenues have grown every year despite these challenges is a testament to Tzuo's leadership and the ability of senior management to handle tough times. Zuora is a tough company to analyze because it's still effectively in a startup stage despite being a public company. Typically, companies with Zuora's financials don't go public but the lengthy bull market meant the Zuora went public a bit ahead of the curve.

This means that the best way to look at the financial of the company is by looking at its revenue and user growth. Profits might not be present right now, but with continued growth, Zuora stands to capture a significant portion of the market.

The simple reason for such optimism is that there is no other company of its size that poses a threat. Zuora moved first and moved fast in this space, and this gives it a clear head start in terms of technology as well as know-how. Low employee turnover has also meant that the company has done a good job of retaining its knowledge.

This experience is reflected in the diversity of its product lines. The original product that Zuora developed was Zuora billing. This is a turnkey solution for companies and large enterprises to easily migrate their existing one-time payment systems to a subscription-based model.

The other product Zuora integrates with its primary platform is Zuora RevPro which handles all of the accounting needs for subscription-based businesses. Accounting poses a particular headache when it comes to SaaS since GAAP rules specify certain methods in which regular payments need to be booked. It isn't as simple as recording the monthly payments that flow in. GAAP refers to Generally Accepted Accounting Principles that all American firms follow. These are guidelines that define how cash flow is meant to be accounted for on a company's books.

The appeal of RevPro goes beyond just tech-based enterprises. With the way payment methods are changing, the model is extending to pretty much every industry out there. A good example of this is Dollar Shave Club, which operates this model when it comes to men's shaving products.

Some of Zuora's other customers include Harley Davidson and Caterpillar. The revenue model is also quite straightforward. Zuora charges a flat fee plus a monthly volume-based fee. The fees are quite cheap and are far more economical for companies to adopt as opposed to designing their own solution.

All of this puts the spotlight squarely back on customer growth. Instead of charging four customers a quarter each to make a dollar, Zuora aims to charge 100 customers 100 pennies to make a dollar. One of the problems with Zuora's stock is that analysts aren't sure how to set expectations, which reveals one of the problems of an emotion-based market.

The company is being valued at its current level because it isn't meeting expectations. These expectations vary wildly, and as a result, the stock witnessed a lot of volatility. Its revenues grew by 15% the previous year, but despite this, the stock tanked 51%. The sole reason is that revenues didn't grow fast enough, not because there's anything wrong with the company.

It's a bit like receiving $100 and complaining that you didn't receive $1,000 when there was no indication that a payment of $1,000 was possible. These emotional corrections will smooth out over time as Zuora continues to grow. Growth is almost guaranteed thanks to the state of the subscription-based billing model. Meaning that Zuora is a solid long term play.

Intuitive Surgical

Market cap - $57.74 billion

52 week high/low - 619.00/350.00

Intuitive Surgical sits at the intersection of technology and medicine. Specifically, as the company's name suggests, it is focused on the field of robotic surgery. This field is a crowded one, and it is rife with competition despite the highly technical and specialized nature of the product.

The appeal of robotic surgery is easy to understand. A robotic arm cannot tire or make involuntary mistakes. Despite the term robotic in the name of the process, this doesn't mean that a robot is the one performing surgery. Instead, it is guided by a human being at all times. It's just that the process removes the possibility of involuntary human error.

The demand for robotic surgery first came from the military, which needed emergency medical procedures carried out on soldiers wounded in war zones. In such places, flying a specialist surgeon out would have put them at risk, and this is how Intuitive Surgical first began life.

It has been around for over 20 years now and continues to make money from defense contracts. Its patented DaVinci surgical system is one of the best in the industry. Intuitive is one of the pioneers that came through the tough times in this industry. Now that it's emerged as one of the leaders of a maturing space, it finds itself the target of competition.

This comes in the form of medical giants Medtronic and Stryker deciding to expand their robotic surgery business. Along with this, Johnson and Johnson have announced a partnership with Google to develop and run a wide variety of robotic surgery solutions in the market. All of these companies are far bigger, and it remains to be seen how Intuitive copes with this competition.

Despite all of this, the company has a well-established moat. Intuitive has network effects giving it a wide level of acceptance amongst surgeons. The DaVinci system is simple to use, by surgical standards, and its precision level is unmatched. The system made waves when Intuitive advertised it by performing surgery on a grape to demonstrate how precise the technology is.

The industry itself is witnessing huge growth, which explains why the giants of the sphere are looking at moving in. Studies indicate that patients who experienced surgery with the DaVinci system experienced lesser complications than those who opted for conventional methods.

In addition to this, regulatory approval for surgical robotics has been increasing, and unlike other fast-growing industries such as marijuana and sports betting, there are no hurdles in this regard. People will always need surgery, and as time progresses, robotics are certain to be embraced as acceptable solutions for this. This doesn't mean there are a few issues with Intuitive.

Valuation

One of the downsides of being valued as a tech stock is that a large degree of expectations of growth are factored into the price. This has been true of Intuitive during this decade. As their technology grew and as tech gained widespread exposure, the valuation of Intuitive rose in line with that of other tech companies.

This meant that the stock has been overvalued for a while now. It took an almighty tumble at the beginning of the year before bouncing back up. In this, it is hardly unique and many stocks have witnessed similar behavior. This means that for the first time in many years, Intuitive stock is priced according to its proper value.

This represents a great buying opportunity for investors. One of the reasons the stock went as high as it did was due to the fact that the DaVinci system has been increasingly adopted and as of this writing, the firm declared profits of $1.4 billion on $4.5 billion in sales.

This amount is more than enough to cover its entire cost of production and operating costs. For a company of its size, this is a truly remarkable achievement. The good news is that this number is only expected to increase over time. Over the past two years, net income has increased by 105%.

Of course, Intuitive needs to redirect a significant amount of money into research and development, and this will pose challenges. Typically, R&D efforts take time to bear fruit, and a wrong decision here can set the company back. However, it isn't as if Intuitive is the only company in this field that is running these risks.

All in all, its fortress-like balance sheet and existing moat make it an attractive investment for the long term.

PayPal

Market cap - $124.3 billion

52 week high/low - 124.45/82.07

We've mentioned Elon Musk a few times, and we're now going to highlight his earliest success. PayPal was created by combining Musk's venture X.com with co-founders Peter Thiel, Max Levchin and Luke Nosek's company Cofinity. The company X.com was renamed PayPal and went from strength to strength in the late 90s.

Shortly after its IPO, PayPal became a subsidiary of eBay. A remarkable fact about PayPal is that almost every single one of its original employees went on to found or become early investors in pretty much every Silicon Valley heavy-weight we hear about these days. In no particular order, companies such as Tesla, SpaceX, Facebook, Sequoia Capital, Flickr, Digg, LinkedIn, YouTube, Yelp and Reddit all trace their roots back to the original employees of PayPal.

All of this has given PayPal an even bigger reputational moat as the years go by. People want to work for the company thanks to the cult of personality that its founders have developed. The company continues to become even more bureaucratic in terms of the way it treats its customers and yet, the sheer weight of its brand name makes it pretty much the only payment processor of choice for a large majority of people.

PayPal is one of those rare companies that has had two IPOs. It was first bought by eBay after its first IPO in 2001, and in 2015, once it became clear that PayPal was eclipsing eBay in terms of sales and profits, the parent company decided to spin it off. Since being detached from eBay, the company has seen remarkable growth.

One of the reasons for PayPal's growth and continued success is the smart acquisition strategy that the company has followed over the years. Let's take a deeper look at why PayPal is such a great investment.

Sector Economics

The digital payments space is set to witness an explosion in activity thanks to the growing unpopularity of cash as a mode of payment. With increasing levels of digitization, governments are finding that extending this to cash and banking transactions helps them recover a greater amount of tax revenues that would have been lost otherwise.

The founding of cryptocurrencies is just the beginning. While cryptocurrencies have not been fully accepted and their exchange is still barred or full of hurdles in many places, governments have taken the hint and have effectively tried to turn their own currencies digital.

Scandinavian countries were some of the first to adopt this tactic. These days a cash payment in those countries attracts an additional cash handling charge at checkout counters. The norm is to usually charge a commission on credit card payments, but here it is reversed. Similar practices are followed in the Netherlands and parts of Western Europe.

The nature of the working economy is also playing a part in this. Clients and suppliers now exist across borders more than ever, and using tired old SWIFT or IBAN bank transfers is a thing of the past. These attract higher levels of fees and also require you to input and set up beneficiaries in your own bank's system. Even after all of this, there is the prospect of the money being routed to the incorrect account.

All of these hindrances have left the payments space wide open for digital solutions to rush into. Banks have responded to this threat by doing nothing and have instead leaned back on their primary cash cow of lending to generate profits. This means that the number of restrictions on digital payments grows less day by day, and cash as a means of transaction will soon be a thing of the past.

Moat

PayPal is the founder of digital payments, and as a result, everyone associates the company with this activity. Small businesses prefer to use PayPal since it's an easy way to receive money without involving tedious bank transfers. Retailers, in general, understand that accepting PayPal is better than not accepting it.

The moat surrounding PayPal is so strong that merchants are willing to accept payments on it despite having to pay high fees. There simply is no other solution at the moment. This is especially true when it comes to the online space. Websites that accept money of any kind integrate PayPal into their structure since users find it best to pay this way.

Acquisitions

As we mentioned earlier, the lack of options in the online payment space is partly because of the acquisitions that PayPal has carried out. One of the best acquisitions PayPal has carried out is with Venmo. Venmo dominates the space of peer to peer payments and is preferred far more than bank transfers.

The app currently has over 40 million accounts and, in the fourth quarter of 2019 handled $29 billion worth of transactions, which comfortably puts it in the lead in p2p payments. This also represents a growth of 56% when compared to the previous year.

While Venmo is used primarily for in-country transactions, Xoom is the platform of choice for cross border transactions. The service is used for far more than money transfers and cash pickups. Xoom also allows its users to recharge mobile phones' balances. Xoom is focused on the phone payments space and faces competition in less developed countries, but as of now, it is the dominant player in South and Central America.

PayPal's acquisition of Honey might not have made waves, but it was a shrewd play to capture a part of the bargain shopping space. The app functions as a browser add-on and as the user shops, it automatically generates coupons that can save money. While the app isn't fully monetized as yet, the tough times that lie ahead certainly bode well for the increase of user numbers.

While Honey didn't make headlines, PayPal's acquisition of MercadoLibre most certainly did. Mercado is South America's largest e-commerce website and far outstrips Amazon in that part of the world. Given the steady rise in users as well as increasing preference for online solutions, PayPal's acquisition price of $750 million seems a pittance to pay for the company.

For comparison's sake, the company generated $1.46 billion in revenue in Brazil alone in 2019.

Digital Nature

PayPal is unique in that, unlike its competitors such as Square, it doesn't have or depend on any in-person interaction. Square is focused more on developing point of sale solutions for merchants, but PayPal has famously stayed away from the business choosing instead to focus only on online payments.

Given the virus outbreak that the world has witnessed recently, this seems like a good decision. While PayPal certainly didn't predict the outbreak, it deserves credit for understanding its business strengths and for sticking to it despite seemingly missing out on an important piece of the puzzle.

While this does increase its exposure to the digital space, and therefore increases its risks. The company is the oldest player in the space and has a wealth of experience to deal with any issues. Its presence around the world is also another sign of strength since it is well versed at this point in handling all regulatory hurdles that authorities put in place.

This places a high cost for newcomers to overcome and allows PayPal to effectively function as a monopoly.

Finances

While Visa and MasterCard are not traditional competitors of PayPal, comparing their financials to PayPal is far more instructive. This is because when it comes to online payments, these three are the only options available for the most part. Given PayPal's focus on the online payments space and the credit card companies' domination of in-person payment methods, you'd expect PayPal to suffer in comparison.

However, this isn't true. Visa carries a far greater debt load on its balance sheet with assets just 1.3x debt. PayPal, on the other hand, is far less leveraged with assets at 7.8x debt. This means it is better suited to handle a downturn. The virus has disrupted the majority of credit card payments due to lockdown measures.

However, PayPal remains unaffected throughout all of this, and even if it were affected, it wouldn't need to worry about creditors. It is in a great financial position.

Small Business

PayPal has been expanding into the lending space and has recently received approval to fund SBA loans through its brand PayPal Credit. This is a major step forward for the company and marks the first time a payment processor is effectively functioning as a bank. While it remains to be seen how PayPal handles the vastly different business, investors don't have too much to worry about.

First off, the size of the business is far smaller than the primary business and given its strong balance sheet, PayPal can afford to take a few risks. Given the economic climate that is likely to exist once lockdown measures lift, there will be a huge demand for loans and being a non-traditional lender will give PayPal a boost in terms of demand.

Risk

A potential risk that PayPal faces is from a phenomenon and not a single company. Blockchain technology has been disrupting existing security measures, and the demand for it grows as the days go by. PayPal is behind the curve with regard to this, and it does face significant security challenges.

This is even more relevant if it's going to be providing loans. The risk here is public perception. While the company hasn't faced any major data breaches, its growing size and reliance on seemingly outdated technology might cause an erosion of trust. As it is, PayPal is not well-liked amongst those who depend on it to receive payments from customers.

The lack of choice is what keeps merchants coming back. If consumers start feeling this way, then the company is in for a tough time. These risks are technological ones and given PayPal's expertise in the space; we do trust that the company will handle it well. Its sheer size as well as its longevity, make it even more likely that PayPal will be a great company for many years to come.

Innovative Industrial Properties

Market cap - $1.24billion

52 week high/low - 139.53/40.21

Marijuana and medical cannabis have made a huge splash in recent years. The legalization of cannabis in select states in the United States and Canada has opened an entire market for investors to benefit from. The first instinct of many people was to invest in cannabis growers.

Initially, the returns were fantastic. Cannabis stocks rose exponentially for a period of two years but the party ended last year. These stocks fell to such an extent that almost all of them are back to their IPO levels. All in all, while the industry itself has been growing, increasing competition and a strangely efficient black market have ensured that individual companies are facing stiff headwinds.

All of this sounds quite familiar to business historians. We've already mentioned how savvy investors got rich during the gold rush. The same 2nd order consequences principle applies here as well. While everyone is scrambling in a mad dash to grow marijuana and sell them to a public that has been demanding it for years, savvy investors recognize the things that all of these companies need.

There really are two needs when speaking of growing marijuana: Fertilizer and land. As far as fertilizer goes, it isn't as if the plant needs anything special, so there's not much of a moat to be found there. This leaves land, and this is what brings us to marijuana REITs. We've mentioned REITs before when speaking of Crown Castle and how these companies are obligated to pay out 90% of their net cash earnings to their investors.

Innovative Industrial Properties (Innovative) has what is probably the most boring name a company can have, but don't let that put you off. It has a simple business model and utilizes its industry advantages well. It leases land to marijuana growers and earns the rent paid on it. The best part is that the high demand for land to grow marijuana on means that the lease payments are much higher than what you would find when leasing farmland or office space.

This is reflected in the high dividend yield that the company offers its investors. As of current writing, this is at 5.8%, which is almost double that of what a diversified REIT would pay. A diversified REIT invests in a portfolio of properties across functions such as rental real estate, commercial real estate, farmland, hospitals. In short, marijuana suited land is fetching almost double the yield of regular real estate. This is truly a spectacular return.

Lease Structures

One of the advantages that strict legislation in marijuana provides is that lease agreements can be changed from what their terms usually are. This means that all of the properties Innovative provides for lease requires the tenant to pay not just the rent but also the property taxes and maintenance. In industry parlance, such leases are referred to as triple net leases.

This leads to Innovative earning an average cap rate of 13% on its properties. Cap rate refers to the cash return REITs make after all expenses are accounted for. For comparison's sake, the average cap rate of a commercial REIT that leases office buildings is 4%.

This allows Innovative to pay off its mortgage within a seven-year period and after that everything is a profit. We must mention that cap rates are this high right now due to the lack of federal legality. This allows Innovative to charge higher than normal market rates for its properties.

We expect that cap rates will return to normal once legality kicks in across the board. For now, though, rates remain high. The structure of the lease also allows Innovative to incur reduced costs on its properties. Typically, REIT companies have to carry out maintenance and upkeep of their properties.

In Innovative's case, their triple net leases mean that costs are low. While this lowers rental payment as well, it isn't as if it sinks to below market price levels.

Risks

Given that the marijuana industry, at least the legal one, is still immature, there are significant risks the company faces. While it has isolated itself from the majority of fluctuations in the business by becoming a supplier, there are risks nonetheless. Strangely enough, legislation is what provides a threat.

Federal legislation will see rents dropping and leases returning to regular terms, and this will reduce the income that Innovative earns. Growth is what will offset this drop, and in this regard, the company has been doing a great job. It owns over 3.8 million acres of rentable property across the United States and given the high cash on cash return the company earns; expansion is not going to be a problem.

As of now, the company not only pays a high dividend but also pays it quarterly. We expect this amount to decrease a bit as time goes on. These are regular risks that all REITs are exposed to. As long as Innovative sticks to its expertise in the marijuana field and resists the temptation to move into something else, its prospects remain great, and it is a great way to get exposure to the marijuana industry, without the risks of directly investing in growers.

Skyworks Solutions

Market cap - $15.34 billion

52 week high/low - 128.48/66.29

This is yet another stock that is going to feel the boost that 5G will bring this year. 5G is one of the most anticipated technological advances the markets have witnessed in a long time, and that's saying a lot. The technology will provide up to 100 times the speeds of current 4G/LTE networks.

Such speeds are necessary for the development of the internet of things related devices such as smart appliances and driverless cars. Skyworks is a company that manufactures RC chips for smartphone manufacturers and home automation manufacturers. In other words, the semiconductor chips that are a part of every 5G electronic device will likely come from Skyworks.

Currently, 5G phones are expected to comprise 12% of the smartphone market, with the number doubling in 2021 as the technology catches on. This means that the best days for Skyworks are yet to come. Currently, it is a supplier to Apple and Huawei, and if you've been paying attention to the 5G political picture thus far, you'll notice that this is a problem.

The trade war with China and the banning of Huawei from doing business with all American entities has meant that Skyworks has seen its revenues take a hit. This has led to its stock tumbling as the current administration's trade war continues to twist and turn without an end in sight.

However, this isn't bad news for Skyworks as far as the long term is concerned. The technology itself isn't going anywhere, and the company remains the leader in its space. It is more likely than not that increasing demand from consumers will lead to more customers for Skyworks and the reliance on Huawei will be a thing of the past.

To offset this loss, the company has begun including smartphone makers Oppo, Vivo and Xiaomi to increase revenues. Its largest customer remains Apple, and this is a double-edged sword. First off, no company wins the business of Apple unless it happens to have exceptional quality, and Skyworks has been the preferred supplier for many years now.

However, its fortunes are joined at the hip with Apple's, and if the latter faces any challenges with its business, then Skyworks will likely sink with it. Given Apple's size, this is an unlikely event but it remains a risk nonetheless.

Valuation

The best part of Skyworks is that the company is in an extremely sound financial position when compared to its other 5G peers. It has virtually zero debt on its balance sheet, and this puts it in prime position to expand and take more risks should the need arise.

It isn't just the past year but in fact, the last five years that have witnessed debt-free growth. The current pandemic has forced some of its competitors to cut back but Skyworks is now free to expand and conduct business as it pleases. The stock has suffered due to overvaluation that all 5G stocks were subject to.

As we mentioned earlier, a lot of 5G stocks were selling at inflated prices, and once the bubble burst earlier this year, all of these stocks came tumbling down. Skyworks is no different. It got caught up in the general hysteria surrounding the sector and is now selling at a very attractive earnings multiple of 19x.

The main strength of Skyworks is its management without a doubt. They are honest to a point and are incredibly frank when discussing the company's shortcomings on earnings calls.

However, this only reaffirms that the management knows what it's doing, and being conservative in what is an extremely popular sector is good for the long run. All of these will stand Skyworks in good stead, and investors will benefit from this.

Skyworks meets all of our investment criteria, and by reviewing all of them, you'll understand why we highly recommend Skyworks as a long term investment.

This brings to an end our look at the 20 best stocks for you to hold for the next 20 years. All of these companies are wonderful investments, and you'll do well to buy into them at fair prices. Speaking of fair prices, let's move on to an important section of this book - How to value a business.

7

COMPANY VALUATION 101

I t's all well and good choosing a great company to invest in, but if you pay too much, then your returns are greatly impacted.

For example, if you buy Disney at $100/share, when the price hits $150, your return will be 50%. However, if you buy at $125/share, when the price hits $150, your return will only be 20%.

Which leads us to the million dollar question: What is a fair price to pay for a company? There are hundreds of different methods of valuing companies, but we like to keep things simple. You shouldn't need to spend hundreds of dollars on advanced stock screening services, when the most important numbers are available for free on websites like Yahoo Finance or MSN Money.

Here are the numbers we take into account when valuing a business, with a brief definition for each one. We use these after we've done our research on a company and decide that it is worth investing in.

This is so we can determine what is a fair price to pay for 1 share of the business today.

Earnings Per Share (EPS): A company's net income divided by the number of shares available. The higher the better.

Price to Earnings (PE) Ratio: A company's current stock price divided by its Earnings Per Share. The lower the better.

10 Year Equity Growth Rate: This is a calculation popularized by investor and author Phil Town. It refers to the EPS multiplied by the projected growth rate of the company.

Minimum Acceptable Rate of Return: This is the annual growth in a stock you would be happy with. For this, we like to choose a 12% return. We settled on 12% as we want greater returns than the market rate (An average of 9.69% over 50 years). If we were satisfied with market average returns, then we would just buy index funds instead of individual companies. We don't go higher than 12% because we need to take the next metric into account. If you are aiming for higher returns, we also recommend using a higher margin of safety.

Margin of Safety: This refers to a share price being below a businesses' intrinsic value. We want prices to be below intrinsic value to minimize our risk. This is in case our estimates were either incorrect or biased. Margin of Safety also accounts for our "weathering the storm" criteria in chapter 4. If you are aiming for higher annual returns, we also recommend using a higher margin of safety.

These 5 factors combined give us 2 important numbers. A 10 year stock price target and a fair number to pay for that same company today.

When we were writing the first (and second, and third, and fourth) draft of this book, this chapter was the most challenging. We found that the biggest problem with investing books is that it's incredibly challenging to give easy to understand valuation examples in book format. Especially inside an eBook with limited screen space. Even if the valuation models are clear at the time, it was tough for readers to use the information to do their own analysis on companies they were researching.

So we found a solution.

To make things easy for you, we've compiled a free company valuation spread-sheet with all the necessary formulas already inserted. So all you have to do is input the corresponding numbers for the company, and the valuation sheet will tell you whether the company is fairly valued, undervalued or overvalued.

You can download your spreadsheet by using the link below. It's completely free; you don't even need to give your email address.

We've also included our free *Company Valuation 101* video course. This will show you how to use the spreadsheet to complement your own research, as well as the free resources we use to find the 5 important company metrics we discussed earlier in this chapter.

Inside the course we also show you examples of how we use the sheet to value some of the companies listed in the previous chapter.

To get your spreadsheet and video course go to

https://freemanpublications.com/valuation101

8

THE TWO MOST EFFICIENT STOCK BUYING STRATEGIES

W hen it comes to investing your money in the market, there are two ways you can go about doing so. The first is to invest everything you have all at once, and the other is to divide your initial investment into smaller portions. The former method is referred to as lump-sum investing (LS) and the latter is called dollar-cost averaging (DCA).

We'll say this right off the bat: Lump-sum investing is always better. However, there are many ways in which investors complicate the process and often end up confusing LS for DCA. Let's begin by clearly illustrating how LS and DCA work.

Lump Sum or Dollar Cost Averaging?

Let's say you have $10,000 to invest. Should you invest all of it at once or should you break it up into smaller investments of $1,000 each and invest these over a period of 10 months? The former method is LS and the latter is DCA.

DCA is not the following: Let's say you receive a steady cash flow of $1,000 per month through your savings after paying for your living expenses. You then invest $1,000 into the market every month like clockwork. This is not DCA. In fact, this is LS investing. We wish to highlight this because many people confuse this for being DCA.

The primary difference between LS and DCA is that with the latter, you're not fully invested in the market. You're setting aside some money as cash at all times. The reasoning behind doing this is that by breaking your investment into smaller parts, you're reducing your risk over a longer period.

For example, if the market declines between months two and six in our previous example, your $1,000 investments over this time will result in you buying stocks at lower prices. This, in turn, reduces your average purchase price, and therefore, you increase the potential size of your capital gains whenever the stock moves upwards.

This works in theory, but it ignores two practical aspects of investing. First, it assumes that the investor practicing the LS method will never invest their money back into the market ever again. Second, it assumes that markets will fall over the short term and that the investor can accurately predict how long they'll fall for.

In other words: If you invest your $10,000 all at once. This is hardly going to be your only stock investment over your lifetime. Who's to say that when you decide to enter the market once again, the market prices will not be low? There's no way to predict this. The DCA reasoning assumes that by investing small amounts over time, you'll reduce your risk.

But what is the appropriate timeline for you to divide your investments into? Should you invest $10,000 over a year? Two years? A decade? This is again, impossible to predict. However, all of this pales in comparison to the real disadvantage of DCA, which is opportunity cost.

Missing Out on Gains

Let's say you invest $10,000 fully into the market. We've already established that the stock market rises by an average of seven percent over the long term. Let's also assume that your investment horizon is 20 years. At the end of this time, your investment will have grown to $38,696.

Now, let's say you practice extreme DCA and divide your $10,000 investment into equal sums and invest it every year for 20 years. This means you'll invest $500 every year. We don't need to run the numbers to prove that this is a losing strategy. With lesser money invested, you're going to be losing out on long term appreciation of capital as well as becoming a victim to inflation. This is where DCA falls horribly short.

You might argue that we're using the assumed return rate of 7% and aren't taking into consideration the fact that the average purchase price might decrease thanks to market declines during this 20 year period. A study that compared the two investing methods using market data from 1960 until 2019 indicates that DCA underperforms lump-sum investing 80% of the time over this period (Maggiulli, 2020).

We must note that DCA outperforms LS during market slumps, as you might expect. However, once the market recovers, LS begins outperforming DCA dramatically and the deficit in performance is erased quickly.

All of this means that instead of asking yourself which method is better when it comes to investing. Focus on having as much of your money invested for as long as possible. This is how returns are earned. This is how you can access greater compounding power. As you know, compounding becomes more powerful the longer you apply it.

Therefore, if you have a large sum of money to invest right now, invest all of it in fairly valued companies. We must emphasize that this doesn't mean putting everything into a single company. You must diversify your investments and use ETFs or mutual funds if necessary. Focus on investing whatever you can, whenever you can. If you have a steady cash flow that allows you to invest money in the market at regular intervals, then do so. Leaving your money sitting on the sidelines doing nothing is the worst possible thing you can do with it.

DRIP

DRIP stands for dividend reinvestment plan. This is a great way to automate your investing and use the power of dividends to boost your returns. They're available on pretty much every dividend paying single, and you're better off opting for them most of the time.

Here's how a DRIP works: When you receive a dividend payment, you can choose to receive it in cash or reinvest that money to buy even more of the stock via a DRIP. By choosing the DRIP option, your broker automatically buys the equivalent amount of shares of stock, and your stock holding increases.

This, in turn, will increase the amount of dividends you'll earn the next time and by reinvesting that sum, you'll increase your stock holding, and this will further increase your dividend and so on.

For example, let's say you own a single share of a stock for $100. This stock pays you a dividend of $2 and you choose the DRIP option. Your broker will buy a fraction of share that is worth $2. Your total number of shares will increase to 1.02 after this. Fractional shares can be bought only via DRIPs. If you receive the dividend as cash and then try to purchase $2 worth of a $100 stock, you won't be able to buy it.

Now that the size of your holding is 1.02 shares, your dividend payment will be slightly greater than before. Assuming the stock still pays $2 per share in dividends, you'll now receive $2.04. If you reinvest this, you'll now own 1.04 shares (up from 1.02). Thus, your dividend payment–as well as your stock holding–increased in number.

The best part about a DRIP is that there are no costs associated with buying these fractional shares. Thus, you get more bang for your buck. Reducing costs has a dramatic effect on overall returns, thanks to compounding. By not paying costs, you'll allow more of your money to compound and are thus capturing greater growth.

The other great aspect of DRIPs is that some companies offer discounts on purchase prices if you choose to invest via a DRIP. Often you can expect a discount of up to 10%. Over time, this will massively boost your capital gains as well as your dividend payment amounts since you'll be able to buy more shares.

In our previous example, additional shares of 0.02 might seem paltry but understand that this assumes prices remain stable. If stock prices decrease, you'll be buying even more shares. When the upswing happens, your gains will proportionally increase. Also, DRIPs work best over time, and this is perfectly in line with the investment principles we outlined previously.

There are a couple of disadvantages you must be aware of when it comes to DRIPs. The first one is that you're not going to be in total control of your money. As long as you've chosen to opt for the DRIP, you're not going to receive the cash into your account. It'll be reinvested all by itself, and this will make some people uncomfortable. If you want to implement a set and forget investment strategy, though, this is the best option for you to choose.

The biggest disadvantage has to do with taxes, but even this isn't as bad as it sounds. Since you won't be receiving money into your account, you might be tempted to think that you don't owe any taxes. However, you will still have to pay taxes on your dividend amounts, and being unaware of this can lead to some nasty surprises during tax time.

Just remember that even if you reinvest the entire sum automatically, you're still liable to pay taxes on your dividend income.

9

MUTUAL FUNDS VERSUS ETFS VERSUS INDIVIDUAL STOCKS

We've only spoken about individual stocks up to this point, but there are other investing options as well. When it comes to choosing which market instruments you want to invest in, you'll typically end up choosing one of these three. There are some differences between them, and you need to learn these in order to make the best choice. Your choice of instrument comes down to your risk outlook as well as your comfort level with respect to backing your stock picks.

Let's begin by looking at what mutual funds are and how they work.

Mutual Funds

Mutual funds are one of the oldest investment vehicles that have been in the market. These are issued by financial corporations. Here's how they work: The corporation creates a fund with a certain investment mandate. This could be anything from capturing dividends in small-cap stocks to buying the largest stocks in a certain country, or to create a well-diversified portfolio that invests in everything.

A single unit in the fund is effectively what a share is when speaking of a stock purchase. The fund invests the money it has into stocks of various companies, and all of these underlying stocks have a certain value. When we add these individual values together, we arrive at the total asset value of the fund.

Dividing the total asset value by the number of units gives us the unit price or NAV. The NAV is repriced at the end of every day. This is because the asset value changes depending on the share prices of the underlying stocks.

For example, if mutual fund A owns one share of stock X and one share of stock Y, both of which are priced at $1 each, the NAV is $2. If the prices of X and Y rise to $2, the NAV is now $4.

Since prices keep fluctuating throughout the day, there's no point in calculating the NAV in real time. This is why it is done at the end of the day. During market hours, you can buy mutual fund units, but you'll be purchasing them at the previous day's NAV. There are a few things you must keep in mind when purchasing mutual fund units.

Their objective is to beat the market, and thus, the manager will charge fees that are higher than the other options listed in this chapter. On average, you can expect to pay between 0.5-2% of gains as fees. In addition to this, there are so-called "loading fees."

A front-loading fee is one that is charged when you buy units. The fund manager will deduct a certain amount from your principal, and this will reduce your potential gains. A back-loading fee is charged when you redeem or sell your units. Some funds charge constant load fees, which is to say that they charge maintenance fees during the lifetime of your investment.

Keep in mind that a mutual fund can either charge all of these fees or some combination of them. Due to investors' increased sensitivity to fees, some mutual funds offer no-load features and have you pay just the fee on whatever gains you make. Typically, no-load funds have higher performance fees.

The best way to get a handle on performance fees is to look at the expense ratio. This number is calculated by dividing the total cost of running the fund by the total assets. Keep in mind that expense ratios don't always include loading fees.

One advantage of mutual funds is that if you choose to buy an in house fund from your broker (a fund that is run by the brokerage itself) you'll likely pay zero commissions on it. This will reduce your investment costs in the long run. Mutual funds don't make the most sense these days as an investment.

Despite certain advantages, this is primarily due to the presence of the next option we'll discuss. However, there are a few exceptional ones you can invest in. It's just that finding them is tough.

Exchange-Traded Funds

ETFs were born from a need to reduce investment expenses. Mutual fund loading fees tend to reduce gains quite a bit. ETFs trade just like regular stocks do in the market. In other words, unlike with mutual funds, you'll see their prices fluctuate up and down intraday.

In terms of structure, ETFs are built just like mutual funds are. They're issued by large corporations and can have a number of investment objectives. In fact, compared to mutual funds, ETFs have a larger number of objectives.

For example, you can buy so-called inverse ETFs. These ETFs increase in price as market prices decline. You can buy an inverse ETF for a particular sector or the entire market. Then there are leveraged ETFs that move in a given direction faster than their underlying stocks. For example, if you buy a 2X leveraged broad market ETF, the ETF will rise at twice speed of the underlying market. On the other hand, it will fall just as fast, so it's not as if these aren't without risk.

You will also find inverse leveraged ETFs, so as you can see, it's possible to get quite complicated with these things. With that being said, you can invest in ETFs that aim to simply capture the average return of an index or a group of stocks. For example, you can buy an ETF that aims to capture the performance of a group of dividend-paying stocks.

ETFs have expense ratios as well, but the ones that aim to capture average market performance have lower expense ratios. These typically are under 1%, so they're a lot cheaper to maintain than mutual funds, and this boosts your gains over the long term. When it comes to ETFs it's best to keep it simple and not opt for ones that have obscure investment strategies.

This is because many ETFs are created by investment banks to find people to take the other side of trades that hedge funds wish to take (Blitz, 2017). For example, if a hedge fund approaches their investment bank (their brokers) and wishes to create a portfolio that they wish to short (profit when the prices decrease). They need to borrow money from the bank to invest in this portfolio. The bank then has to find someone else to take the other side of this trade. If they fail to find any institutional investors to take this bet, they often end up creating an ETF that contains the same underlying stocks and is leveraged. Thus, you might end up buying this leveraged, long ETF while the hedge fund is on the other side of your trade. As prices decrease, you're unlikely to be able to exit this investment since they're not going to be heavily marketed, and thus, fewer people will be trading them.

You can buy ETFs that mimic hedge fund strategies, but you must conduct thorough research to see if these strategies are based on sound investment principles.

FREEMAN INVESTING RULE #11

NOT ALL ETFS ARE CREATED EQUAL. ENSURE YOU KNOW HOW THE FUND OPERATES BEFORE YOU INVEST IN ONE.

Taxes

One advantage of ETFs is that their tax profile is a bit easier to handle than that of mutual funds. Mutual funds often return capital gains as distributions to their investors. Thus, you'll find yourself paying capital gains on your dividends from the fund, even if you haven't sold a single unit. This does complicate the calculation of your taxes when the time comes.

In contrast, ETFs don't distribute capital gains back to their investors. You'll pay capital gains only when you sell your investment for a profit. The interim distributions are taxed as dividends are. For example, if your dividend distribution contains a portion of international stock dividends, domestic dividends, and REIT payments, your 1099-DIV from your broker will break all of this down clearly, and you'll pay taxes on these portions as per IRS rules.

As with mutual funds, you don't have control over the way your money is invested. The fund manager is the one that decides where your money goes. Your comfort level with this depends on the kind of approach you're taking in the market. This is a good time to highlight the differences between passive and active investing.

Passive Versus Active

Passive investing refers to when an investor simply sits back and aims to capture the average performance of the market. In other words, you invest in an ETF that tracks the S&P 500 index, and your investment is tied to its performance. This way, you can capture the broad market performance over the long run. Since the market will increase in size over this time, you're guaranteed to capture these gains.

Your downside risk is also significantly limited since the ETF is diversified. After all, it holds shares in every company that is a part of the index. While a single stock might decrease in value, it's unlikely that every single stock is going to fall all at once over the long term.

The flip side is that you're going to earn whatever the market earns and will not outperform it. However, do keep in mind that this brings ample peace of mind. Contrast this with active investing where you're concentrating your investment into a few stocks with the aim of capturing huge capital gains.

While your potential gains are high, so is your downside risk. As we explained in Chapter 5, with a highly concentrated portfolio, there is a greater risk that all of your investments could decline in value. You'll also need to remain on top of the news surrounding the stock. All in all, both options have their pros and cons, and it comes down to what sort of risk you're willing to undertake.

If you feel that you cannot stomach the thought of long term losses, then you're probably better off following a fully passive model. For most investors, though, a hybrid model works best. This is what we've suggested in this book. You'll be investing in common stocks that have been identified using sound principles for the long term.

By investing in individual stocks, you won't be paying any management fees either. After all, you're investing in them by yourself, so why would you need to pay anyone? If your broker charges commissions, you'll be paying this amount, of course. Best of all, you won't be losing the opportunity to buy an undervalued stock like you would if you invest in an ETF.

"A LOT OF PEOPLE WITH HIGH IQS ARE TERRIBLE INVESTORS BECAUSE THEY'VE GOT TERRIBLE TEMPERAMENTS. AND THAT IS WHY WE SAY THAT HAVING A CERTAIN KIND OF TEMPERAMENT IS MORE IMPORTANT THAN BRAINS. YOU NEED TO KEEP RAW IRRATIONAL EMOTION UNDER CONTROL. YOU NEED PATIENCE AND DISCIPLINE AND AN ABILITY TO TAKE LOSSES AND ADVERSITY WITHOUT GOING CRAZY. YOU NEED AN ABILITY TO NOT BE DRIVEN CRAZY BY EXTREME SUCCESS."

- Charlie Munger

10

THE MOST IMPORTANT INGREDIENT OF SUCCESSFUL INVESTING

What is the key to your long term investment success? It all comes down to your ability to hold onto your investment even when the market declines. This is arguably the most important principle of successful investing, and many inexperienced investors fail this test because of the way they think about the markets.

The Difference Between Realized and Unrealized Returns

A common mistake people make when thinking about their stock investments is that they confuse unrealized gains for realized ones. Realized gains or losses refer to the cash return or loss you incur on your investments. If you bought something for $10 and sold it for $15, you've earned a realized gain of $5.

However, if you've bought something for $10 and its price is now sitting at $7, you have an unrealized loss of $3. In other words, you haven't lost any money as yet. The problem is that most people see the red $3 in their investment accounts and think that they're $3 poorer and hurry to sell in case they 'lose' even more.

FREEMAN INVESTING RULE #12

NO GAINS OR LOSSES ARE REAL UNTIL YOU SELL

People sell for all kinds of reasons, most of them emotional ones. You might switch to your favorite financial channel and see that everything is falling and that 'investors have lost $1 trillion in value' or some such nonsensical headline. These numbers are a picture of the unrealized losses in the market. You will realize them only by selling your investment.

Over the short term, emotions are what drive market prices. The father of value investing, Benjamin Graham coined a term to describe this phenomenon. He created a persona called Mr. Market to represent how the market behaves. Mr. Market is an extremely irrational person, and every day, he comes up to you and offers you prices for his products.

One day he might come to you and tell you that Coca-Cola stock is worth $2,000. The next day, he'll be supremely dejected for some reason and will offer to sell you Coca-Cola for $80. The notion that a giant of a company such as Coca-Cola can have such huge fluctuations in value over a single day makes no sense to him. He listens to his emotions, and that's it.

Many people get carried away by the turmoil that Mr. Market experiences. They believe his words when he tells them that everything is going to fall apart. They believe him when he tells them that COVID-19 is going to result in Chinese hegemony over the U.S for the foreseeable future and that 5G marks the complete destruction of all American enterprise and so on.

They listen to these notions and invest in unknown Chinese stocks and then wonder why they've ended up losing all of their money. We're not saying that Chinese stocks are bad. The point is that following your emotions when investing and not taking a look at the business is a surefire way to lose money.

Law of Averages

The companies mentioned in this book are in a great position to perform well over the next two decades. Will *all* of them fulfill this promise? Probably not. Business is an uncertain thing, to begin with, and no one can ever promise sure-fire returns. However, the objective here is to line up as many factors in our favor as possible and then let the probabilities take over.

One company might not work out. Two might not. But all 20? This is pretty unlikely. The probabilities tell us this. Think of it this way: If you're tossing a coin, you know that you have a 50% chance of calling the result correctly. Does this mean you'll be right every single time if you call heads? Probably not.

However, can you reasonably guess how many times you'll be right over 1,000 coin flips? Yes, you can. You'll be right calling heads roughly 500 times. How about 10,000? In this case, you can be even more certain since the longer you flip the coin, the more you give the probabilities a chance to work out.

It's the same with building a stock portfolio. Invest in sound companies with a long term vision and sit back and let it do its thing.

Emotions are not Facts

On February 19th, Duke played North Carolina in a college basketball matchup that always draws a ton of attention. Duke's star player and future number one NBA draft pick Zion Williamson tried pivoting two minutes into the game and discovered himself on the floor shortly thereafter. It turns out, his Nike shoe had exploded.

By exploded, we mean exploded. It didn't tear or come apart at the seams. One side of his shoe literally burst open, and Williamson was done for the game. The next day, a ton of negative press followed. It turns out that Nike's shoes were making a habit of exploding during critical times.

The press accused Nike of downplaying the incident, and soon, financial news was full of speculation as to whether Nike was now a good short or whether its stock was overvalued. In the hysteria, everyone forgot to ask a simple question: Was this crisis large enough for an entire generation of NBA and sports fans to dump Nike? Would they really dump the brand that owned the Jordan brand of shoes? Can a single exploding shoe really sink a $100 billion-dollar company?

Similar hysteria surrounds Disney at the moment, as we've already outlined. Basing your investment decisions on such short term emotional cues is a surefire way to lose money. Always keep the principles we've outlined in mind before making any decision.

Personal Finances

A good way to minimize your chances of doing something irrational is to avoid any chances of being so. This means you need to have your personal finances in order before investing in the market, as we've already mentioned. If you feel the need to make quick money from the market, you're unlikely to succeed. We refer to our earlier quote about the best way to make $1 million quickly in the stock market. Start with $2 million and go from there.

For example, if you find that you're short of cash to pay your phone bills, you're more likely to sell your investment holdings to raise cash. Eliminating the need for this cash is the best option to pursue. It is best to save at least three months' worth of living expenses along with any emergency cash you might need.

Do not invest money that you might need for the next ten years, at the very least. This way, you'll be able to stay out of your own way and won't sabotage yourself. Do not look at your investments as a savings account that you can tap into in times of need. This will lead you to sell at lows and buy at highs, which is the opposite of what you should do to make money.

Another point to remember is that if your investment principles are sound, and if the original conditions that caused you to invest in the company still exist, then declining stock prices are good news for you. This allows you to get into the stock at discounted prices. Often, investors look at it the other way and see falling market prices as proof that they were wrong.

Use intelligent investment principles, and you'll find that stock market investment will work wonders for you over the long run.

11

WHEN TO SELL

I f you've followed the lesson on unrealized and realized gains properly, you'll have understood that selling is what determines your profit or loss. With this in mind, when should you sell? Most investors get the selling aspect of their investment all wrong and end up selling right when they should be buying.

The question of selling can quickly become a complicated one if you take your life events into account. This chapter aims to simplify the question for you, and by the end of it, you'll have a good idea of how you need to approach this question.

Reasons to Sell

Broadly speaking, there are just three reasons for which you should be selling your stocks:

1. Investment reasons no longer exist
2. Compromised management
3. Better opportunities

Investment Reasons no Longer Exist

You've invested in a stock for a particular reason. Let's say you liked its prospects given the upcoming 5G revolution and think that the company is well placed to take advantage of this. You also notice that the stock is selling at a relatively cheap price, given these prospects and buy in wholeheartedly.

Fast forward eight years and you find that the 5G space has become quite crowded and your company hasn't quite kept up with competition as well as you'd hoped. Its products still have some demand, but there are clearly other ones out there that clients prefer with increasing frequency. In short, the reasons that you based your investment on are no longer valid. Such situations indicate that it's best for you to exit your investment and sell it.

Often, you might find that the core business is no longer relevant. For example, Blockbuster was a great company for many years and was well ahead of the curve when it came to in-home DVD rentals. However, they didn't adapt to the streaming revolution. In fact, Blockbuster turned down the chance to buy Netflix on 3 separate occasions.

As a result, they went bankrupt. You didn't have to wait until bankruptcy to figure out that the company had issues. The warning signs were there early on in terms of decreasing earnings as well as increased expenses. Blockbuster was a behemoth that simply couldn't turn around in time.

Borders is another example of this. The firm was extremely slow to react to the threat that Amazon posed. While its main competitor, Barnes & Noble, struggles on thanks to its brand name and a good location strategy, Borders instead shrunk the floor space it dedicated to books. It began incorporating all kinds of products that had nothing to do with books instead and focused on opening smaller outlets.

Perhaps the worst decision of all was to completely eliminate all seating areas that book lovers prefer within book stores. The company reasoned that this would force patrons to buy more stuff. Instead, patrons simply went to Barnes & Noble instead. All in all, the chances of a bookstore surviving while moving away from books is a bit unrealistic. This alone would have sent alarm bells ringing in the mind of any intelligent investor.

Lastly, we have the most famous case of failure to adapt: Kodak. The company famously doubled down on film roll and neglected the realm of digital cameras. As a result, it's nowhere to be found these days.

Compromised Management

At the turn of the millennium, there was one company that dominated the markets to such an extent that these days, it's unthinkable to imagine. Think of the sort of headlines Amazon, Apple and Google generate, and you'll have an idea of what Enron was like. This company was based out of Houston and was an energy trading firm.

Its business area was sufficiently complex enough for outsiders to worship management as being brilliant, and the firm ticked all the boxes with regard to political connections to be intimidating to competitors. For example, George W. Bush and Dick Cheney were close to the company's chairman Kenneth Lay and the chief financial officer Jeff Skilling.

Given all of this, it came as a huge shock that Enron was bankrupt, and even worse, it had been bankrupt for quite a few years running and had been cooking its books in complicity with its auditing firm, Arthur Andersen (now Accenture). The only reason Lay isn't vilified more than he is for his role in the scandal is because of the supervillain like actions that Jeff Skilling carried out.

An example of this was when Skilling dumped all of his stock prior to an earnings release while still exhorting employees to buy more stock in the company. Skilling even went so far as to abuse an analyst who dared question the financial condition of Enron's books during an earnings call.

Dishonest management will always reveal themselves without prompting. Lay and Skilling's behavior was notorious well before the scandal, and Enron's culture was toxic at all times. However, people ignored this since the company made ungodly sums of money.

Another example of this was the former Wall Street giant Lehman Brothers. This was another case where an earnings call with analysts revealed deep flaws in the company's books. In this instance, the CFO of Lehman, Erin Callan was questioned by the hedge fund manager David Einhorn. In Callan's defense, she wasn't committing fraud. Lehman was just too incompetent to figure out the true nature of the assets they were carrying.

The firm went bust during the credit crisis, and Einhorn was one of the first people to warn of the dangers that banks were running, even if he didn't have a movie made around him. The case of Radioshack's CEO falsifying his academic credentials also comes to mind.

Small lies eventually lead to bigger lies. If you begin to spot inconsistencies in the way management communicates its shortcomings or if it begins to treat everyone else like a bunch of dunces, most likely it is the management that is incompetent. You're best served by getting out quickly.

Better Opportunities

Stocks don't always go up. At some point, they will consolidate, and their prices will remain at a certain level for years. This is not a bad thing by itself. If you do happen to find a better company to invest in and if you've earned at least a 50% gain on your investment, then feel free to sell your holdings and move your money to the new venture. Remember that you will need to pay capital gains taxes when you do sell stocks at a profit. Treat the entire sale as if you're selling a house and buying a new one. Carry out the level of preparation that such a transaction demands.

Alternatively, if you made a poor investment decision in the past (we all do), it's ok to take a loss. Remember to analyze why the stock's price is lower than when you bought. If you don't believe anything about the core business has changed, then keep holding. However, if your initial research was off the mark, or the underlying sector economics no longer make sense, then you are free to sell. It's important to analyze your losses and understand why you were wrong in the first place. This will help you make better decisions going forward. Remember you can write off capital losses come tax season.

Putting It All Together

As we come to the end of this book, you now have a significant opportunity on your hands. While the financial media want you to believe that stock investing is a tough art to master, the best way to get ahead is to use the simple and easy to understand principles you've learned in this book. This is because the simpler your principles are, the less likely you are to overcomplicate things.

Remember to keep the investment principles we spoke about earlier in your mind at all times. These alone will ensure an intelligent investment and will significantly reduce your chances of losing money. Here they are again, briefly:

- The Warren Buffett test - Buy great business at fair prices. See if you can describe the business to a 10-year-old.
- Understand the true business - How well do you know what drives the profits of the business?
- Founder syndrome - How honest and reliable is management? Is there a succession plan in place, or does it all depend on the founder?
- Intangible assets - Does the company have any brand loyalty? Does it have intellectual property like patents or trademarks? Things which don't show up on a balance sheet
- Management quality - How well does management align the business with the economics of the industry? How well do they reinvest capital?
- Sales and marketing - How dedicated is the company to sales and marketing? What is the quality of their teams? How are their key metrics looking year-to-year?
- Long term focus - Is management focused on short term metrics, or does it invest resources for the long run?
- Moat - A moat is a phenomenon that gives a company an unfair advantage in its field. It could be brand loyalty, a superior supply chain, sheer size, etc.
- Can it weather a storm? - How well will the business perform under a stress test?

Ask yourself all of these questions prior to investing in a company. As you can see, they require a high degree of honesty from yourself. It also requires you to stay away from fad and currently popular industries if your sole reason for investment is their popularity. Instead, evaluate the company's fundamental business and management.

Above all else, remember that a share is a slice of the business. You aren't someone only in it for the short run. You're an owner of the company. So, behave like one!

We wish you all the luck and profits in the world and are positive that implementing our Rational Process Investing system will help you earn all the profits you deserve.

One final word from us. If this book has helped you in any way, we'd appreciate it if you left a review on Amazon. Reviews are the lifeblood of our business. We read every single one, and incorporate your feedback into future book projects.

To leave an Amazon review go to https://freemanpublications.com/leaveareview

REFERENCES

Blitz, David, Are Hedge Funds on the Other Side of the Low-Volatility Trade? (January 12, 2017). Available at SSRN: https://ssrn.com/abstract=2898034 or http://dx.doi.org/10.2139/ssrn.2898034

Daszkowski, D. (2019). What's Required to Open a McDonald's Franchise?. Retrieved 16 April 2020, from https://www.thebalancesmb.com/requirements-to-open-a-McDonald's-franchise-1350970

DiLallo, M. (2019). Why Cell Tower REITs Stand Above the Rest. Retrieved 16 April 2020, from https://www.fool.com/millionacres/real-estate-investing/articles/why-cell-tower-reits-stand-above-rest/

Graham, B., & Dodd, D. (1934). Security analysis. New York: McGraw-Hill.

Gupta, R. (2020). How Far Is Netflix From Target Of 100 Million India Subscribers?. Retrieved 16 April 2020, from https://marketrealist.com/2020/02/how-far-netflix-100-million-subscribers-india/

LaRoche, J. (2019). Yahoo is now a part of Verizon Media. Retrieved 16 April 2020, from https://finance.yahoo.com/news/warren-buffett-quotes-from-the-annual-letter-215739887.html

Lewis, M. (2011). The Big Short.

REFERENCES

Lieber, C. (2015). Inside Lululemon's Booming Underground Resale Market. Retrieved 16 April 2020, from https://www.racked.com/2015/3/12/8198483/lululemon-ebay-facebook-resale-secondary-market

Lieber, C. (2018). Lululemon's ex-CEO wrote an outrageous "unauthorized" history of the brand. Here's what we learned. Retrieved 16 April 2020, from https://www.vox.com/the-goods/2018/10/22/18010410/chip-wilson-lululemon-athleisure-book

Maggiulli, N. (2020). Dollar Cost Averaging vs. Lump Sum: The Definitive Guide – Of Dollars And Data. Retrieved 16 April 2020, from https://ofdollarsanddata.com/dollar-cost-averaging-vs-lump-sum/

Martin, E. (2018). Only 23% of millennials prefer investing to cash—here's why they're skeptical of the stock market. Retrieved 16 April 2020, from https://www.cnbc.com/2018/08/01/why-millennials-are-scared-of-the-stock-market.html

Mckenna, B. (2020). Yahoo is now a part of Verizon Media. Retrieved 16 April 2020, from https://finance.yahoo.com/news/3-key-ceo-quotes-zoom-144500599.html

Mitchell, C. (2019). The Two Biggest Flash Crashes of 2015. Retrieved 16 April 2020, from https://www.investopedia.com/articles/investing/011116/two-biggest-flash-crashes-2015.asp

O'Kane, S. (2020). Tesla's record 2019 has bought it some breathing room. Retrieved 16 April 2020, from https://www.theverge.com/2020/1/29/21113987/tesla-q4-2019-earnings-results-profit-revenue-model-3

Orem, T. (2020). 2019-2020 Capital Gains Tax Rates & How to Avoid a Big Bill - NerdWallet. Retrieved 16 April 2020, from https://www.nerdwallet.com/blog/taxes/capital-gains-tax-rates/

Rydon, M. (2020). The Upshot. Retrieved 16 April 2020, from https://www.nytimes.com/section/upshot

Saibil, J. (2020). Disney Is Buying More Land. Is a New Theme Park on the Way? | The Motley Fool. Retrieved 16 April 2020, from https://www.fool.com/

investing/2020/04/02/disney-is-buying-more-land-is-a-new-theme-park-on.aspx

Schwartz, N. (2000). Inside the Market's Myth Machine In pushing Amazon's stock to irrational heights, Wall Street bulls boosted their own careers. Amazon's doubters--even when they were right--haven't fared nearly as well. - October 2, 2000. Retrieved 16 April 2020, from https://archive.fortune.com/magazines/fortune/fortune_archive/2000/10/02/288462/index.htm

Wagner, K. (2019). Facebook almost missed the mobile revolution. It can't afford to miss the next big thing. Retrieved 16 April 2020, from https://www.vox.com/2019/4/29/18511534/facebook-mobile-phone-f8

What is the difference between 4G and 5G?. (2020). Retrieved 16 April 2020, from https://www.justaskgemalto.com/en/difference-4g-5g

Wolfers, J. (2020). The Unemployment Rate Is Probably Around 13 Percent. Retrieved 16 April 2020, from https://www.nytimes.com/2020/04/03/upshot/coronavirus-jobless-rate-great-depression.html

Yuan, E. (2020). Zoom's Use of Facebook's SDK in iOS Client - Zoom Blog. Retrieved 16 April 2020, from https://blog.zoom.us/wordpress/2020/03/27/zoom-use-of-facebook-sdk-in-ios-client/

Zafar, Z. (2020). The Trade Desk: Time Is Running Out For Linear TV. Retrieved 16 April 2020, from https://seekingalpha.com/article/4337232-trade-desk-time-is-running-out-for-linear-tv

BEAR MARKET INVESTING STRATEGIES

37 RECESSION-PROOF IDEAS TO GROW YOUR WEALTH

"WE CONTINUE TO EXPECT THAT MARKETS (AND OUR PERFORMANCE) WILL REMAIN VOLATILE, AND THEREFORE, NEW OPPORTUNITIES MAY PRESENT THEMSELVES THAT ARE SUPERIOR TO INVESTMENTS WE CURRENTLY OWN."

Bill Ackman, head of Pershing Square Capital, after turning $27 million in $2.6 Billion with a hedge against economic growth due to the COVID-19 pandemic.

YOUR WORST NIGHTMARE, OR THE GREATEST OPPORTUNITY OF THE DECADE?

Bear markets are perhaps the average investor's worst nightmare. After all, why would anyone ever want them? These are times of maximum pessimism. Everything financial instrument seems to be going down and entire economies appear close to collapse. The mainstream financial news usually confirms this point of view.

Wall Street slaps the entire market with one big "SELL" rating and if you log in to your brokerage account, all you see is red everywhere. Tough times indeed. Here at Freeman Publications, though, we take a different approach to bear markets. We believe that this is when wealth is truly created.

Making money in a bull market is quite straightforward. A rising tide lifts all boats! When bullish sentiment pervades the market, it looks as if every company's stock rises and investment is a straightforward endeavor. Why does every company's stock rise? This is because in the short term, sentiment is what drives market prices, not fundamentals.

This same sentiment is what makes investing in a bear market so difficult. All of us carry within us a psychological bias called the herd mentality. If you see a large number of people turning their heads to the left, you'll turn left to see what's going on as well. This is an automatic reaction that is deeply connected to our survival mechanism.

Similarly, if you see people selling everything in the market, you'll want to follow suit. It takes a huge amount of awareness and conviction to go against the tide. However, this is where big money is made.

For example, the investor Sir John Templeton made a fortune in the bear markets that preceded World War II (Chen, 2019). Once war was declared, the market slumped thanks to doomsday expectations. Templeton borrowed money and bought 100 shares each in 104 companies that were selling for less than a dollar in the American markets. As a historical refresher, Europe was being subjected to the Blitzkrieg at this point and it seemed as if Hitler's armies would overrun Western Europe entirely (which they did.)

This is when Templeton not only bought shares in companies but borrowed money to finance his purchases! Over the next five years, his portfolio grew by more than 400% and he made a fortune for himself.

This just goes to show that bear markets offer smart investors immense opportunities. The key word to recognize here is "smart."

SMART MONEY VS. DUMB MONEY

The notion of smart versus dumb money has always been present in the markets. The typical line on this is that institutional investors are the smart money while the average retail investor represents dumb money.

This isn't true at all. If institutional investors are uniformly smart, how can one explain the variety of financial crises that have occurred? If they were all smart, Bear Stearns and Lehman Brothers would still be around, not to mention the large number of hedge funds that have sunk without a trace. The real distinction between dumb and smart money lies in the process that each group follows.

Smart investors always have a process that they follow. Their processes are based on rigorous and intelligent principles of investing. Dumb money, on the other hand, has either no process or their process usually boils down to jumping into stocks that are in the news.

Developing an investment process is not a simple thing. You can read all the quotes and listen to all the interviews of famous investors such as Warren Buffett, Charlie Munger or Benjamin Graham, but mere reading isn't going to help you. You still need to work at reigning in your emotions to avoid plunging into some hot stock just because it jumped 12% in a single day.

Helping you develop a rational investing process is what this book aims to do. On the surface, this may seem like a tough task. A study conducted by Bernstein Advisors found that the average active investor realizes just 2.1% per year in gains (Bernstein, 2018). That's less than U.S. Treasury bills! A Treasury bill is a bond that is issued by the American government with a maturity date of less than one year. T-bills, as they're called, are viewed as a safe investment and contain as little risk for the investor as possible. In short, all the investor needs to do is place their money in T-bills and forget about them.

The only asset class that returned less than the average investor over the past 20 years is Japanese equities. So if all that activity in the market produces a return on par with T-bills, is investing even worth it? The answer to this question lies in the study itself.

Bernstein Advisors determined that the abysmal rate of return was caused by investors' timing of asset allocation decisions. Simply put, they bought assets that were overvalued and sold ones that were undervalued. It's easy to understand why this happens.

Many new investors enter the market with the hope of making quick and easy money. They jump into a hot stock that has been promoted in the financial media and hope to see the price rise. They keep checking in every day to monitor the stock price, as if they could influence its movement!

However, that heavily promoted stock has seen millions of people enter at the same time, for similar reasons as the investor in question. In short, the price is inflated well above what it's truly worth. What happens to assets that are over-valued? Simple. Their price corrects back to what it's truly worth.

The result is a decline in price and panic for the investor. The stock is no longer in the news and no one seems to be talking about it. Investors rationalize that they must have been wrong and sell their investments. The millions of other investors who entered for the same reason are doing the exact same thing at this point.

The huge selling pressure results in the stock's price dipping below what it's truly worth. In short, all of these investors sell right when the stock is a bargain. This is how a 2.1% return is made in the markets.

The Social Media Cycle

These days the news cycle is 24/7. Social media is constantly on and the excessive amount of information that is available these days is a double-edged sword. On one hand, you can access a large amount of credible research on obscure companies. On the other hand, too much information can cause you to miss the forest for the trees.

Social media also makes it easy for you to jump in and out of stocks. Company CEOs are present on Twitter these days and anything that they say can upset stock prices. Elon Musk and Tesla are a good example of this. Information is valuable only if you align it with an intelligent process.

Without this, all that information turns against you because you begin to rely on your emotional processes to make decisions. Our objective in writing this book is to help you develop rational processes that will help you filter this information. You'll learn what to pay attention to and what to ignore.

Most importantly, we're not going to focus on things such as market timing or active trading methods. These are not intelligent methods of investing. Instead, if you wish to make money over the long term, you're going to have to develop a strong process for yourself and this is what we're going to show you.

Along the way, we'll also help you eliminate the perception that a bear market is a bad thing. There is no need for you to renounce the US dollar and stockpile supplies or ammo just because the market scenario looks bad. In fact, this is a great time to be investing in the market. This isn't some emotional proclamation we're making, it's grounded in fact, as you'll learn.

You'll discover about a few alternative investments that work brilliantly in bear markets. We'll be discussing gold, as well as cryptocurrencies. These asset classes have been pushed as hedges against the dollar. However, going all-in on these is not an intelligent move. You'll learn exactly what sort of an approach you need to adopt when it comes to such alternative investments.

Above all else, we're pragmatists. Our short-term outlook for the world's economy is less than positive. However, this is not a doomsday book. The long-term view is what matters above all else when it comes to investing, and our view for the global economy is extremely positive.

We might be long-term bulls, but this doesn't mean we cannot take short-term practicalities into consideration. Managing both sides of the equation intelligently is what you're going to learn.

Now that you know what to expect in this book, let's jump in and look at market cycles and what they mean for your investment process.

1

WITHOUT A BUBBLE, THERE IS NO CRASH—A PRACTICAL LOOK AT ECONOMIC CYCLES

C rashes don't occur without assets being overvalued. After all, something that is selling for what it's truly worth is unlikely to see a large price correction. Bubbles are what cause crashes and ever since economies have existed, the markets have witnessed cycles of bubbles and crashes.

The frequency of such events has not been fixed over the years. However, all economic cycles move through certain stages. All of these stages have telltale signs that you can spot in advance. Understanding the mechanics of these stages will help you figure out which part of the boom/bust cycle we're in currently and tailor your investments accordingly.

STAGE ONE: IT ALL STARTS WITH DISRUPTION

Every bubble starts off with a seed of justification. What we mean is that it has a foundation in reality. More often than not, a new process or paradigm makes itself known in the markets and this changes the way things are done. Disruption by itself is not a bad thing.

For example, the past decade has witnessed huge levels of disruption that we're still coming to terms with. Internet companies have existed since the turn of the millennium and going back to the mid 90s. However, comparing the technology and the way in which we communicate these days makes the early 2000s seem like the Middle Ages.

Consider the fact that Facebook and smartphones didn't exist back then and you'll see the level to which our world has changed. Amazon was a bookseller and Google was smaller than Yahoo Search. Disruptions of these kinds cause changes that take time for us to process.

Much like a child learning a new skill, we navigate this new world through trial and error as we feel our way forward. Technology companies have cornered the market when it comes to the word disruption, but the phenomenon has been occurring for a long time now.

For example, the fall of the Soviet Union was an example of an event that disrupted the world's economy. China's decision to open its economy in the late 1970s was another decision that took some time to make an impact. Looking at how strong China is these days, no one will argue against the fact that this was a seminal decision in history.

Disruption comes in two forms. It either occurs through technological advancement or through some fundamental economic change. Often one ties into the other.

Technological Advancement

Technology has always played a huge role in human advancement. You might think we're referring to the dotcom boom or the digital revolution, but our example is more ancient than that. The first huge leap forward that Western economies witnessed occurred in the 1760s.

It's tough to pinpoint the exact moment when it all began, but the invention of the steam engine is usually thought of as the event that sparked change. James Watt managed to greatly improve existing steam engine designs in 1759, and soon wind and labor-powered machines were replaced by steam engines. Suddenly, railroads were a thing!

This in turn led to the creation of factories and other machinery that changed the rate at which countries could produce goods. It also created a huge gap between the haves and the have-nots in the world, and soon imperialism was in full swing thanks to the need for raw materials.

The Industrial Revolution created an advantage for Western economies to such an extent that the world order is still based on the prosperity it produced. While the exact nature of that order has changed, there's no denying that the technological advances witnessed during this period have sustained those economies for a long time now.

The dotcom boom is another example of technological disruption changing the way we look at business. While this is mostly associated with the dotcom crash in 2000, it doesn't change the fact that the explosion of internet-based companies shifted our perception of business and value.

Companies such as Amazon and eBay were born in the mid 90s. Sergey Brin and Larry Page would not have devoted much time to creating a search algorithm if the internet didn't open possibilities to retrieve information. Elon Musk would not have had the money to buy Tesla if he hadn't created PayPal in the 90s along with Peter Thiel.

Over the past decade, the development of the Software as a Service (SaaS) business model has disrupted revenue collection models. A SaaS model asks the consumer to pay a monthly fee for accessing the software instead of having them pay once for purchasing it.

In the early 2000s, you could buy McAfee's antivirus, or Adobe's Photoshop software with a one-time payment. Which would then grant you lifetime access to it. These days, you pay these companies a monthly fee for usage and get access to automatic updates. This represents a smaller upfront payment to the consumer, and increased lifetime revenues for the provider. The SaaS model has moved into brick and mortar industries too. Tesla has brought some elements of the SaaS model to the automobile market with its cars receiving software updates via the cloud.

Fundamental Economic Change

The other major source of disruption is when fundamental economic disruptions occur. Communism versus capitalism was the heavyweight bout that gripped the world from the second World War till 1990. Everything in the world revolved around what America and the USSR were involved in.

Wars were started, space was explored, man stepped on the moon and countries' entire economies were dictated by which brand of politics they preferred. Thus, in 1989 when the USSR fell, no one was quite sure of how things would play out. The opening up of Russia's economy provided massive opportunity to a certain group of people.

For the first time in a long time, Eastern European countries had to stop worrying about a big brother being present and govern themselves. It was a monumental shock to the world's system, in other words.

Lending standards have always been a reliable indicator of fundamental economic changes taking place. The invention of mass consumer lending in the 1920s and the relaxation of credit standards in the early to mid 2000s are examples of financial changes that disrupted the way economies ran.

The disruption stage is characterized by optimism and opportunity. This is when things are beginning to boom and investors are beginning to take notice. They typically begin moving capital into these economies or opportunities.

STAGE TWO: THE BULL MARKET

Once more and more people begin to recognize the disruption, the amount of money that is piled into these opportunities increases. The result is a boom that is backed up by performance. A good example of this is the tiny emirate of Dubai.

Dubai belongs to a country that is composed of seven separate kingdoms. These kingdoms together form the United Arab Emirates (UAE) and the country has been in existence in its present form since 1971. From that time till 2000, the emirate of Dubai was a stopover town between two other kingdoms, a glorified rest stop of sorts (Brook, 2016).

Things changed around 1995 with the appointment of a new crown prince. Quickly things began moving in the sleepy emirate. First, a fancy new hotel called the Burj al Arab was constructed by the coastline. Its design is considered futuristic to this day, so one can imagine the splash it caused when it was completed in 1999.

Property construction began in earnest and land values began booming. At the turn of the millennium, when Western economies were being affected by the dotcom crash, Dubai's economy was about to enter a rapid bull market. A man-made island in the shape of a palm was constructed and investment poured in.

There was justification for this boom. The government was rapidly expanding and modernizing its economy and tourism was growing almost tenfold every year. From 2002 to 2008, property values quadrupled. Given that the kingdom's economy was not tied to oil prices, this was some achievement.

The only comparable boom like the one Dubai has witnessed occurred during the Second Industrial Revolution back in the late 1800s and early 1900s. This was when Germany under Bismarck and the United States rapidly industrialized and joined the big boys' table.

Germany is particularly notable because in the matter of a decade it went from being a primarily agrarian economy to a fully industrialized one. While it faced a lot of hostility from its European neighbors, this hostility was a mark of how potent Germany's boom was.

Justified Bullishness

Technology has fostered huge booms since the turn of the millennium. While there was a massive devaluation in between, this was primarily because of large misunderstandings when it came to value. Companies such as Amazon and Netflix survived the dotcom bust primarily thanks to their businesses providing consumers with real value.

In the early portion of the previous decade, Google and Facebook grew from fledgling startups to behemoths of the industry. All of these examples, including the ones highlighted previously, have something in common. The products and services that were developed are truly valuable and thus the rise in prices is justified.

One of the key changes that occurs during this time is the perception of value. After all, new services and goods have been created and the definition of value changes. For example, the narrative around business valuation before technology companies began to dominate was that profits drove valuation.

However, Facebook and Amazon proved that it was not profits but users that drove valuation. The result was the creation of a completely different philosophy of investing. Where investors once looked at profits and margins, they were now looking at user numbers and growth and didn't care about profits.

A lot of people found this incongruous. How could a business not care about profits at all? Over time, this philosophy has fleshed itself out more and the connection between users and profits is now well established. However, it took everyone a while to get there!

This period is also home to a large number of innovations that facilitate change. For example, the early 2000s saw the transformation of a boring financial derivative called the mortgage bond into a driver of profits. The mortgage bond market was pretty boring at the best of times (Lewis, 2008).

However, between 2003 and 2007, Wall Street banks turned this relatively unknown instrument into the very basis upon which their businesses were founded. This was done in reaction to the great prosperity that Americans were experiencing and the availability of easy money.

Notice that in all of these examples, the transition from the first stage to this one is different. In the case of Dubai and Germany, the process played out over a few years. In the case of the internet companies, it took close to a decade. With mortgage bonds, it took less than two years.

The key is to identify the qualities that underlie these phases instead of getting caught up in how long the stage lasts.

STAGE THREE: BUBBLE

The bubble phase is characterized by euphoria. The bull market has been going on for so long that no one remembers the bad times anymore. People can get adjusted to riches pretty quickly! As a result, complacency sets in because money becomes easier to make.

All of these disruptive companies or sectors have long since moved from being risky to can't-miss territory. The general public now becomes aware that they can make lots of money by investing in certain sectors or in certain assets. A good example of this is provided by the tulip mania that gripped the Netherlands in the early 1600s.

Tulips were viewed as an exotic flower, given that they had to be imported all the way from Istanbul. With prosperity levels growing in the Dutch economy, people began coveting them. Wearing a tulip was a mark of belonging to high society. Soon, Dutch farmers recognized this opportunity (Stage Two) and began growing them.

As people began buying more tulips, the price rose to high levels. The general public caught on to the fact that there was money to be made in tulips and began buying them in bulk to resell them. Soon enough, farmers could not keep up with the demand for tulips and prices skyrocketed (Hayes, 2019).

A secondary market popped up where people sold and bought the rights to buy a tulip. In some cases, the price of the right to buy a tulip was worth more than an entire house. People still bought them though, since there was always someone who would buy it from them.

In short, demand was driven by the fact that there was a greater fool to buy the asset. They were not correlated to the underlying asset's value anymore. Everyone wanted to get in on this thanks to the riches that could be gained and a bubble was formed.

FOMO and Complacency

This stage is mostly characterized by the investing public's fear of missing out and complacency with regards to the disconnect between price and value. The average investor believes that prices can only go up. Pretty much everyone jumps in on the hot new trend because of this.

This decade has witnessed behavior like this. How many people became crypto traders once Bitcoin hit $20,000? How many people bought cryptocurrency at this price in the hopes of making a quick profit? They probably heard stories of someone who bought it at $13,000 and resold it for $18,000 in a few days.

The get-rich-quick mindset prevails during this stage. It's safe to say that this mindset has never made anyone any money. The ones who do manage to make profits usually have luck to thank. This sort of thinking also leads to overvaluations for every asset that closely or even remotely resembles the original disruptor.

Once Bitcoin's price rose sharply, so did the prices of every other cryptocurrency. This led to the rise of a large number of initial coin offerings (ICOs). An ICO is when a new cryptocurrency is launched to prospective investors. The boom in ICO offerings led to outright fraud being perpetrated on the public with shady promoters offering the promise of huge profits with very little justification for them.

The confounding thing is that investors often recognized that there was very little value in the offering but invested their money in them anyway. This highlights the complacency with which they valued the asset to begin with. Everyone was getting into it and the pull of the herd mentality was hard to resist.

The technology world also witnessed some ridiculous overvaluations as well. The social media company Snapchat went public for a price of $24 per share (representing a market cap of $33 billion) despite not having any viable monetization strategy or a platform that lent itself to doing this. As of current writing, the company's stock is still trading at these levels.

A bigger disaster was the massive valuation of the coworking company WeWork. It was thought to be a disruptive company, simply because it positioned itself as being the Uber of office space. At its height, it was valued at $50 billion. The problem was that the company never had a hope of posting a profit. The bigger it got, the larger its losses. What's more, WeWork declared in its SEC filings that it didn't hope to make a profit in the foreseeable future. Currently, it's valued at a far more sober $8 billion.

Zoom was another company whose valuation rose to an eye-watering 63 times revenue (note that's not 63x earnings, we're talking purely on sales numbers). This was despite the fact that the company had never turned a profit. Pretty much everyone jumped in on Zoom and other tech companies because it's what everyone was doing!

Divergence from Fundamentals

At this point you may hear maxims such as

"Value investing doesn't work any more"

"If you'd have just bought every tech IPO in the past 10 years, you'd have outperformed the S&P 500"

"Warren Buffett has lost his touch"

All of these are rooted in a certain degree of truth. However, just because something works in the short term, does not make it a reliable method for the long-term.

As a rule of thumb, if you ever hear the dumbest person you know begin to talk about stocks and the market, that's the time for you to get out.

Another factor in the FOMO-driven stage of the cycle is leverage. Leverage rises massively during these times as people borrow money to get in on the excitement. This is what happened in the case of Dubai's economic boom as well.

By 2008, demand for property was so high that people could buy property and flip it within a month. Developers began waiving down payment requirements since speculators were interested in flipping properties to someone else, without having any interest in owning them. Thus, a person only needed to make a single monthly payment to receive the title to the property.

Such behavior was justified due to the fact that prices were constantly increasing. banks began providing personal loans that were duly used to purchase multiple properties through low monthly payments. Sellers knew that no buyer had any intention of using the property, but they didn't care. All that mattered was the fact that everyone else was doing the same thing.

Smart Money Exits

The bubble stage is when smart money exits the market. Remember that retail investors are also a portion of the smart money group, just as institutional investors can be dumb money. Since the disconnect between value and price is unjustified, these investors recognize the warning signs and cash out their investments.

This is mostly done because having cash during bad times is a huge advantage. It allows an investor to quickly seize opportunities and invest in them while the rest of the market is reeling from the shock of the drop. At this stage the bubble hasn't burst yet, but savvy investors are getting ready for it.

Having said that, even the smartest of investors can get caught in these bubbles. Warren Buffett and Charlie Munger were famously caught out by the credit crisis despite seeing the signs. They managed to steer clear of subprime mortgages in their insurance businesses but didn't foresee the damage that some of their portfolio companies such as Wells Fargo and Moody's took. Recently, they managed to lose money investing in airline companies as well.

STAGE FOUR: EXTERNAL SHOCKS

This stage is when the bubble pops. Just as every great party ends with an external force stopping it dead in its tracks (the lights come on or the cops show up), the bubble is burst by an exogenous event. The shock itself might have nothing to do with economic events, but it causes markets to tumble and it gives pessimists an excuse to begin dumping stocks.

Given the huge disparity that has been created between price and value, there isn't much propping these eye-watering valuations up. As a result, a crisis ensues where prices begin tumbling downwards. Something that catches out a lot of investors is trying to predict what the shock will be, instead of preparing for the occurrence of a shock.

In other words, some investors try to time their exit from the market by looking for signs of specific events that indicate a fall. This is a lot like trying to time your entry into the market. It's a pretty pointless game to take part in since you can never predict what will cause a shock.

The current COVID-19 pandemic is a great example of this. The markets had been fueled by cheap money for a while. While the pandemic caused businesses to shut down, the state to which things have fallen shows how overvalued assets were.

Consider that the American unemployment rate is currently a few points below what it was during the Great Depression (Iacurci, 2020)! The unemployment rate spiked from 2% to 20% in just a few months. It's hard to fathom how this could have happened without businesses being overly reliant on cheap debt that was widely available.

Previous economic crises have also had seemingly innocuous beginnings. The credit crisis of the previous decade is thought to have begun when an obscure hedge fund that was run by Bear Stearns failed in late 2007. To the outside world, no one knew what The High Grade Fund was or what it did, but it began a snowball that would eventually claim its parent firm and a few other notable ones.

The odds of the average investor or even the average institutional investor being able to predict this event as the catalyst for collapse is pretty remote.

Leverage

This stage is marked by the failure of overleveraged companies. Leverage here refers to debt that companies carry on their balance sheets. During the previous stage, companies often borrow cash to finance their businesses. This decade has witnessed unprecedented amounts of leverage being used in American businesses.

After the credit crisis dissipated in 2009, the government began printing money in order to provide lenders with more money. This was followed by Quantitative Easing (QE) measures. QE is a fancy name for the American government buying toxic assets from lenders to prevent them from going bankrupt.

The money to buy these assets came from newly printed dollar bills. This approach was followed by pretty much every central bank in the world. In an effort to kickstart their economies, interest rates were cut to the bone, with Europe even experiencing negative interest rates.

This created an environment where businesses borrowed money for next to nothing to finance their businesses. While some level of debt is good on a balance sheet, cheap money led to excessive levels of debt being carried. In the past, such levels of debt would have resulted in companies going bankrupt.

However, these days governments have shown that they're willing to step in and prevent the collapse of companies. A good example of this was the sale of Bear Stearns that was orchestrated by the U.S Government. The propping up of RBS by the UK government is another example.

It isn't just the financial sector that has been propped up. The likes of General Motors and Chrysler also received bailout money from the government. While bailouts are a recent phenomenon, this particular stage is characterized by some spectacular bankruptcies, thanks to leverage.

Bear Stearns was bought out by J.P Morgan with the government's assistance, but the firm was allowed to fail as much as possible. The firm became aware of the risks it was running in late 2007 but as the value of its assets dipped, its leverage levels became alarming. A week before it went bankrupt, the stock was trading as high as $100 per share.

Another spectacular collapse from that time was Lehman Brothers. In this case, the government did not intervene and allowed it to fail. Lehman's fall was also characterized by huge levels of leverage. While this was the reason on the surface of it, the real reason was massively overvaluing the assets it was carrying. This was the case with Bear as well.

This overvaluation of assets occurred primarily because both companies were still caught up in the frenzy of the previous stage. They honestly believed they could sell worthless mortgage bond-backed derivatives to other investors and carried these assets on their books for the prices they thought they could get.

Much like the investors who placed their money in the rights to buy tulips, they soon found out that the underlying assets were worthless and the money they had borrowed to buy them was now due.

The same pattern is playing out now with the COVID-19 crisis. A large number of businesses have had to let go of staff and shut down because of not being able to service the debt on their balance sheets. While there hasn't been any high profile bankruptcy yet (other than Hertz) as of this writing, highly leveraged balance sheets might cause further bailouts and even more money printing.

STAGE FIVE: DISGUST

As reality sets in, we will witness people come to terms with what's going on. The financial media, which is ever present to jump into hysterical overreaction, begins using terms such as "worst crisis" and "lowest point in history" and so on.

None of them pointed out or even came close to uncovering what was going on during the previous stages but now, all of a sudden, they begin talking about how the signs were always there. They trot out the appropriate talking heads on their shows and manufacture outrage at how things could get so bad.

New celebrities are born. These are people who managed to correctly call the bubble. The most notable example of this in the previous recession was Michael Burry, whose work was the basis for the book (and subsequent movie) *The Big Short.* Burry was an obscure Hedge Fund manager who rose to prominence in the late 2000s after his Scion Capital firm made investors more than $700m after betting against the sub-prime mortgage bonds which caused the Financial crisis. Burry's fund returned 489.34% in an 8 year period compared to 3% for S&P 500. Burry himself argued that many people had access to the same data he had, and that he was not merely a "supremely lucky flipper of coins." (Burry, 2010).

This is also the time when the tide truly runs out and fraud is uncovered. Following the credit crisis, the biggest scandal that emerged was Bernie Madoff's. Madoff had been running the world's largest Ponzi scheme, which defrauded investors of more than $64 Billion.

The previous recession, the dotcom bust, was also followed by one of the biggest frauds of all time being uncovered in Enron. This was a company that was supposed to be the smartest in the energy trading markets and it turned out that everything had been falsified. What was worse was that the management of the company (chairman Kenneth Lay and the CFO Jeff Skilling) had been dumping company stock while telling their employees to buy more.

The scandal even managed to sink the firm that had audited Enron's books, Arthur Andersen. The damage to their reputation was so bad that they had to change their company's name to Accenture. All of these bleak news items lead to massive distrust in the government and in the established political order.

Following the previous bear market in 2009 we saw protests break out demanding reform. Movements such as Occupy Wall Street began and the common investor, who has probably lost their shirt by now in the markets, was ruminating over how they had been duped by the system.

The stock market is unfair and is loaded against the little guy, such investors think. All this while, the smart money has read the signs and is identifying opportunities that will soon make themselves known.

Prices of companies will be at lows. These might not be historical lows, but they certainly will be near five to 10-year lows. This results in a number of great companies being sold for a fraction of their true value, and slowly but surely, we return to the first stage all over again.

We should note that these five stages describe the overall economy. However, individual sectors will run at their own pace. For example, technology might be experiencing a stage five crisis but healthcare might be in stage three.

When buying individual stocks, it's important for you to focus on the economic cycle that a particular stock or sector is subject to, instead of worrying about the broader economic cycle.

"INVESTORS HAVE LOST MORE MONEY BY TRYING TO ANTICIPATE CORRECTIONS, THAN THEY'VE LOST IN THE CORRECTIONS THEMSELVES"

- Peter Lynch

2

BEAR MARKET TIMELINES AND EMOTIONAL MANAGEMENT

T his book is going to focus on stages three to five of the cycle from the previous chapter. A common mistake that many investors make is to fall into the trap of trying only to value a company with as much accuracy as possible. The truth is, it's far more important to control your emotions during such times.

No matter how rational you are or how aware you are of your emotional state, it's tough to go against your evolutionary instincts. If the whole world tells you that things are going to pieces, you're going to believe this to a certain extent. Your investment decisions will reflect this as well.

Recall from the introduction that most investors earn abysmal returns because they end up making the wrong asset allocation decisions. They end up buying when they should be selling and selling when they ought to be buying. Your objective is to maximize your good decisions in bull markets and minimize your bad ones in bear markets.

It's a simple thought process, but it works brilliantly. It helps you focus on avoiding large errors when times are bad. This alone will keep you from making a bad situation worse and will put you in a better situation to take advantage of the bounce that will inevitably occur as the market moves back to stage one of the cycle.

There are a few points you can keep in mind to help you maintain this framework.

THIS IS NOT THE END

During bad times you're going to hear a lot about how everything is going to fall to pieces and how we're all going to go back to a hunter-gatherer society. There will even be a group of people who will actively look forward to this and they're bound to receive more exposure in the media.

This will lead you to think that the established paradigms of this world are coming to an end. A common thread through all financial crises that have occurred in the United States has been the thought that America is no longer the force it once was. In 1929, the Great Depression was thought to have dampened the fastest growing economy in the world. Following the crash, common thought was that all the economic power America had gained over Europe following World War I had been squandered.

This sentiment carried on throughout the following two to three years until the recovery began in 1933. As we know now the Great Depression, even as bad as it was at the time, was just a very large speed bump in America's ascension to the top of the economic pile.

Doomsday predictions are a dime a dozen during the final stage and you should be very conscious of avoiding that train of thought. Yes, it might look like you'll need to stockpile food and other necessities, but this hardly means you'd be justified in doing so. The current COVID-19 pandemic has proved this over and over again.

When the disease first broke out in China, the rest of the world reacted by dismissing it as nothing more vicious than the flu. As the disease spread and its true ramifications came to be known, people began panicking and storing up on supplies. Even governments began overreacting and implemented lockdowns in ham-fisted ways.

The government of India gave its citizens all of four hours to prepare for a 21-day lockdown (Kettleman & Schultz, 2020). This led to panic buying and gave businesses no time to prepare for the increased demand as consumers stockpiled necessary goods. It also led to large quantities of essential provisions stuck at state borders due to lack of communication between local governments.

In the United States, the President went from suggesting that the disease was nothing to be worried about, to insisting that all Americans lock themselves down to defeat the virus, to refusing to wear a mask, to suggesting that people inject disinfectants, to inciting people to rebel against local government lockdowns, to vowing to reopen America. The world anxiously awaits the next stage of this sequence.

Throughout all of this, what has been missed is that human beings are remarkably adaptable. Across the world, people have adapted to new circumstances and have gone on with their lives. While there's no denying that times are tough, a lot of the hysteria that has been generated has prevented people from focusing on the few positives that have emerged.

The world is not going to go back to the Stone Age. So relax and focus on what's truly important to you.

THE LONG-TERM APPROACH

What does short-term or long-term mean to you? To some people the short term signifies the next few weeks. For some particularly fast-paced folks, it could mean the next few hours. It's important to gain the right perspective when it comes to these terms and investing.

In order to be successful at investing, you need to focus on the long term. How long is the long term? This is typically at least a decade long. Your money needs time to grow and it works best when you stand aside and let it compound. Interfering with it constantly by reacting to short-term news cycles is only going to decrease its growing power.

How long is the short term? By stock investing standards, the short term refers to the next two years at the very least. Remember that successful stock investment is not like trading, where you jump in and out of stocks repeatedly. You need to buy and hold for long periods of time in order to allow your investments to grow.

This is because in the long term, a company's stock price grows at the same rate that its earnings do. Like Benjamin Graham said, in the short term the market is a voting machine, but in the long term, it's a weighing machine ("The Voting and Weighing Machines," 2020). You'll need to overcome a variety of short-term sentiments for the long-term trend to assert itself.

A good illustration of this occurred when the credit crisis was beginning to unfold in 2007. Things were falling apart, and in the middle of all this Warren Buffett repeated his oft-quoted investment mantra for the common investor in his annual letter to Berkshire Hathaway shareholders: Buy a cross section of America and hold.

What Buffett meant was that even at the height of pessimistic opinion, the average investor needed to simply invest in an index fund that would give them exposure to the broad stock market. He even said that this simple investment would outperform the best hedge fund over the next decade (Floyd, 2019).

To put this in context, Buffett made this statement when home prices were tumbling across the nation and firms such as Countrywide Financial were in danger of going under. No one fully knew the extent of the crisis and how bad things would get. There wasn't even talk of a bailout yet! The climate was grim and many people around the country were being foreclosed on.

Buffett's bet was taken up by Protege Partners, a hedge fund based in New York, and the terms of the bet were modified a bit. Buffett would place $1 million of his own money into a low-cost index fund that tracked the S&P 500 broad stock market index while Protege would invest the same amount in a basket of hedge funds.

As 2007 turned to 2008, Buffett's investment was hammered. The market kept tumbling to new lows. By mid 2008, the market had tumbled 20% and it kept getting worse. By mid 2009, Buffett had lost 50% of his original value. Protege partners did very well during this time.

The exact numbers are not known, but their basket of funds earned an admirable 10% during this time. When compared to a tumble of close to 50% in the overall market, this was a stellar return indeed. It seemed as if Buffett was wrong to back a simple and cost-effective strategy.

Fast forward to 2017 and Buffett's simple investment had averaged 7% per year while the hedge fund basket had averaged just 2.2% per year. What's more, Protege Partners had given up the bet in 2015, conceding defeat and remarking that there was no way they could hope to beat Buffett's bet within the short time remaining on the bet!

This is remarkable considering the head start that the hedge fund basket had in the beginning. Buffett likened this scenario to the famous fable about the hare and the tortoise. While the hedge funds practiced a form of investing much like the hare, by jumping around into different asset classes and looking to time their entries into the market perfectly, Buffett's tortoise-like bet simply stayed the course and remained steady.

In the end, he came out ahead, just like the tortoise does in the fable. Without the clarity that focusing on the long term brings, this would not have been possible.

Rallies

During bear markets, at some point the news cycle shifts from pure outrage at the state of events to hope. Market observers begin to hype good news and celebrate every single uptick in the market. You'll often hear news such as "markets rallied 21% this month to finish their best month since the crisis" and so on.

While such news might give investors some solace, the fact is that they conceal more than they reveal. Let's consider an example to demonstrate how this works. We're going to highlight some sample returns the market provided within a three-year period. The time in which the returns below are earned are different.

In some cases, the return is earned over a month and in some it's six months. Whatever the timeline is, take a look at these numbers and ask yourself: Do these numbers make it seem as if the entire market is bullish or bearish over the course of these three years?

- 48% gain
- 12% gain
- 21% gain
- 27% gain
- 35% gain
- 72% gain

You'd be forgiven for thinking these came during a bull market. In fact these returns were earned during the worst three-year stretch that American markets have ever faced. That's right! Our sample three-year period runs from the height of 1929 right before the crash till 1932, which is when the market hit the bottom.

The market during this time lost 90% of its value. $10 invested in the beginning of this period would have been worth just $1 at the end of it. But just looking at those gain numbers, you don't get the feeling that they could have been produced during one of the worst times in American stock market history, do they?

This is precisely how rallies are reported in the media. A rally refers to an upward movement in a bearish market. Markets don't decline in a straight line. They go up and down, with the longer-term trend being down. The media might breathlessly report those numbers, especially the 72% rally, and give you the impression that the worst is over.

However, they neglect to mention that the market has declined by close to 90% from its highs and that the 72% rally is measured from the most recent low. For example, let's say the market price is currently $70 and that it has declined from a high of $350 to this level. That's a decline of 80%.

Before it rose to $70, the market had made a low of $40.70 and has now rallied to the $70 price. This is a rally of 72%. Clearly, it barely takes anything out of the overall decline. Don't get carried away by such gaudy rally numbers. The way they're measured causes investors to lose sight of the big picture.

By the way, those numbers aren't made up. They're real numbers that the Dow Jones Index hit between 1929 to 1932. The 72% rally was a rise from a low of around 41 to around 72. The index fell to these levels from a high of 380.

UNCERTAINTY AND OPPORTUNITY

Information is widely available these days. Be it on social media or through websites such as Seeking Alpha, you can access credible research reports on any company out there. There are also a large number of research firms that operate entirely on the internet, and by subscribing to their newsletters, you can access quality research material on everything from microcap stocks to behemoths.

This is a double-edged sword. You have huge access to this treasure trove of information. However, so does everyone else. The news that you've read in your newsletter has been read by other subscribers as well. If enough people get there ahead of you, the price of a company's stock will rise or fall to reflect its intrinsic value. It might even become overpriced.

This has led many market spectators to posit that the markets these days are far too efficient. The Efficient Market Hypothesis (EMH) has been around for a long time. EMH is a theoretical financial principle that says that all information surrounding a business (and its stock) have already been factored into its price.

For example, if Walmart is expected to announce bumper earnings, the price at which its stock sells in the market will be priced to reflect this fact ahead of time. As a result, when the bumper earnings announcement does come through, the stock won't witness a huge jump upwards.

EMH has always been used as a model to figure out the intrinsic value of a stock and plays an important role in valuation models that are a part of corporate finance courses. So what does all this have to do with you? It turns out that EMH has been a pretty terrible way to value stocks for a long time now.

This is primarily because information has never been widely available about a company in the past. A company in China that sells fertilizer and is listed on the New York Stock Exchange is unlikely to have its price account for all factors affecting the business. There's just too much of a gap.

To be more accurate, we should say there *was* too much of a gap. As information has become more freely available, market prices have become more efficient. The speed of the average market transaction has increased exponentially and, as a result, prices adjust to available information quickly.

In an efficient world, the only way to gain an advantage is to spot inefficiency. During normal times, doing this is close to impossible. Everyone is in the market and everyone is paying attention to all relevant news items. The number of casual market participants is high and institutional presence is also high. Thus, the average investor doesn't have much time to capture any inefficiencies.

An underreported company's stock might sell at a discount for a short period of time, but that mispricing isn't going to last for long since word will get out, and quickly. This dynamic changes during a bear market.

During these times, markets are a bit more inefficient. This is because the primary nature of news is pessimistic and no one likes listening to Debbie Downer. The average investor has probably witnessed their principal reduce massively and is therefore disinclined to take further part in the market.

In short, everyone's hurting and this is where your opportunity arises. There will be inefficiencies present in every sector and your task is simply to filter the news that is available. The saturation of information works to your advantage in these times because fewer people are willing to act upon it.

Successful bear market investing requires you to adopt a contrarian approach. You might believe that overcoming your inbuilt psychological mechanisms might be impossible. However, if you adopt this mindset of looking for diamonds in the rough when everyone else has given up, you'll manage to invest your money successfully.

Another important element of success is to avoid the traps that many investors fall into. These traps can come in the form of extremely negative news. It can also come in the form of flat-out misjudgment of the opportunity that's presented to you. You need to monitor your actions and be aware of your biases at all times.

While this isn't easy, viewing uncertainty as an opportunity for you to get ahead reduces your risk of making a mistake.

OVERVALUING BOUNCES

Previously we addressed this topic in brief, and it's worth taking a deeper look. The real reason the media and commentators scream with joy every time the market bounces is because people get used to trading in one direction. As long as things are going up, our brains are happy because their reward centers are being stimulated.

The minute things start going down, alarm bells start ringing and it feels physically uncomfortable for us to watch what's going on. During the COVID-19 pandemic, we've seen the effects of this discomfort. People have been pushing to get the American economy open quickly and get things back on track as soon as possible.

While livelihoods are at stake, the idea of making the pandemic go away just by reopening the economy is a head scratcher. Are governments and their people really willing to risk lives in order to reduce the unemployment rate? While there are significant numbers of people who are suffering, surely a more balanced approach is needed.

This mindset has led to a skewed manner in which market movements are reported. The markets declined precipitously in February and March 2020 as the world grappled with the true extent of the virus. April saw a huge rally and this was reported as being almost as if the crisis had come to an end.

However, the rally represents less than half the drop the market suffered from its highs. The fact is that such overly bullish news is great for retail investors. It simply means the opposite is happening and that there are great opportunities for you to unearth.

IRRATIONALITY IN THE MARKETS

John Maynard Keynes, one of the few economists who was also a successful investor, remarked that the markets can remain irrational longer than the investor can remain solvent (O'Brien, 2012). Investigating this quote a little bit more provides us with a cautionary piece of advice that every bear market investor must pay heed to.

Keynes, whose career spanned the decades before and after the Great Depression, was famous for remarking that the stock market was a lot like a beauty contest. Imagine a contest where you had to pick the six best-looking contestants out of 10 on stage. The catch is that you don't win a prize unless the large crowd agrees with your picks.

Success in this contest thus depends on how popular your picks are, irrespective of whether you believe your picks represent the six best-looking people. Stocks are pretty much the same. Their valuations are often driven by euphoria, and towards the end of bubbles many rational investors lose sight of this.

They believe that the bubble must have run its course and that the existing valuations are too far removed from reality. As a result, they begin to act upon their biases and fail to recognize one simple fact. Their opinion doesn't count unless the market backs it up. The markets, as Keynes pointed out, can remain irrational for far longer than one can expect.

With regards to present market conditions, consider that there have been voices remarking that the market was overvalued all the way back in 2016. Bill Gross, the famous bond investor and trader, is one such example (Heaton, 2016). Gross was in fact bearish on the economy since 2014!

Considering that the market was exhibiting signs of overheating all the way back then and is turning bearish in 2020, one can appreciate just how much patience and room for error there is when it comes to investing in bear markets. An investor who built their entire investment thesis without taking irrationality into account would have probably lost patience long before the markets began nosediving.

In some cases, bad news might come pouring in yet the stock price continues to rise. There's also the danger of underestimating irrationality after an initial fall. You might see the stock price fall and heave a sigh of relief thanks to expecting this for a long time. However, the price might immediately recover and continue back up to make new highs.

The markets are unpredictable and this makes it extremely important that you always cover your downside. This means you need to ground your investment thesis in facts and not according to your biases. Extreme rationality is also a bias. You're effectively saying that every participant in the market is rational and always acts on the basis of provided information.

This is a lot like what EMH hypothesizes and it's never fully worked despite some of its tenets proving true in recent times. It sounds strange to say this, but your investment process must take irrationality into account. Both your own and that of the other investors in the market.

"TRUTH - MORE PRECISELY, AN ACCURATE UNDERSTANDING OF REALITY - IS THE ESSENTIAL FOUNDATION FOR PRODUCING GOOD OUTCOMES."

Ray Dalio, who started Bridgewater Associates in his apartment. It became the world's largest hedge fund within 25 years.

3

THE ONION - ADOPTING THE RATIONAL PROCESS INVESTING MODEL FOR A BEAR MARKET

S o what is Rational Process Investing anyway? More importantly, how can you create a process to serve you through both bullish and bearish markets? The best way to think of this process is to use an analogy Jim Chanos regularly uses when he teaches investment at Yale and the University of Wisconsin (Koster, 2018). With regards to your long-term investing process, this is the most important piece of information in this book, so make sure you understand it thoroughly.

Chanos likens the company analysis process to peeling away the layers of an onion. Most investors begin from the outside in. They peel the outer layers of the onion and then progressively go towards the inner core. Presumably by the time they reach the inner kernel of the onion, they're weeping their eyes out and don't take their time with it.

According to Chanos, intelligent analysis is done the other way around. The investor needs to work from the inside out. They need to begin with the most painful part of the process and then progressively move towards the less tearful bits.

In Chanos' analogy, the inner core of the onion contains the information provided by the company that cannot be fudged. These are the 10-K filings along with other legally mandated filings that every public company has to provide to the SEC.

One layer removed from this inner core are the press releases put out by the company. These are fairly reliable, but their tone and message can be gilded, depending on how well the PR firm handling the issue massages words. Companies will typically not lie outright in these, but this doesn't mean that everything presented is 100% true either.

The third layer is the earnings calls that management conducts with analysts. These calls are usually held right after earnings announcements are made. Here, investors can listen to analysts that cover the company ask management questions about certain areas of their business and financials.

These statements are then used by analysts to create company analysis reports and these form the fourth layer of the onion. By the time this report has been published, it contains a ton of projections and estimates that may or may not be true. Most anomalies in reports have been explained away by management and analysts tend to toe the line with what management says.

The final layer of the onion is your neighbor Bob. Bob does nothing but trawl social media all day and isn't afraid to let people know his stock recommendations. He's a self-proclaimed expert on the financial markets despite his experience with it amounting to standing next to the Broadway bull. Your family members and all of your social media contacts fall into the Bob category.

Unfortunately, this is where most people begin and end their investing journey. Instead of doing this, do the intelligent thing and begin with the deepest, most uncomfortable, yet most accurate layer.

We should note, that simply hearing about a company on social media or from family and friends is not in itself a bad thing. The issue arises when buying decisions are made solely from this layer five level "research", if you can even call it research.

No matter where you hear about a company or potential investment, start at layer one and work your way outwards. We'll now explain each layer in depth.

LAYER ONE—LEGALLY MANDATED FILINGS

Why should you start with these filings instead of say, the analyst calls or research reports? Think of it this way: By reading these reports, you're getting the worst-case scenario in many ways. This is because the SEC thoroughly regulates the language contained within these filings.

Companies cannot conceal any facts or exaggerate any other elements in their financials unless it happens to be an opinion. Such opinions are noted explicitly in these filings. Do note that not all legal filings fall into this category.

Wall Street gets pretty breathless covering 10-Q releases. The 10-Q is a quarterly earnings statement that is filed by all public companies. It contains all of the financial information pertaining to the business in that quarter. Sounds pretty important, doesn't it? There's just one catch.

10-Qs are not audited! The company can literally enter any figure and pass it off as real. If the number is completely nonsensical, companies will release an amended 10-Q that contains a more realistic number. However, for analysis purposes, 10-Qs should be taken with a grain of salt.

The report that investors should be reading is the 10-K. These are the annual report filings that companies make with the SEC.

The 10-K

Do not confuse the 10-K filing with the annual reports that you can find on companies' investor relations websites. The latter are slickly produced and contain a large dose of propaganda. The SEC filing on the other hand is dull as ditchwater and looks like every high school student's worst nightmare.

It contains many pages, doesn't have any pictures and is written in small type. It also contains language that is forcefully neutral and is filled with legalese in certain areas. It has paragraphs that go on and on and is seemingly written by the most boring person in the world.

All of this is great news for you!

Believe it or not, this dull language serves a very important purpose. It stops you from getting carried away in the euphoria surrounding a company. There are a number of sections that do this brilliantly in a 10-K. The first section that is invaluable in a 10-K is the "Business" section.

This is where a company discusses their history and explains their business in detail. If they happen to have a subdivision of a subdivision hidden away in Wichita, you'll learn about it here. Companies can get a bit one-eyed over here and talk themselves up a bit.

To tone this down, the SEC mandates that the "Risk Factors" section come next. This section lays out all of the worst-case scenarios facing a business. For example, here are some gems from market favorite Tesla's 10-K (Tesla, 2020):

- *Any problems or delays in expanding Gigafactory Nevada or ramping and maintaining operations there, could negatively affect the production and profitability of our products, such as Model 3, Model Y and our energy storage products. In addition, the battery cells produced there store large amounts of energy.*
- *Any issues or delays in meeting our projected timelines, costs and production at or funding the ramp of Gigafactory Shanghai, or any difficulties in generating and maintaining local demand for vehicles manufactured there, could adversely impact our business, prospects, operating results and financial condition.*

Both of these points explained a lot of Elon Musk's latest tweets surrounding the lockdown. Mind you, these are just the headings of these sections. The company expands on both of these points in a lot of detail within the report.

Last but not least is this item:

- *We are highly dependent on the services of Elon Musk, our Chief Executive Officer.*

There are many ways of interpreting that particular line. On one hand you could argue that Musk's personality is the company's biggest strength. On the other hand, for a company of Tesla's size to be so heavily dependent on one man could be concerning. This book isn't providing stock recommendations, so we'll just leave it at that.

Our point is that you're unlikely to read such things in the company's press releases and certainly not in Musk's tweets. The company has to disclose all of its risk factors to investors. In addition to this, it also has to list all legal proceedings that it currently faces as well as all property it owns or leases.

The next section that is highly informative comes a little later in the report. This is titled the "Auditor's Report" or some equivalent name. This is where the auditing firm provides an opinion about the veracity of the financial statements as well as its opinions about the company's finances. It also highlights any accounting changes that have been made recently.

For example, here is what PricewaterhouseCoopers LLP notes about Tesla's financial statements:

As discussed in Note 2 to the consolidated financial statements, the Company changed the manner in which it accounts for leases in 2019 and the manner in which it accounts for revenue from contracts with customers in 2018.

This by itself is not an alarming note by any means since companies do this often. However, it alerts the investor to take a look at Note 2 in order to understand the basis of these statements better. Again, this isn't something you'll learn about by following social media.

Then there are the financial statements themselves that provide a lot of insight into a company's situation. Management discusses and highlights some of these numbers in a separate section that is quite illuminating as well.

Overall, the 10-K contains a wealth of information that every serious investor must read. It's best to read 10-Ks going back a few years since this gives a better picture of how the company has evolved over time.

Despite the high level of transparency in the 10-K, there are a few things to watch out for and pay attention to.

Notes to the Statements

The notes to statements are often treated much in the same way the bibliography of a book is treated by the average reader. Naming this section as being the "notes" is unfortunate. A better name, such as "the keys to understanding the statements" might get more investors to read them.

The notes are where companies are required to come clean about every little thing on their financial statements. This is where they describe their revenue recognition process, explain how they accounted for various line items and explain all off balance sheet financing measures.

That final term is something that Jeff Skilling of Enron was particularly fond of, and Enron was disclosing its less-than-honest scheme of earnings recognition in the notes of its 10-K long before the general public got wind of it (Ponzio, 2007).

The notes are also particularly illuminating when it comes to looking at the stock options that are being awarded to management. These days, stock options are expensed from income, but this wasn't always the case in the past. While you don't need to worry about excessive stock option awards these days, it pays to take a look at the sort of incentives management is being offered.

The notes also contain special items that are relevant to the way in which the company has accounted for certain one-off charges. You don't have to be an expert in accounting to understand these items. While they are heavy with jargon, they're not as difficult to understand as a lot of investors think.

Often, the notes will contain amendments to revenues that the company has recognized. This typically happens when the company has taken advantage of certain revenue recognition loopholes. SEC rules mandate that companies clarify all of the instances of this. The notes are where they disclose them and unfortunately most investors don't read them.

Revenues and earnings are at the center of a lot of controversy when it comes to accounting principles. These are the next topic of our discussion.

GAAP and EBITDA

Businesses are complex things and companies typically have complicated revenue streams. For example, when should a company recognize revenues on their books? For a small business, it makes sense to recognize them when cash enters their bank account. However, it's not so simple in the case of a large business.

Let's take the case of a retailer. They might have sold goods in December, yet face a raft of returns in February, thanks to a 90-day refund policy. Assuming their financial year ends in December, a cash-based revenue recognition system would result in massive ups and downs. It won't paint a clear picture of the way the company earns money.

Another example is that of companies that make sales towards the end of quarters or reporting periods. Let's say they land a huge account a few days before the reporting period ends. The customer is surely going to pay, but their cash will arrive a few days after the period ends. For all intents and purposes, the money is in the bank.

If a cash-based recognition system is followed, this will skew the numbers between the two reporting periods. You'll see a large peak in one period preceded by a much smaller peak or even a trough. Some companies receive payments for services a few years down the road thanks to payment plans and other agreements they have with their customers.

All of this makes revenue recognition a headache for companies. This also happens to be just one of many accounting issues that they deal with. To solve these issues a bunch of smart accountants got together and created a set of principles called the Generally Accepted Accounting Principles or GAAP (Tuovila, 2020).

GAAP is a lot like democracy. It isn't perfect, but it's the least worst system we have. There are loopholes in the GAAP framework and the SEC recognizes them. This is partly why the notes to the statements exist. GAAP rules are widely used in North America while the rest of the world follows the International Financial Reporting Standards (IFRS) protocol.

IFRS and GAAP are pretty much the same when it comes down to it. If you're looking at American companies, you'll be dealing with GAAP. One of the biggest grey areas in the GAAP framework is the recognition of revenues. The rules state that revenues must be recognized when there is substantial evidence of the work being complete and of the certainty of payment.

This is up to the discretion of the company and its auditors. The burden of proof is on the company, and the independent auditor must enforce standards when preparing the 10-K. Companies typically don't violate this rule because the consequences of doing so are too large. They could face a public backlash from their investors that sends their stock price tumbling.

Besides, GAAP now mandates companies to release a cash flow statement along with the income statement and balance sheet. The cash flow statement clarifies a lot of points that can be raised with regards to revenue recognition, and as such, there isn't much room to fudge the numbers.

There are a few loopholes, but these can be detected by reading the notes to the statements. The bottom line is that GAAP is a reliable framework for creating complex financial statements. There might be a few issues, but these are handled easily by intelligent investors.

Somewhere in the mid 80s, Wall Street began realizing the huge potential of the investment banking model. Previously, they earned fees only when companies wanted to merge with one another and the primary mode of exchange was equity. Somewhere along the way banks started figuring out that instruments such as junk bonds and convertible debt could be used just as effectively.

As the phenomenon of the leveraged buyout and hostile takeover became more mainstream, these banks ran into a problem. GAAP earnings often posed a problem when it came to financing these takeovers. A typical corporate raider would approach the bank to borrow money (junk bonds) to finance a takeover.

However due to GAAP income being too low or too high, financing would not always pass through a lender's underwriting requirements. The specifics of this process are not important. What you need to understand is that Wall Street, ever considerate of its clients' needs, created a solution.

This solution was called Earnings Before Interest, Taxes, Depreciation and Amortization or EBITDA (pronounced e-bit-da). This is a metric that makes a lot of sense on the surface, but in typical Wall Street fashion the devil is in the details. Here's how the reasoning goes: companies deduct a large number of non-cash-related expenses from their revenues.

Depreciation, for example, is a non-cash charge that companies take to reduce the value of the assets on their books. A desk that you bought five years ago is not worth the same amount you paid for it. You're still using it so you don't know what its market value is. The solution is to reduce its value by a certain percentage until you reduce it to zero.

Amortization works the same way. Let's say you're renting a home and the land-lord tells you that you need to pay the entire year's rent before moving in. This will lead to a huge cash hit upfront that will make it seem as if you've run out of money. This is inaccurate. The solution is to report the rental expense as 12 monthly payments over the course of the year. You amortize that single huge expense over time.

Then we have interest and taxes. Wall Street never quite explained the rationale behind including these in EBITDA, but it's included, so let's roll with it. By subtracting all of these non-cash expenses, taxes and interest, you gain a clearer picture of what the company's earning power is. At least that's what the proponents of EBITDA claim.

There is some merit to this. Buffett and Munger have spoken in the past about calculating owner earnings and that calculation also adds back non-cash expenses. However, EBITDA is a very different animal. For one thing, it's a non-GAAP measure.

This means companies are free to fudge it as they please. Here's a brief summary of what can be done (Mercer, 2020):

1. E - Earnings can be recognized for practically anything. If the company signed a memorandum of understanding (MoU - not a sales agreement), they can theoretically recognize that as proof of revenue.
2. I - Interest expense is excluded and this flat-out makes zero sense. It's a bit like saying a person's mortgage, car and credit card payments are not real expenses.

3. DA - These two items are prone to fudging even with GAAP. Companies can accelerate or decelerate their rates of D & A to boost earnings. With GAAP gone, companies can add as much as they please to EBITDA and claim it comes from D & A.

Over and above this, companies can claim any expense they like to cook EBITDA right up to the levels they want it to be. Enron was exemplary in this regard and one wonders what Jeff Skilling might have achieved had he directed his creative skills towards art or music.

Enron regularly hyped its EBITDA numbers and created a buzz on Wall Street. This boosted its stock price and earned its management hefty stock option compensation. A typical model that Skilling used to boost EBITDA was to recognize MoUs as evidence of revenue collection (Segal, 2020).

Of course, this being Jeff Skilling there was an added dash of creativity applied. The MoUs were signed between Enron and offshore subsidiaries of Enron. Imagine if a car maker's Japanese unit agreed to buy cars from its American unit and then cancelled the order once the reporting period passed. This is pretty much what was going on with Enron, amongst other equally nonsensical measures.

EBITDA can be manipulated to the extreme and is a Wall Street creation. It has never made sense and you ought to ignore this. GAAP has a few loopholes but is a far tighter regime. This is what you must pay attention to. 10-K filings are GAAP based.

LAYER TWO—COMPANY PRESS RELEASES

While the 10-K is pretty hard to put a spin on, press releases offer a bit more leeway in this regard. Here companies are bound by regulations from the SEC but have control over the words they use. Thus, with some decent word-smithing, they can potentially downplay the impact of adverse circumstances.

The size of the company in question also plays a role in how press releases can be used. Smaller companies often use press releases to tout their earnings and this can cause stock prices to rise. There's also selective disclosure that is practiced.

Larger companies have an army of lawyers who protect them from disclosing too much in their releases. The idea is to promote the good and minimize the bad as much as possible. Consider this recent press release from Tesla that is exemplary in its optimism ("Tesla Q1 2020 Vehicle Production & Deliveries," 2020):

In the first quarter, we produced almost 103,000 vehicles and delivered approximately 88,400 vehicles. This is our best ever first quarter performance.

The quarter referenced above is the first quarter of 2020. "Best ever" quarterly performance! Sounds great! The press release continues below.

Model Y production started in January and deliveries began in March, significantly ahead of schedule. Additionally, our Shanghai factory continued to achieve record levels of production, despite significant setbacks.

"Ahead of schedule," "record levels of production"—all of this sounds great. "Significant setbacks"? Well, record production levels offset that! Tesla has seemingly managed to overcome the challenges of a global pandemic.

At least, that's what the management wants you to think. The point here is not to say that Tesla is hiding things. Every company practices this sort of communication. It's important for you to look at what lies beneath these statements.

Note the point about record levels of production from Shanghai. If you glance at the most recent 10-K (reporting results from 2019), Tesla notes that the factory was scheduled to open in January 2020. Thus, "record levels of production" are to be expected in Q1 2020 if there is no previous record to compare it to!

While Tesla's form of communication is the most prevalent, there are instances where companies will simply lie on their press releases. This usually happens when the company is unaware of the situation and is often the result of incompetence and not malice.

A good case in point was the Cambridge Analytica scandal that Facebook was involved in. Facebook data was being used to create user profiles and this was used to deliver targeted political ads to them. Facebook did provide a disclosure saying that users' data might be misused.

However, it adopted a "don't ask, don't tell" policy when it came to data misuse by third-party companies. As far as it was concerned, the way other platforms used data it provided was none of its business. Facebook's argument was a bit like saying that if you lend someone money and they end up causing harm using that money, it isn't your fault.

Except, Facebook knew what Cambridge Analytica was doing with user data. In the previous example, it's like knowing what the other person was planning to do with the money before you gave it to them. This was the basis of the SEC's argument ("Facebook to Pay $100 Million for Misleading Investors About the Risks It Faced From Misuse of User Data," 2019).

Frustratingly, the company got away with a $100 million fine, which barely moves the needle, given its size. It also did not admit any wrongdoing. All Mark Zuckerberg had to do was appear on C-Span and repeat that he was sorry to a group of appropriately outraged senators.

Throughout the scandal, Facebook's press releases touted how it "valued" users' privacy. Once the scandal ended, it announced that it was "turning the page" on the scandal and was focusing on the "future."

LAYER THREE—EARNINGS CALLS WITH MANAGEMENT

Once a company releases earnings reports, it typically holds an earnings call with analysts covering the company. These calls are an opportunity for analysts to question management about the recent results and any other issues that surround the company. In practice, what really happens is that management receives a bunch of softball questions that are easy to handle without saying much of value.

One of the more famous earnings calls transcripts occurred in 2015 when the CEO of Marriott was questioned by an analyst about expected changes to the holiday season spending patterns. The analyst enquired whether there was anything investors ought to know about Q1 2016.

The CEO responded by saying that New Year's Day would fall on January 1st. The CFO responded that Easter would fall on a Sunday. Everyone chuckled and moved on.

The reason for such inanity occurs because analysts are heavily dependent on the very managers of the company they cover. Wall Street analysts are expected to provide thorough and intelligent sounding reports to their clients. However, these reports cannot be thorough without gaining access to company documents.

These documents are provided by management and there is an unspoken quid pro quo that occurs here. If the analyst provides a bad review of the company, you can bet that their levels of access will be curtailed or that important information might be withheld.

It isn't entirely the analysts' fault, to be honest. It's their job to have an opinion. However, not every client appreciates an honest opinion despite what they might say. This is typically the case with hot stocks such as Tesla and Netflix that everyone loves. A sell rating from an analyst usually results in prices dropping.

This enrages existing investors and they direct their ire towards the analyst who made the call. As a result, the analyst loses client support and, coupled with the loss of company access, it's a death knell for their career.

Earnings calls therefore are a meet and greet between old friends. Some companies hold themselves to a high standard of honesty and transparency. The majority of them don't.

LAYER FOUR—WALL STREET ANALYST REPORTS

Despite being a different layer, the same issues plague this layer as well. We're still in the world of the analyst and it's close to impossible to receive an honest opinion from them about the companies they cover. Once the earnings reports have been released and calls done, it's the analyst's job now to put some spin on things.

If everything is fine with the company, the analyst doesn't have much to do. All they need to do is repeat what management says and their job is done. This keeps both the company as well as the clients happy. Things become more difficult when the company is facing a tough time.

In such situations, the analyst relies on future earnings and projections. In particular, there is one nonsensical metric that is often put forward. This is the forward price to earnings ratio (PE). The PE ratio is calculated by dividing the stock price by the earnings per share. It is a measure of how cheap or expensive the company is.

All sectors have different standards by which the PE is defined as being expensive or cheap. Technology companies typically have high PE ratios while utility companies have low PE ratios. The forward PE uses projected earnings per share in its calculation.

To calculate the projected earnings of a company, the analyst uses all kinds of estimates and other data provided by management to arrive at an estimate. The fact that this is an estimate gets lost on them at some point and forward PE ratios are treated as gospel. It's not uncommon to witness stock prices drop after an analyst projects a lower forward PE.

Thus, according to the market and the average investor, a good analyst has to be a psychic as well.

Apart from this projection nonsense that happens, there are deep conflicts of interest that are rife within the industry. Analysts typically work for large investment banks. These investment banks earn hefty fees from companies for carrying out all kinds of work with regards to restructuring, going public etc.

It's a brave analyst who issues a sell rating for a company that is a lucrative client of the highly paid investment banking and trading division. Analysts who do this are immediately sidelined and fade away from the Street after a few years.

Lastly, every analyst has their own system of weighting and standards. A buy rating from one analyst might equate to a hold from another. For example, if analysts from Barrington's Research and C.L. King expect a company to outperform the S&P 500 by 9% over the next year, the former would rate it as a strong buy while the latter would issue a hold rating on it ("Guide to Analyst Recommendations," 2020).

Analyst reports are not completely useless. However, you do need to keep the inherent conflicts of interest and bias in mind when reading them. They can give you insight into select data from within the company. Just don't rely on them entirely and definitely don't pay any attention to ratings.

LAYER FIVE—MAINSTREAM NEWS, SOCIAL MEDIA CHATTER AND STOCK TIPS FROM FRIENDS AND FAMILY

There is a wide variety of media that is contained within this layer. Think of how the average person makes stock investment decisions and you have an example of this layer. Tips from friends and family, your coworker, social media, mainstream media and so on are examples of layer five sources of research.

Calling it research is a bit of a stretch. In this layer there is almost no insight. At best, you might find some funny memes and that's about it. Unfortunately, this layer has an outsized impact on stock price. We say unfortunate because it indicates the number of people who confine themselves here.

As an intelligent investor, this is a huge advantage for you. Social media chatter will lead to some amazing buying opportunities in companies. After all, you cannot receive bargains with inefficiencies existing and social media is one huge inefficiency when it comes to company analysis.

Knee-jerk opinions? Check. Lack of nuance in analysis? Check. A desire to one up the other person instead of solving an issue? Check. These behaviors aren't native to just social media. The mainstream media is adept at this as well. Prominent financial reporters make a name for themselves by breaking news about companies. It's just that the sources of these news items come from within the company itself. There hasn't been any mainstream media outlet that has broken news of fraud or of any other form of financial inappropriateness. Even worse is the habit of financial shows bringing expert investors on the show to lend an air of credibility.

Famous investors typically recommend stocks on air and this ends up driving prices up massively. While the recommendations might be solid, it doesn't change the fact that a company's stock is a bargain at a certain price. Buying a loaf of bread for a few cents is a great deal. Buying it for five dollars is a bit of a stretch.

Opinions at this stage are simply a collection of the herd mentality. You're unlikely to receive any insight here. Even hotshot CEOs who use their Twitter accounts as propaganda tools rarely provide any insight. Elon Musk famously fires off on Twitter all the time.

One tweet of his caused a drop of 10% in Tesla's stock price to $700. The media reported this by saying that $14 billion had been "wiped" off Tesla's market value. Musk is unlikely to have cared because he inhabits another planet and he's unlikely to have sold any of his stock. Intelligent investors spotted an opportunity and Tesla's stock duly hit $1,200 within the next 3 months.

Most investors begin their analysis at this level and work backwards through the layers. By the time they get to the most important layers, they've formed a strong opinion of the company and are now subject to their own confirmation bias. They're looking for evidence that supports their point of view instead of remaining neutral. Herein lies the danger of working from the outside in, rather than the inside out.

A classic example of a level 5 trap is that of Luckin Coffee. The Chinese company was a social media darling for much of 2018 and 2019. A media narrative focused on technological disruption and being dubbed "The Chinese Starbucks", drove stock prices up 20 fold from the IPO price.

However, smart investors would have noticed a lack of transparency in financial reports, dubious claims about how sales were actually recorded (all sales were recorded within the company's own mobile app), and growth numbers which were completely divergent from the "eye-test" of the number of people physically present in Luckin Coffee stores.

So it was of no surprise to us when less than a year after the IPO, Luckin disclosed that 75% of their 2019 revenue was fake. Share prices tumbled 83% in a single day, and it was retail investors who felt the brunt of this (Han, 2020).

This didn't stop many retail investors from sensing a get rich opportunity. So we saw significant buying from retail investors when Luckin hit $5/share. This buying spree wasn't based on fundamentals, or intrinsic value. Instead it was based on greed and hope. We've seen a similar situation with Hertz as well.

Hope is not a process, and imagining that if a stock like Luckin only recovers to 30% of all time highs, you'll still make a huge profit" does not change poor management and bad finances.

We live in the greatest investing age ever. Because anyone with an internet connection can now access the most unbiased financial reporting on any public company within minutes. Therefore, it's imperative your process starts from the inside out, and deals with the most uncomfortable information first. Doing so will not only make you a better investor, it'll help you sleep a lot better at night as well.

The Onion Model: Most investors start from the outside in, and never get past layer 5 before making their decision. The best investors start from the inside out, and make a decision before even acknowledging layer 5.

"ONCE WE REALIZE THAT IMPERFECT UNDERSTANDING IS THE HUMAN CONDITION THERE IS NO SHAME IN BEING WRONG, ONLY IN FAILING TO CORRECT OUR MISTAKES,"

George Soros, who made over $1 Billion in a single day in 1992 after shorting the British Pound during the UK's attempt to withdraw from the European Exchange Rate Mechanism.

4

NAVIGATING THE FLAWS IN HUMAN PSYCHOLOGY

You learned about how the confirmation bias skews your ability to properly analyze an opportunity. The fact is that human beings are subject to a wide range of biases that cloud our ability to judge situations. These flaws are deep-seated evolutionary instincts and it's close to impossible to get rid of them. In fact, you might not even want to do this.

The good news is that you can become aware of them and choose to ignore their call in a given situation. Money and investing is an intensely emotional process. In order to be successful at it, you have to keep these biases in mind and guard against them. Making money over the long term often boils down to avoiding mental traps as opposed to coming up with a genius-level plan.

This chapter is going to introduce you to some of the most common flaws in human thinking and show you how you can navigate them.

THE BLOOD IN THE STREETS PROBLEM

"Be fearful when others are greedy and be greedy when others are fearful."

Out of the thousands of Warren Buffett quotes regularly touted by the media, this one, more than any other, has received the most airtime lately. Like many of his statements, there is a lot of nuance to it that is often lost on the wider public. Even investors who study his methods fall prey to this kind of thinking.

They assume a default position of looking to buy stocks the minute the market begins to fall. They wear contrarian badges proudly and neglect to realize that they're being overly greedy in this scenario and aren't investing intelligently.

Buffett's statement is a good philosophy to adopt, but it isn't something that should be applied at every turn. Not every low-priced stock is a good buy and not every high-priced stock is a potential sell. You still need to do the work and analyze what's going on underneath.

Believing in this philosophy blindly will cause you to fall victim to your confirmation bias. You'll spot a low-priced stock and automatically believe that it's a great opportunity. Your analysis will now be colored by this thought and you'll filter out information that proves the opposite case.

The best way to guard against these situations is to use Charlie Munger's advice and recognize that truly outstanding opportunities occur very rarely in life. The majority of the opportunities you receive are going to be below par. As a result, even if you miss them, you're not going to lose out too much. The important stuff has a way of finding you, and you'll be able to recognize it when it comes.

The partnership of Buffett and Munger has worked well for the both of them. Why not use their philosophies to form a partnership in your mind to help you as well?

Another behavior that often occurs by believing Buffett's philosophy to an extreme is when investors become obsessed with calling the bottom of the bear market. They're impatient to enter the market and as a result, begin thinking of every bottom as the moment when prices are about to swing the other way.

This only results in them investing in short rallies. The market drops ever lower and they keep losing money by exiting and reentering even lower.

Stay away from this kind of behavior if you wish to make long term profits. Instead, evaluate every situation on its own merit and be aware of your propensity to believe in this philosophy a little too much.

LEARNING TO APPRECIATE A CRISIS

We've touched upon this sentiment previously. Bear markets offer investors a huge opportunity to enter some of the best companies in the market at bargain basement prices. Crises often inject a lot of emotion into the markets and people overreact to such announcements.

For example, the COVID-19 pandemic will have a significant impact on businesses. However, the extent of the initial fall in the markets was grossly exaggerated. There were some truly excellent companies that were available at 20-25% discounts from their true value. Many of them were companies we already held such as Starbucks, Berkshire Hathaway and McDonald's. Needless to say, we loaded up on them to lower our cost basis.

The reasoning behind buying even more of these companies wasn't that their prices had dropped. It was that their underlying economics hadn't changed. These underlying factors were the reason for investing in them in the first place. As long as these remained intact, the only logical thing to do was to buy more of them.

If you can act rationally while the markets are irrational, you'll make a lot of money. This is why a crisis offers a huge opportunity for the intelligent investor. Emotions run riot during these times and inefficiencies pile up to create huge discounts between price and value.

STOP CHASING MOMENTUM

During bull markets, buying high-momentum stocks is a popular strategy. The stocks that have historically exhibited higher growth levels than the broader market typically rise a lot quicker when times are good. Many momentum investors bring this philosophy to bear markets as well.

They reason that if stocks that rise higher than the market provide gains in bull markets, stocks that fall faster than the rest will make them money in bear markets. This sounds great on paper, but unfortunately it doesn't work this way. Shorting everything in sight isn't a strategy. Shorting refers to when an investor can sell a stock first before buying it back for a lower price.

Bear markets usually witness lower participation from people. This is because no one likes it when markets go down and the average investor is uncomfortable with the shorting process. Bull markets witness huge levels of involvement and as a result, pretty much every stock tends to rise. You can get away with buying everything in sight because there are large numbers of other investors who are doing the same thing.

Due to volumes being lower in bear markets, this effect doesn't carry over. To modify what Tolstoy once wrote, all stocks rise for the same reasons, but every stock declines for different reasons. Some might drop in an unjustified manner while some will drop for fully valid reasons.

You'll need to examine them individually to determine what the reason for the drop is. Assuming that bear market irrationality carries over to each and every individual company is the wrong thing to do.

Then there's the other side of the coin. Some investors believe that once the market has fallen low enough, every stock in it is a worthwhile buy. This is just as much of an error as shorting everything is. They feel that since everything that has fallen must rise at some point, every company is a reasonable buy.

There are investors out there who are still buying companies such as Luckin Coffee, airlines and cruise ship operators just because their prices have dropped a lot. In Luckin's case, the drop was caused by financial fraud. In the case of airlines and cruise ship operators, it's still unknown how they'll recover from the restrictions imposed by the pandemic.

Companies go bankrupt all the time. The good times lead investors to forget this crucial fact. They forget that businesses will face tough conditions at some point in the road. The ones that prepare for them beforehand are the ones that survive. The ones that load themselves up with leverage tend to be exposed when the music stops.

Perhaps the most egregious example in the current market is that of Hertz. Retail investors were buying up huge amounts of stock, even after the company declared Chapter 11 Bankruptcy. In a 6 day period in March 2020, the stock price went from $3.38 to $8.21. An increase of 148.04%. A similar trend occurred in June 2020 when the price went from $1.50 to $5.53, an increase of 268.67%.

Most alarmingly of all, these trends continued after Hertz issued $500 million in new shares. The share release prospectus (an SEC mandated 8-K filing) including the word "worthless", alluding to future stock values, a staggering 7 times. For day traders, these wild fluctuations in share price might be a positive. But for long-term investors, we can't think of a worse company to buy right now than one currently going through bankruptcy procedures, and facing a delisting from the New York Stock Exchange.

Just because stocks are cheap, does not make them a worthwhile investment. Stocks can and do go to zero.

So stop chasing trends in bear markets. Whether the trends are up or down, don't buy or sell stocks just because the strategy worked in a bull market. This is how you'll lose money.

DON'T OVERREACT TO NEWS

Bear markets cause most market participants to lose their heads. They see doomsday warnings everywhere and this causes huge price movements in the markets. This is referred to as volatility. Volatility is a measure of how fast and how far a particular instrument in the market moves.

Bull markets witness volatility but of a different kind. Due to the abundance of good news and due to everyone jumping into the market believing it's going higher, the market moves quickly in one direction (upwards.)

Bear markets experience a different kind of volatility. Due to uncertainty and fear pervading the markets, prices jump up and down to a huge degree all the time. This results in a lot of investors getting cleaned out. Take for instance the shenanigans that surrounded the price of oil recently.

Due to lockdowns being imposed, the demand for oil crashed to lows. As a result, the price of oil moved into negative territory for the first time ever. Oil is traded through futures contracts. These contracts are valid for a month and anyone who buys them is effectively locking in a purchase of oil for that month.

Prices moving into negative territory was a quirk of the futures market. Physical oil was still selling at positive prices. However, a few investors reasoned that the quirk of pricing in the market could be exploited. There were a number of news outlets that jumped on the hysteria as well and screamed that "oil was negative!" and so on.

A large number of investors bought oil-related instruments in the hope of witnessing a positive jump. However, they underestimated the degree to which they understood the oil market. As a result, they ended up getting cleaned out. It wasn't the bear market that caused them a loss. It was their lack of understanding of the instrument they were investing in.

This lack of understanding came about because they'd put their blinders on and were convinced they'd spotted an opportunity. They treated it as the deal of a lifetime. If they'd instead followed Charlie Munger's advice as highlighted before, they'd have been able to get rid of their confirmation bias and would have stepped aside.

There are a lot of market participants out there who have no idea what they're talking about. In this age of social media, you're going to be bombarded with all of their opinions and they'll likely sound very convincing and smart. Of course, they'll still be wrong for the most part.

Going bargain hunting in sectors or assets you do not understand is the easiest way for you to lose money. We'll cover this in more detail shortly. The COVID-19 pandemic is already witnessing a raft of intelligent-sounding social media discussions and media coverage when it comes to companies in the pharmaceutical sector.

Almost every drug maker is now working on a potential cure that is extremely promising. The expected bump upwards in share prices duly arrives shortly after such announcements. Popular themes tend to be used in this way by companies to boost their share prices.

The best example of this is a small beverage maker based out of Long Island, NY. The company's name was Long Island Iced Tea after the famous adult beverage. Despite the name, it sold iced teas with a small degree of success. However, in 2017 it announced that it would change its name to Long Blockchain corp and would begin to explore opportunities in blockchain technology (Cheng, 2017). Which sounds like a perfectly reasonable thing for a beverage maker to do.

Shares of Long Island Iced Tea duly jumped over 200% and eventually settled at 183% above the opening price before the announcement. There was no reason for this jump other than the word "blockchain" being added to the name. No one stopped to question why on earth a reasonably successful beverage maker was switching its focus to blockchain.

Instead, its share price rose thanks to the millions of uninformed investors thinking this was a bargain of a lifetime and the chance to get in on something great. Needless to say these shenanigans got the company into trouble and it was eventually investigated by the SEC.

STOP HUNTING FOR SHORT-TERM SUCCESS STORIES

As human beings, we love believing in optimistic happy endings. Even the most hardcore pessimists among us love to believe that things will turn out fine in the end. While this applies to the big picture, it doesn't necessarily apply to every single entity within that picture.

For example, the market might recover well in the long run, but there's no guarantee that all of the current companies in the market will recover along with it. Most investors don't extend their thinking beyond the most obvious of consequences that a company might be facing.

This illustrates the importance of second order thinking. This is in contrast to first order thinking. For example, if you're hungry and someone gives you a bar of chocolate, you reason that the chocolate will satisfy you. Hence, you arrive at the conclusion that eating the bar of chocolate is good for you. This is first order thinking.

Second order thinking requires you to go a bit further and ask "then what?" Once you've eaten the chocolate, then what happens? You'll feel full, but is this really the best option for your health? Will it cause you harm thanks to all of the other chocolate bars you've eaten? Thinking in this way will get you to reason that a healthier snack might be in order.

The right decision often comes from engaging in second order thinking. This is especially true when the first order choice is negative or distasteful. You might not feel like waking up in the morning and exercising because you slept late last night. However, if you keep sleeping in, you'll not hit your fitness goals and this will cause even bigger problems down the road.

When it comes to investing, first order thinking is prevalent everywhere. This is what causes the stock price of companies like Zoom and Netflix to rocket upwards. At one point Zoom was selling at a PE ratio of 1000! This is more than sixty times the price of comparable companies in its sector.

The reasoning behind such a large price rise is due to evaluating first order consequences. People are going to be confined to their homes a lot more and will therefore use both apps increasingly. However, what are the second order consequences of being at home for longer?

Is Zoom capable of cashing in on its newfound fame? It is an app designed primarily for B2B communication. It has already faced a crisis when users discovered security flaws within its structure. While the company has dealt with this admirably, is there some other danger that Zoom is exposed to because of this new army of users?

Then there's Netflix. The company has witnessed higher user numbers. However, it's producing original content at a much faster rate and is investing the same amount of money into creating it as Disney currently is. Disney has revenue streams and valuable trademarks to backup its investment.

Netflix has nowhere near this kind of cushion. Can it sustain profits despite investing this much into content creation?

Often, the worst consequences come from decisions that have positive first order effects and negative second and even third order effects. For example, let's say a new CFO joins a startup and, in a bid to make a great impression, decides to do away with free snacks and meals.

The first order effect is huge cost savings for the company and a boost to its bottom line. The second order effect is older employees getting disillusioned and jumping ship because things aren't the same. The employees who joined the startup are who made the company what it is, so this will leave a mark.

A third order effect might be the startup's competition realizing the importance of free snacks and they might begin offering this to their employees. As a result, talented employees jump ship to the competition and the startup struggles to attract talent, let alone grow.

Short-term success stories are typically the result of first order thinking. Believing that everything will be fine and that things will go back to the way they once were only causes you to look for positive first order consequences. For example, with the pandemic having enforced a new normal in people's lives, everyone wants to go back to the time when things weren't this way.

However as the pandemic has proven, the world was extremely fragile in 2019. Is this really a state we want to spend our lives in? In a world that is on the verge of being turned upside down without adequate support? Where excess leverage is rewarded and where economic prosperity is just an illusion?

Considering second order effects gets you thinking in this manner, and in the markets it will make you money. An added bonus is that you'll have less competition to deal with!

EVALUATING YOUR CURRENT PORTFOLIO

Bear markets bring significant shocks to the system and your portfolio is going to feel these effects. Before making a move to get rid of any of your current holdings, ask yourself if the underlying economics of the business has changed. Have any of your original investment considerations changed at all

If the answer is yes, then you should exit your investment. However, if there hasn't been any change in the underlying business, you should be buying more. If the business was a good buy at $50, it must be an even better buy at $30.

By forcing yourself to look at the underlying business in a logical manner, you'll end up acting in rational terms. You will stick to your original investment thesis and avoid haphazardly jumping in and out of stocks.

If price shocks really bother you and if you're looking to lock in your unrealized profit, you can use what is called a trailing stop loss order. A stop loss order protects your downside risk on your investment. This is a sell order that you place with your broker and instructs them to sell your investment if the market dips below a certain price.

For example, if you buy a stock at $100 and place a stop loss at $80, your maximum loss on this order is $20. Now if the stock moves up to $120, you've earned an unrealized paper profit of $20. If you would like to lock in some profit, you could place a trailing stop loss order that is $10 away from the current market price thereby locking in 50% of the price rise.

As the stock price keeps rising, your stop loss order keeps rising with it and "trails" the market price. This allows you to lock in whatever profit you've made. If the market moves back down too swiftly, you'll exit your investment at the trailing stop loss level and will keep your gains.

DON'T WATCH WHAT PEOPLE SAY—WATCH WHAT THEY DO

Many investors turn to the mainstream financial press and their favorite blogs during bearish times in search of guidance. This isn't a bad thing by itself. After all, you do need to remain up to date with what's going on in the markets. The problem occurs when you begin to use these sources as justifications for investment actions.

Thanks to the media's obsession with finding a bottom for the bear market, you'll hear statements from hedge fund managers proclaiming that they're now bullish. A few others will come out and say that they're bearish. Eventually these two opposing parties will be brought on air to argue against one another.

At the end of the day nothing gets decided and the market does whatever it wants to do. A lot of these arguments are set up by the media and these hedge fund managers often don't believe the things they proclaim. The best way to figure out where someone stands is to look at what they do, instead of listening to what they say.

If an investor is bullish, have they been buying anything? What does their portfolio look like? If the investor doesn't offer proof for their statements, there's no need to listen to them. Examine their statements for consistency as well.

One website that offers a look at the portfolios of famous investors is gurufocus.com. On the site you can see the current portfolios of investors like Warren Buffett, Carl Icahn and Bill Ackman, as well as other businessmen like Bill Gates. For example, did you know almost 10% of Bill Gates' portfolio is in utilities company Waste Management (NYSE:WM)?

Opinions change all the time. However, you can't invest on the basis of someone changing their opinion every other day.

In fact, take everyone else's opinion with a large grain of salt. You don't know what their motivations are and where they're coming from. Evaluate their words objectively, watch what they do and see if those actions make sense for you. If they don't, feel free to ignore them.

YOUR STOCK DOESN'T LOVE YOU

Or perhaps we should say, your stock doesn't love you as much as you love your stock. You cannot hold onto your investments just because you've developed an emotional bond with them. Many investors become attached to their holdings and fall right into the trap of the sunken cost fallacy.

This is an emotional bias that we develop. If you've invested money into something, you're now deeply affected by its prospects. If it declines, you think that you'll simply ride out the bottom of the curve and wait until it gets back to where it was. Besides, pulling the trigger and cutting the investment loose will cause you to lose money.

That's painful for a lot of investors. As we mentioned earlier, you need to objectively evaluate your reasons for investment and check if they're still valid. If the underlying business has changed, you need to let go of your investments and cut your losses (if any) as quickly as possible.

You know you're a rational investor when you have the confidence to short the very stocks you once bought!

246

AVOID NARRATIVE INVESTING

Every one of us loves a good story. Unfortunately, successful investing doesn't care much for your stories. It relies on facts and logic. If a company isn't successfully hitting its targets with its product, that company is going to decline. If it doesn't follow good business principles, it's going to decline.

This example is a bit old, but it's worth pointing out. Concorde was and still remains the only fully functioning supersonic commercial airplane. It was developed in 1969 and was an engineering marvel. Calling it an engineering marvel is an understatement in fact ("When Did Concorde First Fly to North America?," 2020).

The plane was never significantly updated in terms of technology until its retirement in 2003. Despite this, it was still faster than any modern commercial airliner. Concorde could fly from London to New York in an average time of three and a half hours, with the fastest flight time coming in just under three hours.

Modern airplanes cover the same distance in just under eight hours. The plane had an average cruising altitude of 65,000 feet. This meant passengers could look at space up above if they peeked outside their windows. They could see the curvature of the earth as well. Concorde wasn't a plane as much as it was an experience.

It was also a monumental flop, as such things sadly are. Despite the wonderful experience every passenger had, the plane was commercially unsuccessful. British Airways and Air France never earned a profit on Concorde flights. The plane was fuel-efficient at supersonic speed. However, getting there meant it had to accelerate to Mach Two over populated areas.

This meant that all houses over Concorde's flight path were subject to sonic booms. European governments soon outlawed mainland continental Concorde flights due to this. Not that it mattered anyway. Concorde needed long flight distances to truly stretch its legs and New York to London was the only route at the time that had sufficient demand.

A tragic accident in Paris in 2000 that involved an Air France Concorde, but was not caused by any faults in the plane, sealed its reputation in France. It never flew from France again. British Airways struggled with it until finally pulling the plug in 2003. A marvelous engineering feat that showed what humanity was capable of was put out of action with little ceremony.

As emotional as people became over Concorde, there's no denying that it was never going to succeed and it didn't make sense to invest in it (assuming you had the chance.) People get emotional about the products their portfolio companies make as well.

You can invest in a company that is making a product that is going to change the world. However, if this product isn't going to be commercially successful, that company is going nowhere. Investors form such world-changing narratives in their minds and this causes them to ignore facts. Concorde should have been put out of its misery in the 1980s, but sheer emotion kept the flights operational. British Airways and Air France had their confirmation bias blinders on fully and only looked at the positives.

One of the worst mistakes you can make as an investor is to retrofit your emotional investment thesis to sound rational. For example, you might like the way Tesla's cars look and believe in Elon Musk's drive and energy. You might also believe that electric cars are going to take over the world. You thus decide to invest in Tesla stock without looking at the numbers and underlying business.

When someone asks you why you invested in Tesla you then say something about how Musk is disrupting thought and how Tesla is disrupting the automotive sector and the internal combustion engine and so on. By doing this you've given your emotional decision the veneer of logic.

Our point is not to say that Tesla is a bad investment. It's to say that you need to be careful and avoid falling into narrative traps such as these that aren't backed by facts. During bull markets, the majority of companies rise in value thanks to the overall mood of optimism. This means narrative investing works very well in such times. However, it falls apart in bear markets.

KNOWING YOUR CIRCLE OF COMPETENCE AND AVOIDING TOURIST TRAPS

A tourist trap is a stock that draws investment into itself purely because of headlines that highlight how cheap it is (Summers, 2020). Oil ETFs were a tourist trap recently thanks to the price of oil dipping below zero.

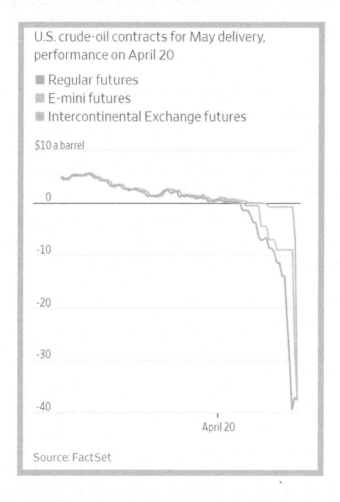

U.S. crude-oil contracts for May delivery, performance on April 20

■ Regular futures
■ E-mini futures
■ Intercontinental Exchange futures

$10 a barrel

Source: FactSet

We've already highlighted the example of investors who poured their money into buying oil-related instruments and were burned by the market. This occurred due to them straying away from their circle of competence. The circle of competence is a fancy term for explaining all of the things you know well.

For example, a medical doctor's circle of competence extends to their field and practice. It probably does not include knowledge on how to build a rocket. An NFL athlete's circle of competence extends to his sport. He might be above average at another sport, like baseball, but it's no guarantee that he'll be elite at it or be able to play professionally.

In real life, most people stay away from things that call for specialized expertise. If a pipe bursts, you call a plumber. However, put someone in front of a trading screen and suddenly they're experts at evaluating everything from a utilities company to a technology company.

This behavior gets really bad when people begin investing in certain exchange traded funds (ETFs). ETFs are a great, low-cost way to invest, but a lot of the market surrounding them has misled people. They are convenient, but ETFs are effectively hedge funds for the everyday investor. Each fund has a particular strategy that the fund manager follows. There are simple ETFs such as SPY that track the broad stock market by owning all of the stocks in the S&P 500.

However, the common misconception is that ETFs work this way. Many ETFs do not own the underlying asset. This is the case for many ETFs which retail investors buy to get exposure to non-equity markets like commodities or precious metals. For example, the USO ETF attempts to mimic the price of oil by trading oil futures. Investing in futures contracts means that the fund has to utilize leverage (borrow money).

Once the oil market went into meltdown, this put USO in a very bad situation. Its assets were deteriorating and its creditors were turning up asking for their money. So with oil prices hovering near zero, many traders felt that USO would be a good buy. What these traders didn't realize is that because they were trading in futures contracts and not the spot price of oil, prices could go negative. This happens as the fund itself would have to pay others to take the futures contracts off their hands. This is exactly what happened, as prices crashed to -$37.63. However for many retails investors, their investment platform showed positive prices on the screen, likely due to the way the software had been programmed. It wasn't until the following day when they realized that they had suffered catastrophic losses.

This was because USO practiced what is called a next month rollover. A rollover happens when an investor shifts their position from the current month futures contract to the contract that expires one month after that. USO had religiously rolled its contracts over every month for the last 10 years when the current month futures expired.

With the current month price near 0 and the next month's price at $12, investors figured they could capture that huge price swing. All they had to do was buy USO and wait for the rollover.

Except the rollover never came. USO announced it would be restructuring its contracts and that the rollover was being modified. This meant that all investors who had bet on the rollover lost their shirts. Was this legal? Yes. This was the point that these investors missed. USO was not bound to rollover their contacts in the first place! It was entirely up to management to do so. Professional firms knew this and profited handsomely, but it was retail investors who paid the price. According to the Wall Street Journal, Interactive Brokers had to pay more than $100m to cover for traders whose "holdings" ended up in the negative.

These investors' losses were caused by not understanding what they were investing in. as well as playing in areas that were well beyond their circle of competence. When investing in ETFs, especially ones which are non-equity focused, don't let greed cloud your judgment. Always read the prospectus from the fund's website before buying and understand how it functions before putting money into it. If you find that you can't understand how the ETF works and what the investment strategy is, stay away from it.

"IF YOU FIND YOURSELF LOSING SLEEP OVER YOUR INVESTMENTS, SELL DOWN TO THE SLEEPING POINT"

Jesse Livermore, often referred to as the "Father of Day Trading"

5

HOW TO CAPITALIZE EFFECTIVELY IN A BEAR MARKET

Y ou've learned that bear markets offer huge opportunities for the intelligent investor. How are you supposed to take advantage of them exactly? Every investor could do with a primer of sorts before we get into the details of bear market investment, and this is what you'll learn now.

These points are a mix of tips and best practices for bear markets. They'll help you prepare for those times and will also keep you safe.

OPTIMIZE YOUR ACTIVITY LEVELS

How active should you be in a bear market? Given that there will be more opportunities for you to invest in, it stands to reason that you'll be more active in bear markets than in bullish ones. However, being active merely for the sake of it doesn't make any sense.

Some investors understand that bear markets offer huge opportunities but get carried away with the thought of finding them. This causes them to put their confirmation bias blinders on, and they soon find themselves buying into investment ideas that have no merit.

It's important for you to always keep the basic principles of investment in mind. Just because a market has turned bearish, this doesn't mean you're obliged to find opportunities. Some investors might have their egos hurt and think they're missing out on huge opportunities.

They might begin to question their analysis process and think they're being far too conservative. They might end up modifying or loosening their criteria, and the next thing you know, they're buying the likes of Luckin Coffee because they cannot think of anything else to buy.

Remember that there's no rule saying that you have to invest in a bear market. Whether bullish or bearish, the principles of sound investment are the same. You need to evaluate companies within your circle of competence and you need to understand what their business is all about.

If you cannot understand something, you need to stay away from it. This applies to all forms of investment, by the way, and all asset classes as well. A good example to highlight here is the case of Warren Buffett. He famously avoided technology stocks for the majority of his career.

Even after the dotcom crash in 2000, he stayed away from investing in technology companies despite the presence of some huge bargains. He could have theoretically bought Apple, Microsoft, Amazon and Intel for pennies on the dollar in terms of their true worth.

What's more, this wasn't the first time Buffett passed on Intel. The founder of Intel, Bob Noyce, approached Buffett for startup capital after being introduced by a mutual friend. Buffett passed on the offer because he didn't understand the business or its economics (Schroeder, 2008).

Ordinary investors who get burned in bear markets routinely think and fantasize that they could have bought this or that for cheap when the market crashed. They don't pay attention to their circle of competence and get carried away with make-believe numbers they could have earned as a return.

These investors mistake activity with productivity. It's a lot like the office worker who is constantly busy but gets nothing done on time. The issue isn't with their energy levels. It's the efficiency and method of working that's the problem. As an investor, your job is to look at and source opportunities that fit your style of investing.

Your style is defined by your philosophy about the markets. If you happen to understand one particular sector better than others, then dive deeply into it. If you happen to understand the casino business very well and can reasonably predict what might occur next, then find the best casino stocks to invest in.

Don't go around chasing biotech stocks because someone told you they're the future. Or 5G stocks or any such companies whose business you don't understand.

Another mistake that investors make when the market begins to decline is to look at small cap stocks exclusively in the hopes of unearthing bargains. Small cap stocks refer to companies that are between $300 million to $2 billion in size. These stocks have potential for greater returns than large cap stocks, but they're also extremely risky. After all, these are tiny companies and they face a lot of obstacles. The investor chasing them reasons that in bear markets not only will good small cap companies decline in price, they'll also have a large runway to grow.

This means the investor can earn huge returns. By doing this, the investor is trying to find the next Amazon or next Google. Typically, such investments go nowhere. Instead of beginning in this manner, start with what you know and work forward from there.

If your circle of competence happens to include a small cap company, then go ahead and analyze it further. Don't feel compelled to invest money into a company just because you feel you need to be doing something in a bear market.

PREPARE FOR DIPS

Remember what Keynes said about markets? About how they can be irrational for a lot longer than the investor expects? Well, this is going to affect your portfolio. The average bear market investor can expect the value of their portfolio to almost certainly decline in the short term.

This is because very few people manage to invest at the exact moment when the market turns back up after hitting their lowest low. There's a saying in investment circles that bear markets test your stomach more than your brains. You need to mentally prepare yourself to watch your investment sink in value.

This can be difficult because potential loss affects us more than potential gain. Cognitive Psychologist Daniel Kahneman first brought this idea to the stock market sphere in his seminal work *Thinking Fast and Slow*. Kahneman explains that this loss aversion is why we tend to act more based on perceived losses (panic selling stock), than we do after perceived gains (buying more).

There will also be the onslaught of television and social media constantly telling you how investors "lost" one billion or one trillion or whatever number they come up with. You need to understand that these "losses" they're talking about are all on paper. If you bought a share of stock at $100 and watched it decline to $50 and have still not sold it, you've not lost anything.

You'll realize the loss only when you sell it. The same applies to when markets rise. If your investment rises to $200, you've not gained anything anywhere, other than on paper. You realize gains and losses only when you sell. If the underlying business is great and if you continue to hold onto the investment, you'll see the price rise back up at some point.

A good analogy that explains market movements was provided by Benjamin Graham. He created a fictional character called Mr. Market. Mr. Market was quite a character. Some days, he'd offer you $100 for your stock, which was right about what it was worth. On other days, he'd get depressed and offer you $20 for it. On some other days he'd suffer from a dose of euphoria and would offer you $300 for it. There was no rhyme or reason to what Mr. Market would do. All you had to do was receive his offer and decide whether you wanted to take him up on it.

This analogy doubly applies to bear markets. On some days you'll find that your stock has been in a rally and it's up by a large amount. Everyone will be cheering about the end of the bear market. You might even be looking forward to seeing green in your portfolio after a long time.

However, as with most bear market rallies, it will end and you're going to be staring at red again for a while. During these moments, it's best to remind yourself that all of these movements are just on paper. They're not real unless you decide to sell.

To clarify, we're not recommending you keep holding onto an investment in the hopes that it will rise. The point is to analyze every investment in your portfolio objectively and figure out which ones are still good businesses. You must hold onto or add to only such investments. The rest should be sold immediately.

A good way to prepare for such moments is to simply not check the prices of your investments. Focus only on following the relevant news surrounding your businesses and keep track of news releases and legal filings. The 10-Qs might not be the most reliable, but it will give you something to focus on in between 10-K filings.

If you have capital to invest, you should also be looking for further investment bargains.

MAINTAIN HEALTHY CASH RESERVES

If you're going to take advantage of mispriced assets in the market you'll need to have cash on hand to invest. When setting aside cash to invest, it's extremely important for you to plan well in advance. For starters you should not be investing cash that you'll need anytime soon.

This rules out any emergency money that you need for your living expenses, money for your kid's college tuition, money that needs to be put towards a down payment and so on. You need to invest money that you will not be needing for a long time in the future, for the next 10 years at the very least.

The first reason for this is any investment carries a certain degree of risk. You don't want to be risking money you need to survive. If you end up losing 50% or even more of your capital and this money was meant to pay the bills, you can imagine the chaos that would ensue in your life.

The second reason is that stock market investments need time to flourish. When speaking of bear markets, no one knows how long they'll last. They might last for two years, or they might last for five. Your investment needs time to grow because companies don't turn into behemoths overnight.

By remaining invested for a long time, you're also giving yourself the best chance of compounding your investment. Compounding refers to your money earning a steady interest rate over time. For example, if you invest $1,000 into a company that rises by 10% every year for 10 years, you'll have $2,593 at the end of this time. That's a 159.3% return despite the sum of the yearly interest adding up to 100% (10% multiplied by 10 years).

Compounding allows you to earn an additional 59.3% of your principal for free. The catch is, you can't touch the sum and need to remain invested. The best part about compounding is that your overall return increases the longer you remain invested. In 20 years your $1,000 would have grown to $6,727. That's a 572.7% return despite the sum of yearly interest adding up to 200%. You've earned an additional 372.7% return for free!

The method is very much like a snowball. It begins with little additions, but as it starts rolling downhill and collecting more and more momentum, its size increases. Soon, you've started an avalanche.

Something that can accelerate your returns is leverage. Brokers offer margin accounts that allow you to borrow money to buy stocks. You might be tempted to follow the example of Sir John Templeton and borrow money to buy shares in companies you like. Unless you are already very experienced, do not do this.

Bear markets tend to fall a lot faster than bull markets rise. This means you'll have less time to figure out what's going on and when things go bad, they'll go bad quick. You'll be hit with a margin call, which is when a broker asks you to deposit more money to cover your losses, and risk being cleaned out.

It doesn't matter how attractive the price is or how sure a shot you believe the opportunity is. You need to cover your bottom-line risk first. While Templeton made his money by using leverage, there have been plenty of other investors who haven't needed its power to earn huge returns. If they didn't need it, you don't either.

Plenty of investors focus far too much on the rewards on offer and don't think about the risks they run while investing. The stock market is a risky place and companies go bust all the time. Especially in bear markets. It is possible for you to make a mistake and lose your investment.

Instead of trying to hit home runs all the time, try to avoid poor decisions. Limit your risks and only invest what you can afford. The ultimate test of successful investment is whether you can sleep at night.

PLAY EARNINGS SEASON CORRECTLY

For the average investor, planning purchases around earnings season is usually not a great idea. Stocks during this time will experience high volatility and they'll be subject to the market's perceived first order risks. For example, some investors think that a company might not meet its earnings expectations and they'll plan on buying it at lower prices around earnings announcements.

To their dismay, they might find that not only does the stock price remain stable, it rises. This might be because the company's earnings aren't as bad as everyone thought they might be. The reasons for your entry should never depend on capturing a price around earnings seasons.

If your investment is going to be that price-sensitive, you're probably looking at too short a time horizon for your investment and are speculating on the price. For example, if you plan on buying a stock at $100 and holding it for just a month, it's unlikely to move far beyond $110 or $90 in that time. These are 10% movements, and most stocks don't move that much even in volatile markets.

Should your purchase price be $105, this reduces your potential profit quite a bit. However, if you were planning on holding this stock for 10 years, the potential ceiling for the price is unlimited. Who knows how far it could rise? If someone told you that the price of this stock would be $500 in 10 years' time, would you care about $100 versus $105?

Chances are that you won't. You should care about price in relation to value. When buying a stock, you need to have a good margin of safety built into the purchase price. A margin of safety is simply a buffer you build for yourself against adverse price movement.

For example, when you prepare a budget for yourself, you probably add a "Miscellaneous" line in there to account for unexpected expenses. This is the margin of safety or buffer you've given yourself. Similarly, if you determine the fair value of a stock to be $110, you want to buy it at a fair discount so that, even if you're wrong, you still have some room for yourself.

The exact amount of the margin of safety depends on your temperament as an investor. Whatever this might be, if you're worrying about a dollar here or there, you're probably not building a big enough buffer for yourself. For example, if your safety margin is 20%, you'll look to pay around $88. If you end up buying at $90 or even $95, you've still got yourself a good deal.

The problem starts arising when you're buying at $105 or $108. You're pretty close to fair value and as a result, you're far more price-sensitive.

Coming back to earnings season, stocks will have their first order consequences factored into their price. As a result, you won't witness huge levels of volatility unless something unexpected happens. Stay away from trying to time your entries according to earnings expectations.

If a company's business is solid and if you're not price-sensitive, then how does a difference of a few dollars on entry matter to your investment? In percentage terms, it's going to be a very small portion of your projected gain. Be aware of earnings but don't use them to time entries.

EXAMINE YOURSELF: HOW ARE YOU WRONG?

Charles Darwin had an interesting mental approach when it came to publishing his work. His method was quite simple at first glance (Parrish, 2020). After he was done postulating a theory for publishing, he would go for a walk. On this walk, he would contemplate all the ways in which he was wrong and why his theory was false.

He would conduct a debate within his mind and would fervently argue for the opposite side, trying to poke holes in his own theory. This approach is something that many successful people have adopted, from Charlie Munger to Reed Hastings, the CEO of Netflix.

Hastings in fact encourages his staff to practice the method as well. When two managers within the company disagree with each other over a point, Hastings has them debate one another. The exception is that each person argues for the other side. This allows them to view all the holes in their own argument and brings more empathy to the process.

This simple thought process is quite difficult to practice in reality. We love our own ideas, and if they happen to be particularly insightful or contain even a morsel of insight, we jump on board and refuse to look at anything else. Confirmation bias kicks in and we rationalize everything else to fit our model.

The bias is so strong that even when we nominally sit down to consider the other side of the argument, we often focus on the negatives and ignore the positives. After this cursory process, we go right back to what we believe in. This sort of thinking favors no one.

Take the time to draw an argument for the other side. Poke holes relentlessly in your own theories. Remember Munger's advice about the majority of opportunities not being worth your time. When analyzing an investment opportunity, have it prove itself worthy of your time and attention.

This doesn't mean you set up barriers that are far too high to be breached. Instead, adopt an attitude of slight disinterest in your mind. Imagine that Mr. Market has brought you this proposal and you know how he behaves on a daily basis, with his constant drama and manic depressiveness.

Adopt this air of detachment and you're not going to get sucked into believing you're infallible. When you've formed your thesis fully, argue for the other side. The point isn't to launch ad hominem attacks at yourself. Instead, imagine that another person with your qualities is looking at this idea and it's your job to let them know why it might not work.

It's tough to do this objectively, but once you start doing it, you'll find that it's a foolproof method to verify and validate a lot of information you receive, not just investment related. If you find there's no compelling evidence against your idea, you know you're onto something good.

6

HOW TO HEDGE YOUR CURRENT PORTFOLIO

I n our research for this book, we found that the majority of retail investors we spoke to had 2 things in common. Number 1, their portfolio was long only, which is to be expected during the conditions we experienced in the previous decade. The more alarmingly commonality was that 100% of their portfolio was in equities, so they were not holding bonds or precious metals. If they did have alternative investments, it was mostly in cryptocurrency.

This becomes an issue during bear markets as equities, especially in high-tech sectors tend to get crushed. For example, between October 2007 and February 2009, the S&P 500 fell by over 50%. Over the same time period, Gold was up over 50%, and 20-year treasury bonds were up 16%. Smart investors hedged their equity portfolios with precious metals and bonds, while the average retail investor saw their holdings get decimated.

So now that you have a good handle on the mental aspects of bear market investing and have gained a good idea of what you need to do before deploying your money in such investments, it's time to look at asset classes that tend to perform well in bear markets.

These asset classes are where you will have the most opportunity. Along the way, you're also going to learn all about some of the assets that don't do well during such times. You need to be aware of these assets because you'll likely find people jumping into them.

The media will also be touting them as being "hot," so it's imperative for you to understand why they won't provide you with good opportunities.

GOLD

There is a lot of debate surrounding gold and its value. Gold as a commodity doesn't offer any notable value to the economy or to any industrial process. Instead its value derives from the fact that everyone else thinks it is valuable. On the surface, it seems to be exactly the kind of investment asset that the intelligent investor ought to avoid. However, 5000 years of history give us a different perspective.

The primary argument for investing in gold is that it's a great hedge against inflation. The interesting thing about this argument is that it's incorrect over the short term but plays out quite well over the long term. For instance, a study conducted by professors at Duke University's Fuqua School of Business found that gold doesn't always work as an inflation hedge (Emspak, 2020).

That study also tried to determine the primary movers of gold prices but came up short. There's a good reason for this. Gold prices are moved mostly by fear. While intelligent investing should prioritize rationality, there's no doubt that human beings are emotional creatures. If there is an opportunity to capitalize on these emotions, it is irrational to ignore it.

Gold has risen in value over time (the past three decades) primarily due to huge levels of demand from India and China, where it is seen as a safe asset. One can understand this point of view. The people of those countries aren't that far removed from times where their currencies were devalued and the nation fell into default.

In India's case, the current working class demographic would have vivid memories of financial instability and times where the government was the only source of stable employment. China is more removed from highly unstable times, but the memories of those times don't fade away soon.

In short, gold is a very effective hedge against those local currencies, even if it doesn't always correlate to the relatively stable dollar and other Western currencies that have enjoyed generations of stability. Bear markets tend to increase fear in market participants and, as a result, gold always comes into the news.

However, it doesn't move when you would expect it to. Typically, gold spikes when the economy *exits* a downturn, not when it is entering one. The credit crisis proved this pattern during the previous decade. Gold witnessed a huge spike in 2008 but it managed to consistently rise and spiked to new highs throughout the bear market before peaking in 2011.

In fact, thanks to Quantitative Easing, and central banks printing money, the value of currency has declined. As a result, gold is seen as an asset that holds its value better.

This is because the more dollars a government prints, the less valuable its existing currency becomes. Gold on the other hand, cannot simply just be "printed" and yearly additions barely add to existing volumes.

There is a lot that doesn't make sense when it comes to gold, but given the way fear dominates in bear markets, these moments provide great opportunities for the intelligent investor. A research report from Bank of America projects that by October 2021, gold will likely hit a price of $3,000 per ounce (Wink, 2020). Others are even more bullish, with famed precious metals commentator Jim Rickards expecting long-term prices to hit $10,000 per ounce. This is due to the expected money printing that all central banks are expected to carry out to combat the downturn caused by the pandemic.

While $10,000 or even $3,000 per ounce might be a bit hyperbolic, there is no doubt that gold is expected to rise in value thanks to negative or close to zero interest rates present all around the world.

Due to these facts, and because of gold's historical utility in providing as a hedge against falling asset prices, we recommend all investors hold 10% of their portfolio in precious metals, with a priority given to gold holdings.

Ways To Invest in Gold

There are four major ways to invest in gold. These are:

1. Physical gold
2. ETFs which track the price of gold
3. Mining company stocks
4. Streamers

Physical gold, also called spot gold, allows the investor to touch and feel the gold they've bought. Some investors prefer the security that owning physical gold brings. After all, in case total economic collapse occurs, physical gold can still be used to trade for items. This might be an unlikely event, but it suits the mindset of certain investors.

There are many places you can buy physical gold from. The most obvious place is a jewelry shop, although in the West you're going to find a preponderance of diamonds in such stores. There are reliable online sources such as APMEX, J.M Bullion and wholesalecoindirect.com.

There are different kinds of spot gold you can purchase. Typically bullion is the most sought-after since this is pure gold, often 99.1% and above. Other forms of gold are usually alloyed with nickel or zinc to benefit certain industrial processes. The purest form of gold an investor can buy are Canadian Maple Leafs. These are 99.9% pure and are usually in the form of coins.

When buying physical gold, look for the name of the manufacturer, the purity and weight to be stamped on its face. Reputable mints include the Royal Canadian Mint, Valcambi and Perth Mint. The United States Mint also produces bars, but its major product happens to be coins.

Coins are a bit different from bars and aren't always the purest. Some coins, such as the US Mint American Eagle, are 91% gold but have a higher value than pure gold (per ounce) thanks to its desirability as a collector's item. When buying coins, you're also purchasing the desirability of the coin and you should thoroughly evaluate its merits and demerits.

We should also note that contrary to popular belief, you *can* hold physical gold and silver with a self directed IRA or a 401(k) established with a trust company. You cannot buy physical gold with a conventional IRA, because they do not allow for "special circumstances" assets like precious metals. Although you can transfer your current IRA to a self-directed one.

When buying physical gold, it's better to buy workable sizes instead of one huge size. For example, it's better to buy 10 one-oz. bars than to buy one 10 oz. bar. This way you can sell portions of your investment into the market should the need ever arise.

A second way of investing in gold is via ETFs. ETFs vary in terms of the strategies they apply and you should carefully evaluate what these are before investing in them. A lot of ETFs invest in gold futures while some invest in mining companies and so on. Still some more invest in physical gold.

There are a few risks of investing in ETFs. For one thing you won't own the metal directly. In fact, you'll typically be at least two steps removed from it. You'll own shares in a fund that invests in futures contracts. As a result, you might be exposed to the type of price action that oil experienced in the early part of 2020.

Investing in futures also involves what is called counterparty risk. A futures instrument is a contract where one party promises to deliver an asset to the other at a certain price at a certain date. If the counterparty doesn't live up to their end of the deal, there isn't much the other side can do.

Sure, you could go after them, but if they plead bankruptcy, this isn't going to do you much good. Smaller investors won't face such risks because of their investment sizes being small. This is not the case with ETFs that are investing billions in the market. While default isn't something that occurs a lot, there's no denying that during extraordinary times, as most bear markets are, counterparty risk increases significantly.

Another aspect of counterparty risk is the byzantine process by which ETFs actually buy gold. GLD is one of the most popular ETFs when it comes to gold investment.

Here's how the buy chain works. An investor buys shares in GLD. These are delivered by an Authorized Participant to you. This Authorized Participant then buys equivalent shares in the SPDR Gold Trust. The Trust then buys physical gold and stores it with a custodian, in this case HSBC Bank. HSBC also helps source the gold for the trustee. When it comes down to it, the investor is completely dependent on HSBC. Now because most investors buy gold to insulate themselves from financial meltdowns. If there is a meltdown, you can bet that a global bank like HSBC is going to be involved in it somehow. Therefore, investing in gold via an ETF hasn't provided any insulation at all.

The biggest disadvantage to investing this way is that you don't own any physical gold and instead you're investing in the trustee. If there ever comes a time when you need to cash in your gold, you'll be doing so in dollars, which makes you dependent on the monetary system.

Despite the risks, gold ETFs can be good investments. Our point is to highlight the risks to present a well-rounded picture. If you cannot practically buy physical gold, then investing through an ETF makes sense.

An even more indirect way to invest in gold is to buy shares of mining companies and streamers. Let's look at miners first. As the name suggests, these are companies that mine gold and sell it on the market for a profit. Gold mining has very little output and the global supply of gold is pretty low.

South Africa happens to be the largest exporter of gold and it also perfectly illustrates the advantages and disadvantages of investing in miners. On the positive side, you have the fact that you're investing in a company whose product will always have demand. People have been drawn to gold ever since it was first discovered and this is unlikely to stop, no matter how many times Warren Buffett proclaims that gold is useless.

By investing in a miner you're placing your money as close to physical gold as possible. This puts you in a better position than investing in an ETF. The company's prospects are tied quite closely with the price of spot gold since they're selling the raw material for the finished product (gold ore).

The downsides are quite significant, though. You're still intimately tied to the prospects of the mining business. Mining is a capital-intensive business, and it isn't uncommon for mining companies to have low levels of cash the deeper they get into a project. This causes them to seek loans and that builds debt.

While a leveraged balance sheet can produce huge returns for shareholders when things go well, it does open you up to significant downside risk. For example, let's say you buy 1 share of a $100 stock by placing $1 of your own money and borrow the remaining $99. If the stock price increases by one percent to $101, you've just earned a 100% cash on cash return.

However, if it declines by just one percent (to $99), you've lost all of your investment. There's no margin of safety in this case. While the example highlights huge amounts of leverage, the point still stands. A leveraged balance sheet puts the miner at risk. If the ore in the mine doesn't live up to market standards or if a global meltdown happens and secondary effects impact the economy of the industry, the gold miner will likely go bankrupt.

Then there's country risk as well. South Africa, which is where the most prolific miners are located, happens to be particularly unstable when it comes to mining strikes. Workers' rights is a huge issue and it also happens to be racially charged, like everything else in that country. Buying mining stock exposes you to this risk.

Keeping these risks in mind, most miners seek to avoid leveraging their balance sheets. They still need cash, though. This leads them to approach streaming companies or streamers. We highlighted one particularly good streamer in our other book *20 for 20* called Sandstorm Gold.

Here's how streaming works: The streamer provides the miner a loan that is collateralized by the ore that is recovered. The miner agrees to sell the ore at a discount to the streamer. The streamer in turn can either sell the ore or refine it to create pure gold. Since they've bought it at a discount, the streamer realizes significant profits the minute the mine begins producing.

The biggest advantage of the streaming model is that the payouts are connected to the potential of the mine, not the miner. In other words, the miner might run out of cash to refine the ore and could struggle to sell it in the market. This does not concern the streamer since they're receiving the product no matter what.

The streamer thus acts like a bank and receives physical products instead of interest. This aligns their interests with that of the miner without creating heavy dependence on the mining business. As an investor, this is a huge asset for you. This doesn't mean the streaming business is without risks.

For starters, the company might misread the mine's potential output. Secondly, macroeconomic factors might make financing tough for a streamer. These companies typically borrow money from banks, and if banks tighten lending standards far too much, then streamers might not be able to provide miners with financing.

Despite these risks, streaming remains the best method of investing in gold after buying physical gold. There are quite a few companies in this field, but as we have mentioned, Sandstorm Gold is one of the best candidates for investment in this area.

Storing Gold Safely

One of the biggest headaches with gold investment is the storage needs it imposes on investors. This is often why a lot of people prefer investing in ETFs. Gold storage can be tough, but it's hardly a reason for you to stay away from investing in it. The first option is to buy a fireproof safe.

When buying this safe, it's best to pay with cash and install it in your home yourself. The reasons for this should be obvious. Store your gold within the safe at home and you'll always have access to it.

Yet there are downsides to this method. For starters, it's in your home and this makes home security paramount. The very presence of a safe in your home might attract less desirable consequences and your overall peace of mind might be disrupted. After all, your home is a place to relax and feel safe. Storing gold within it might not suit the mindset of most people.

Safety deposit boxes in banks are a favored option. They are cheap and convenient. Most safety boxes cost around $50 per year to maintain and offer large-enough sizes for you to store all the gold you want. But these have significant drawbacks to them. For one thing, these boxes can technically be seized by the government at the stroke of a pen.

This is what happened in 1933 when an executive order signed by President Roosevelt mandated that all gold held in private safety deposit boxes would be seized and that Americans were forbidden from owning gold. The rationale behind this was that people were hoarding gold during the depression and this was making things worse. For people who did comply with the order, the government paid them $20.67 for every ounce of gold that was turned in. But then, shortly after the deadline, Roosevelt raised the price of gold to $35, essentially stealing nearly half of the wealth of those former gold owners.

As far as legally mandated thuggery goes, this act is right up there and there's no reason why it won't occur again. The United States and most Western economies have a checkered record when it comes to this sort of thing. In the name of clamping down on money laundering Americans are now subject to more financial surveillance and heavy-handedness than ever.

For example, the money in your bank account can always be seized by the government and it's technically not yours. If you fall behind on your tax payments, the IRS can seize the money in your account even if this leaves you with nothing to pay for your living expenses.

Aside from the way governments behave there's the fact that the Federal Deposit Insurance Corporation (FDIC) does not insure safety deposit boxes. The FDIC typically insures bank balances for up to $100,000, but safety deposit boxes are not provided this insurance. This leaves you vulnerable to any misfortune that might befall the bank.

There are private repositories that store gold for you in the United States and offshore. Repositories in the United States are required to comply with income declaration guidelines. This is another way of saying that the government will have full access to your gold much like they have access to your bank accounts.

People who are especially mistrustful of the government can consider offshore storage options. If you're an American resident, your options in this sphere are severely limited. For example, Switzerland offers a range of brokerage and storage services, but many Swiss institutions will not accept American clients due to the demands that income declaration laws place on them. These institutions have built their business on privacy protection and offering governments access to client assets is unlikely to help them.

The best options for American residents (and citizens) is Singapore. The country is a stable financial jurisdiction and its infrastructure is in fact decades ahead of the West. Singapore does not offer the highest levels of protection in terms of privacy, but it does offer you secure storage and a number of companies that offer brokerage services.

Le Freeport in Singapore is an option that many investors utilize. The company has two branches, one in Luxembourg and another in Singapore. Upon visiting you will be guided through a facility that resembles something out of a high-tech spy movie. Costs reportedly start from a few hundred dollars per month for the smallest storage options.

Another storage option exists in Vienna, where investors can have their gold delivered to companies such as Das Safe. In contrast to Singapore, this option adheres to old-school European banking values. One might wonder how much privacy an EU country can provide, but Austria happens to have one of the world's highest priorities in terms of privacy laws.

The costs of offshore storage are higher than what you would have to pay with a storage repository such as Brinks. However, if privacy is a concern for you and if you're really planning for a doomsday scenario, these options are great. Make sure you don't plan on liquidating your asset before you invest in these facilities since they're not the most accessible, thanks to their locations.

A reprint of Executive Order 6102 which gave the US Government the legal right to confiscate gold owned by private citizens. The law was in place for 41 years until it was repealed by President Ford. A similar order was signed regarding silver deposits in 1934.

SILVER

Along with gold, silver is another famous precious metal that catches investors' eyes. Unlike gold, silver actually has many industrial uses and has sizable demand from industry. This means its price fluctuates according to supply and demand principles to a larger extent than gold's does.

For this reason, many famous investors recommend silver as being a better investment than gold. Warren Buffett is famous for his disdain of gold but has invested in silver in the past. Historically, silver has been regarded as the second most valuable metal in the world.

Back in the 1800s, the economies of countries were pegged to the levels of silver and gold they held in reserves. This era is often referred to as the bimetallic age. Countries determined how much money they should print on the basis of some combination of the amount of gold and silver they held. This also meant that silver prices were fixed to gold and both metals fluctuated in a correlated manner.

The ratio of gold's price to silver was 15 (Banton, 2020). While the bimetallic method was good in theory, in practical terms it didn't always work out. During this age, European economies were the most advanced in the world and, given the number of conflicts they had with one another, the bimetallic standard was almost never adhered to.

A good example of this is Austria. These days the country is primarily known for Mozart and Freud, but in the 1800s it occupied a position much like America does in the world today. The country went through a century of prosperity in the 1700s and this meant it was embroiled in conflict with its neighbors throughout the 19th century.

The economic history of Austria during this time is a succession of promising to stop printing money and then printing it anyway, followed by head scratching as to why this was done in the first place. War costs money and the economic depression that sets in after it requires money printing.

Since gold and silver reserves were largely fixed, this meant that the Austrian Florin was out of touch with the bimetallic standard. Eventually in 1870, Austria gave up pretending it was following the standard and other European countries followed suit. The constant wars had taken a toll on Austria and the country never recovered its former status in world politics.

The bimetallic era gave way to the gold standard since gold was viewed as being more precious and this gave countries more leeway in terms of how much money they could print. With silver now freed from gold, the gold to silver ratio began to fluctuate.

Over the years, as the 20th century unfolded, the ratio went higher and higher and even reached as high as 100 in 1991. These days the ratio hovers around 50. Of course, countries gave up the gold standard in the 1970s and this has meant the ratio is even more volatile than ever.

Traders seek to take advantage of the gold to silver ratio by adopting mean reversal strategies. This means when the ratio falls far out of line with historical averages, they bet on it moving back to the mean. This isn't an investment strategy, and we won't be focusing on this as a result.

When buying physical silver, you will find that the premium you will be charged over the spot price will be a lot higher than what you'll find in gold. The reason for this is the demand for silver is higher than what exists for gold. The reason silver prices don't go charging up is because silver supply is also relatively high.

Bullion dealers are aware of the fact that silver's industrial usage means demand is strong. Compare this to the situation in gold, where demand is mostly driven by emotional buying. The buyer can always reason that they'll buy it later since they're going to be storing the gold anyway and not putting it to practical use.

This isn't the case with silver. The metal is used in a variety of industrial processes such as in soldering LED chips, creating alloys, creating RFID chips, semiconductors, photovoltaic cells and so on. The metal also has medicinal qualities and is witnessing a surge in nanomedicine.

All of this contributes to you having to pay a higher premium when you invest in it. Historically, there have been many commodity traders who have viewed silver as a better inflation-hedged asset than gold. Their thinking is that since the metal has practical use, it is a better hedge against money printing activities.

This line of thought illustrates the danger of putting too much importance on a fully rational process without taking emotions into consideration. The most famous example of this was the Hunt brothers' corner of the silver market in the 1970s (Beattie, 2019). H.L. Hunt made his money in oil, and upon his passing his sons inherited his considerable wealth.

The Hunt brothers were convinced that silver prices were going to increase rapidly thanks to a weakening dollar and renewed energy crisis concerns. With the United States facing a shortage of oil and inflation at an eye watering 14%, there was a lot of sense in the Hunts' theory. However, much of their execution was flawed.

For starters, it was gold that began rising, not silver. This goes back to our point in the previous section where we mentioned that gold rises in fear. Silver is at a disadvantage in such a scenario. It rises on some occasions and stays flat on others. For example, in 2009 silver began rising along with gold as the credit crisis began hitting home. However, it didn't do so after the dotcom crash.

Either way, the Hunts poured their money into silver and were rewarded with rising prices. Taking this to be a sign, they borrowed money and leveraged their trades. By buying up monstrous amounts of silver in the market, they briefly managed to become the richest men in the world.

However, they created a situation where there were very few counterparties left to trade with. Even worse, the government noticed what they were up to and decided that they were attempting to create a monopoly in silver and strong-arming the economy. This led to a crackdown of biblical proportions, and given the small number of counterparties to their trade, the Hunts had no leverage when it came to negotiating price.

They were forced to declare bankruptcy and were dragged in front of Congress as well. It took them 10 years to get rid of their debts and set things right with their creditors. Don't worry, though. The Hunts made good and became billionaires once again thanks to their oil holdings. They reportedly stayed away from silver after this debacle.

This episode illustrates the irrationality that often afflicts the best investment ideas. The Hunts' thesis specified that things were going to fall apart and didn't account for the government stepping in and changing the rules. While it is unlikely that you'll be playing on the same level as they were, it is something to take note of.

Silver has a lot of things going for it, but just like gold, it is subject to irrationality. Bear markets are highly irrational times. While you can take advantage of this, it might also turn around and bite you if you're not careful.

Let's look at a few ways for you to invest in silver.

Silver ETFs

Like with gold, silver has a number of ETFs that track its price. Just like with gold, there are risks associated with these ETFs. The primary investment reasoning for silver is that it functions as a great hedge. However, with an ETF you're not really gaining much of a hedge. All you're doing is speculating on the price.

The risks associated with silver ETFs are the same as with gold ETFs. We highlighted these risks when looking at the case of GLD in the previous section. Given that silver has a large number of industrial uses, the number of strategies that you'll find in the silver ETF space are high as well.

For example, the iShares MSCI Global Silver and Metals Miners fund (SLVP) tracks a composite basket of silver futures and mining stocks. Buying this ETF will bring you exposure to the entire silver market, but it's a pretty indirect way to invest in the metal itself.

A more direct way is offered by the iShares Silver Trust. This fund functions exactly like GLD does and holds multiple custodian relationships for the storage of silver. However, the risks here are high. Typically, such funds have complex relationships with the custodians of physical silver and in some cases, they might even hire sub-custodians.

These sub-custodians might be located in less than savory places, and as a result there is the danger of fraud occurring. Remember that at the end of the day these ETFs are still funds that operate at the manager's discretion. If the manager decides that the silver market is far too volatile and that palladium offers better opportunities, they can legally shift operations there.

This leaves you in a vulnerable position. When investing in an ETF, what you're actually doing is investing in managerial prowess, not the underlying commodity.

Another silver ETF that is popular is the Global X Miners Silver ETF (SIL). This is an index fund masquerading as an ETF. It tracks an index of silver miners. While this reduces the risk inherent in silver investment considerably, you're still not following the price of silver directly or owning any metal. What's more, this particular ETF has far less liquidity than the others.

Liquidity refers to how readily an instrument trades in the market. An instrument that has just 100 active traders will be less liquid that an instrument that has 1,000 active traders. You're more likely to receive a fair price for your asset if it's liquid. The greater number of traders present will ensure that there will be more prices available for you to buy or sell your asset.

The bottom line is that silver ETFs present a large degree of risk and you should carefully consider your other options before choosing to invest in them.

Mining and Streaming

Like with gold, silver offers a number of opportunities to invest in mining and streaming companies. By investing in these companies you're going to gain exposure to the finances of the individual company and not the metal directly. Silver prices might increase, but if the company mismanages its investments, you could be stuck with a dud.

There's also location risk as we highlighted in the previous section when talking about gold miners. Silver mines are located in even riskier locations across the world. While the world's highest producers of silver are located in Mexico, Peru and China—places that aren't all that unstable—the case of Tahoe Resources illustrates just how risky things can get.

Tahoe Resources, which is now a part of Pan American Silver, was a company that owned and operated a mine named Escobal in Guatemala (Chamaria, 2018). Given the political history of that country and shifting lines of power, it was no surprise that Tahoe had managed to gain access to it under questionable circumstances.

These circumstances perhaps allowed it to operate with impunity for a while, but soon it ran into trouble. A local NGO raised questions about the circumstances under which it was granted a license and soon the case landed in the Guatemalan Supreme Court. This took place in early 2017.

There were other issues as well, mostly to do with the red tape that Tahoe had to navigate. While its mining license was reinstated, its export license that was issued by another ministry was not. This left it in the curious position of being able to mine silver but not being able to do anything with it.

The case was brought to the Supreme Court and the process was expected to take 18 months conservatively. This meant that Tahoe would be offline till the end of 2018. This was a best-case scenario estimate. Ultimately, the management had enough of dealing with third world courts and decided to sell itself to its primary competitor, Pan American, which had a stronger balance sheet and could withstand these shenanigans.

Tahoe's case underlines the importance of doing your due diligence. Companies might have a list of diversified mine locations, but all it takes is for one crackpot government to throw things completely out of shape. In such investments you're dealing with a company that is effectively a foreign stock. After all, the bulk of their assets are outside the USA and in such cases, they're subject to foreign laws.

The company's 10-K will list the production capacity of every mine it has control over. Pay close attention to where it derives the bulk of its production. Mining is a tough business that is constantly plagued by allegations of exploitation and environmental concerns. This is doubly true when operating outside of Western economies.

You want to reduce your risk of exposure towards one particular political climate or zone of the world and invest in companies that have diversified assets. A good candidate for investment is First Majestic Silver (TSE:FR). Despite the word silver in the name, the company derives close to 40% of its revenues from gold mining operations.

Since 2011, the company has been steadily moving away from gold dependence and has been expanding into silver. It was founded back in 2001 by the current

CEO, Keith Neumeyer. He's been in charge for this whole period and it's safe to say that he knows how his company runs, backwards.

Stable management is a good sign of a well-run company and First Majestic checks this box. It has a strong balance sheet, which is a great thing for a mining company to possess. The CEO owns close to two percent of the company, which is also a great indication of strength in the company.

Speaking of ownership, the investment case for First Majestic is boosted by the fact that Renaissance Technologies owns this company. Renaissance is a hedge fund that is run by a bunch of math geniuses, and over the years their investment record is unparalleled. A vote of confidence from institutional investors of such pedigree is always a good sign.

2019 was a record-breaking year for First Majestic. A key metric that all mining companies track is the recovery rate. This measures the efficiency of their mining operations. It's a measure of how much metal they could recover from the raw ore. In 2019, First Majestic's recovery rate was an astonishing 86%.

The income statement of the company doesn't provide pretty reading. Critics will point to operating losses in both 2018 and 2019 as well as EBITDA losses of 150 million in 2019. However, dig a little deeper and you'll find that these losses were caused mainly by non-cash expenses such as mine depletion allowances (depreciation for mines).

After accounting for these items, the free cash flow from operations stands at $140 million for 2019, which was up from $33 million in 2018. All of these numbers point to the possibility of a great investment. Given that the pandemic caused by COVID-19 will possibly result in the price of silver rising, this might be a good investment.

Streaming companies are also a good bet in this area. One particularly good company is Wheaton Precious Metals Corp (NYSE:WPM). The economics of silver streamers are the same as those that govern gold streamers. In fact, much like mining companies, streamers tend to invest across both asset classes, so you might end up gaining exposure to gold and silver through these investments.

The bottom line is that there are good opportunities in silver. Remember that ETFs don't always offer the best opportunities. You should look at streamers and a few miners that are well capitalized to take advantage of the potential rise in silver prices.

A historical comparison of the returns of Gold (dark line) vs. Silver (light line) over the past 22 years. A spike in the silver market in 2011 was caused by a supply shortage, rather than the inflationary concerns we saw in the 1980s.

The gold:silver ratio, the number of ounces of silver you can purchase with 1oz of gold. This is a historical indicator going back to Ancient Greece when Alexander the Great fixed the ratio at 12:1. In the modern era, the ratio was initially fixed at 15:1 by the US Government. As countries moved away from the Bi-Metallic age in the late 19th Century, the ratio moved in favor of Gold prices. In the past 20 years, the ratio has been as low as 30:1 during the silver boom of 2011. In the past 12 months we have seen a spike of over 100, a ratio not seen since 1991.

SHORT SELLING

"I've seen more stocks go to zero than infinity."

— JIM CHANOS

Let's say you take a look at a company during your analysis and notice that instead of being a gem, it resembles a turd. There's nothing it has going for it and management is incompetent. It's in a business that is stuck in all kinds of difficulties and its competition is pulling ahead.

You'll often come across such companies, and the average investor will simply sigh and move on. After all, there's no point buying these companies. Just because these companies aren't a good buy doesn't mean you can't profit from their situations. This is what short selling is.

The traditional way to make money in the market is to go long. You buy a stock and wait for its price to rise and sell it for a profit. You buy first and sell later. Short selling flips that sequence around. In this method of placing orders, you sell first and then buy. You'll make money if the selling price is higher than what you can buy the stock back for.

Shorting seems like a complicated process, and behind the scenes it is. However, this complexity doesn't need to affect you as an investor. As far as you're concerned, you can sell first and buy later (called covering your short.) You'll need to pay attention to a few things with regards to your account balance, but with prudent risk management, it is possible to do this quite easily.

The biggest qualm most people have with shorting is that they think it's immoral. They think that by shorting you're rooting for someone to fail. This is an uneducated opinion and adopts a very black and white view of the world. A company that is strong and well-run cannot be shorted successfully.

It is impossible for a single trader to ever force prices in the market in a particular direction. As we highlighted earlier, the Hunt brothers managed to buy almost all of the silver in the market and even this didn't allow them to prop prices up. The market is bigger than everyone else.

If the market witnesses unjustified shorting it will react with even greater long pressure. In order to short, you need to have a very strong justification for doing so. It isn't a question of "I don't like the CEO's face hence I'll short." There are urban legends of institutional money managers using shorting as a means of forcing management to bend to their will, but this is mostly false.

Management typically hates short sellers and they're the ones who often peddle the immoral line. Their compensation is tied to stock prices (thanks to options) and any potential reduction in them hurts their wallets. Good management typically doesn't care about shorting activity. It is bad management that always blames shorts for everything.

Some of the most famous investors have made billions shorting. Jim Chanos famously shorted Enron when it was trading at $90 and cleared $500 million from his bet. Going back in time, one of the most famous short sells ever was when Jesse Livermore spotted the signs of the stock market being overvalued in 1929 and shorted the entire market.

Livermore, who is something of a cult figure amongst traders, began by shorting the biggest companies in the Dow Jones index and kept shorting other industries as the malaise spread. By the end of it he had amassed profits of more than $100 million. What is often left out of the story is that he was $6 million in the red before his bet worked in his favor.

In this perfect example of how the mainstream media and uninformed public views shorting, Livermore was blamed for the crash and received death threats. Shorts are simply the messengers of bad news, not the creators of them.

Another example of this comes from 1992 when George Soros shorted the British pound. He cleared $1 billion from this trade and earned the undeserved moniker "the man who broke the Bank of England." This suggests that he somehow bankrupted England by causing a devaluing in the pound, but this simply wasn't the case. If anything, Soros was the one who highlighted the cover-up efforts that the Bank of England was undertaking by trying to smooth over deficiencies in the economy.

There are other notable examples, such as Paul Tudor Jones shorting the American market before the crash of 1987 and Sir John Templeton (him again) shorting the dotcom bubble. While there are many investors who choose to go short, shorting and investing have been viewed as polar opposites thanks to the words of Warren Buffett.

Buffett famously avoids shorting. His reasoning is simple. Stocks can go up infinitely but they're always limited to the downside by zero. Chanos' retort to this is that he's seen many more stocks go to zero than infinity. It just goes to show that sticking to your circle of competence is extremely important in investing.

Many famous investors are conscious of the bad optics that announcing a short brings. As a result, they almost never announce their short positions. In fact, an announcement of this kind by a famous investor can be considered as evidence of financial foul play by the SEC. For example, if Warren Buffett announced he was selling shares of Goldman Sachs, the stock price would tumble.

However, this didn't faze Bill Ackman when he announced his short of Herbalife, Inc. According to him, the company was running a pyramid scheme. He proclaimed that he was going to donate his profits to charity once he was proved true. Ackman appeared on CNBC shortly after this proclamation and reasserted his conviction behind his bet.

This prompted Carl Icahn to phone into the show, and a highly entertaining mudslinging match began between the two rivals. Icahn declared he was going to buy shares in Herbalife just to prove how wrong Ackman was and the stock price of Herbalife began soaring. Other hedge fund managers quietly allied against Ackman as well, with Dan Loeb of Third Point Partners, who was thought to be Ackman's ally, joining Icahn.

Amidst all this drama was the fact the market deduced that Herbalife was not running a pyramid scheme and Ackman wound up being wrong. He never fully disclosed how much he lost, but one assumes he could afford it (Monica, 2018).

The Basics of Short Selling

As we mentioned earlier, short selling is a straightforward process as far as the investor is concerned. From a bird's eye view, it does get complicated. Here's how it works: You initiate a short by clicking the sell button in the software provided by your broker. If you don't own the stock, your broker has to borrow the shares from someone else to allow you to sell them.

The act of borrowing brings interest with it and your broker will pass this cost onto you. Different countries treat the payment of this interest in different ways. In the United States, the interest is added to the price you pay to enter your trade. If you hold onto your trade for multiple days, your broker will debit the interest from your account.

To close or cover your position, you press the buy button and your broker will take the borrowed shares back and will return it to the source they borrowed it from. This is usually from another trader's margin account or from their own inventory of shares.

If this process sounds confusing to you, think of it this way. Replace shares with money. Let's say you want to borrow $100 (the money that represents a sale of stock). Your broker borrows this amount from another trader or from their own wallet and lends it to you (they've synthetically bought the stock for you).

After a while, you return the $100 back to them (by covering your position you pay them money that represents how much it costs to buy) and the broker returns the borrowed amount to the original source plus interest ("Who Benefits From Loaning Shares in a Short Sale?," 2020).

This is how short selling works on a retail level. At the institutional level, it involves sales and agreements between two counterparties, with the broker acting as an intermediary. In some cases, the broker might take the other side of the trade, but this is done only if the broker evaluates the risk as being worthy of accepting.

Institutional brokers are the big Wall Street banks and typically they don't assume counterparty risk. The exception is when the asset is already on their books and they're looking to get rid of it.

As a retail trader, short selling is extremely easy for you to carry out. The first step you'll need to take is open a margin account with your broker. Margin accounts usually attract higher minimum account balance requirements. Brokers in the United States usually place a threshold of $10,000 for these accounts, but this varies from broker to broker.

Discount brokers sometimes provide margin accounts for as little as $5,000. Opening a margin account is as easy as applying for one through your broker. There is no additional documentation needed beyond what you already provided them when you opened your trading account. Once you have a margin account, you'll be able to not just short sell but also trade futures and options.

Before you proceed to begin trading your margin account it's important for you to understand that Pattern Day Trader rule or PDT. PDT is an SEC-mandated designation that came about because too many retail traders were running huge risks using margin accounts.

If you place more than four trades over the span of five days in your margin account, you'll be slapped with a PDT tag. There is nothing additional you need to do in this case except maintain a minimum balance of $25,000. If you do not comply with these requirements within the mandated time (as defined by your broker), your broker will liquidate your positions and might even freeze your account.

Therefore, if you're going to short sell, be very careful about the PDT rule. If you have that much capital, then you don't have anything to worry about.

The amount of money placed in your account is referred to as the margin you have available. Margin is the sum of your cash balance and the market value of all open positions in your account. If you have a cash balance of $500 and two current positions worth $4,000, your margin is $4,500.

The cash balance is referred to as free margin by some brokers since it represents how much liquid cash you have. Your margin levels are extremely important when it comes to short selling. Let's say you spot a short opportunity that you'd like to use the $500 on.

SEC Regulation T or Reg T specifies that the investor must maintain 150% of the value of short sale in their account as initial margin. In our example, $500 is the value of the short sale and 150% of this is $750. Your account currently has $500 as cash and $4,000 as equity margin. Therefore, you can initiate a short sale.

Once your position is live, maintenance margin requirements go into effect. Maintenance margin refers to the amount of margin your account is supposed to have at all times when the position is open. Currently, the authorities mandate that maintenance margin limits be a minimum of 25% (Kagan, 2020).

However, this is just a minimum. Some brokers will impose maintenance levels of 30%. Coming back to our example, let's say the price of the stock rises (which is bad for a short) and the value of your short position increases to $600. Assuming your broker requires 30% as maintenance margin, you will need to have at least $180 in your account as margin.

Note that this is margin, not cash. Since the other two positions in your account add up to $4,000, you're well above the limit. If you didn't have these two positions in your account, you would have had nothing in your account and would have been hit with a margin call.

This is a notice from your broker asking you to deposit more margin in your account. If you don't do this, your broker will liquidate the position and recover their money from the proceeds. If there were other positions in your account that could allow the broker to recover the maintenance margin amount, your broker will sell those as well.

You need to be very careful of violating maintenance margin requirements. All brokers have an indicator that clearly shows how much equity is left in their account and how close they are to a margin call. Some brokers use a ratio to display this amount. However your broker chooses to depict this, make sure you understand what the indicator means. If you happen to receive a margin call and don't deposit money quickly enough, your broker will sell your investment holdings (even the long ones) and you'll end up losing money.

The Poor Man's Short: Utilizing Inverse ETFs

As you can see, shorting involves a few risks that some investors might not be comfortable with. On top of this, you are not allowed to hold short positions within an IRA because of "undefined risk" rules.

So to aid investors who want to hedge their long-term holds but can't or won't short stocks on margin, many investment managers began offering what are called inverse ETFs. These ETFs, which you are allowed to hold in an IRA, move in the opposite direction to their underlying asset.

For example, ProShare Short QQQ (that's the name; the ticker is PSQ) is an inverse ETF that rises as the NASDAQ 100 falls. If the NASDAQ 100 rises, it falls in price. Another example of this is the ProShares Short Financial Index (SEF). This ETF moves in the opposite direction to the Dow Jones Financial Index.

So if you think financial companies are going to get hammered, you can buy this ETF and put your strategy into action. This is a great way of shorting stocks without requiring a margin account or worrying about maintenance and initial margin requirements.

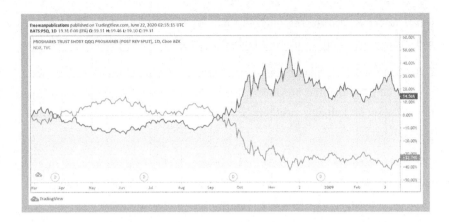

The correlation between the ProShare Short QQQ inverse ETF and the NASDAQ index between Mar 2008 and Mar 2009. During this volatile period, the inverse ETF returned 14.56% while the index lost 32.74%.

We should note that unless you believe an entire sector is dying, these inverse ETFs are not designed as a long term hold, merely as a hedge against temporary dips in the market. For example, over the past 5 years, the NASDAQ is up 165.82% whereas the inverse ETF is down 65.41%.

Which means you should be wary of such ETFs. When choosing inverse ETFs, stick to the ones that are heavily traded and are the inverse of popular indices. If you find an inverse ETF of a single stock, then run far away from it.

This is because there are many inverse ETFs that are issued by hedge funds. In effect, they're taking the other side of the trade from you. This means you won't have any liquidity when you want to sell and if the position moves against you, you're going to get squeezed.

You'll also find what are called 2x ETFs. These instruments move in double units of their underlying. For example, if the underlying index or stock moves by one dollar, the 2x ETF moves by two. They achieve this through leverage. You'll also find 2x inverse ETFs. If the underlying moves up by one point, the 2x inverse ETF will move down by two.

Stay away from these because leverage ensures you'll get cleaned out quickly. Worst of all, you're not in charge of the leverage and you never know when things might go bad for the fund. In some cases, the government steps in and halts trading in certain instruments if things get out of hand.

For example, in 2008, the government halted trading in SEF, the financial inverse ETF highlighted previously, since all bank stocks were tumbling after the collapse of Lehman Brothers and the credit troubles of the insurance giant AIG.

This means that sticking to broad index inverse ETFs is a good idea. Be on the lookout if things get too grim with a particular sector. It's best to cash out early than risk governmental action that will throw your best-laid plans into a ditch.

The 1 Chart Pattern You Should Know for Short Selling

This isn't a book about technical analysis, but even if you've never utilized charts in your investing philosophy, there is one technical indicator that you should be aware of, and that's the death cross.

The death cross refers to when an asset's short-term moving average crosses its long term moving average. The most common time period for this is when the 50 day moving average falls below the 200 day moving average. In a bull market, both moving averages will rise as there are more buyers than sellers. When the cross happens, it indicates that sellers have recently gained the upper hand and that short-term downwards movements are likely.

The death cross has been a consistent predictor of a number of bear markets including the 1929 crash, the dotcom crash in 2000 and the 2008-9 financial crisis.

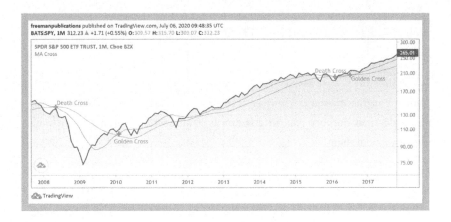

For example a death cross occurred on the SPY ETF in mid 2008, at that point the market already had dipped slightly from previous highs, but the index then fell almost 50% from 144.35 to 72.48, and it took almost 18 months for the 50 day moving average to move above the 200 day moving average. This reversal is known as the golden cross.

Another death cross occurred in early 2016, which preceded the small pullback in stock prices over the next 3-4 months. As you can see from the above chart, the death cross is not a 100% accurate predictor of bear markets, and should not be relied upon by itself. If the 50 day average only stays below the 200 day average for a couple of days, then a prolonged bear market is unlikely.

But when it stays there for multiple months, as we saw in 2008, the likelihood of a bear market significantly increases. For example, if you had waited 3 months after the death cross occurred in 2008, you would still have been able to exit SPY at 135, rather than seeing it plummet to 72 within the next 6 months.

We should reiterate that the death cross is not a short term instrument, so you won't be able to day trade on this pattern alone. Nor will you be able to predict events such as COVID-19. Instead it's a tool for long-term investors to take profits before a prolonged bear market is about to begin. Remember, no one ever went broke by taking profits.

INDUSTRIES THAT TRADITIONALLY DO WELL IN RECESSIONS

While shorting is a way for you to take advantage of market weakness, not every company in the market is going to suffer from weak earnings. There are some businesses that do very well in downturns. This section is going to introduce you to a few of them.

Please note that while we'll mention the names of a few companies in this section our objective isn't to provide stock recommendations. It's merely to highlight a few characteristics that we'll be discussing. The focus here is the characteristics, not the companies themselves.

Low Capital Requirements

A bear market places immense strain on all companies in an economy. Cash is hard to come by since lenders have a habit of turning off the supply of money right when people need it the most. In such times, companies that have low costs thrive and ride out the storm far better than the ones that have high costs.

There are two kinds of costs that companies encounter. These are fixed and variable. A mining company, for example, has high fixed costs. Real estate development companies have high fixed costs as well. Variable costs are tied to top line revenues.

For example, the more sales a bakery needs to make, the higher its costs are going to be. Variable costs aren't bad by themselves as long as they're being backed up by higher revenues. The problem arises when companies need to spend additional money to achieve growth. In bull markets such businesses do very well. However, during bear markets such businesses stagnate.

Given that access to financing is so important to these companies, they usually carry high levels of debt in their balance sheets. This comes back to bite them when they cannot earn the same level of return on their investment in a bear market. The aforementioned baker can create all the cakes they want, but try as they might, sales are going to be down.

In bear markets you want to focus on businesses that are service-based and don't require additional investment to provide such services. In-person service businesses tend to do well, but it really depends on the kind of service being offered. Debt consolidation services boom but shoe shining services probably won't.

The COVID-19 pandemic has thrown in-person services into disarray thanks to social distancing requirements. However, as businesses reopen, expect to see a rebound in these sectors. Services these days are provided online as well and these companies have perhaps the best bear market business model.

SaaS or Software as a Service is something we've highlighted previously in this book. By capturing steady monthly payments or by locking in subscriptions for a year, SaaS companies have a strong economic moat. They can scale their business up without having to invest too much into expanding their platform.

For example, the business marketing platform Hubspot is going to encounter similar costs whether 10,000 or 100,000 people use their platform. As user numbers increase they will need more rack space (the technical term for server and data storage space), but these costs reduce on a unit basis over time as more growth is achieved.

These companies also have lower fixed costs. Their business is conducted over the internet which means that the need for physical office space is less. While they will have an office building, the business doesn't depend on having a physical location. Remote work is perfectly fine in such industries and it's no surprise that these businesses have been carrying on as normal (or close to it) during the pandemic.

Traditional businesses will have higher fixed costs than SaaS companies, but this doesn't mean it's a bad thing. It's the ratio of costs to revenues that you want to look at. Retail outlets tend to have high fixed costs, and rent payments make up a large portion of their gross margins.

Even with the move to eCommerce models, the need for inventory storage is high. While the likes of Amazon can thrive thanks to their diversified businesses, the prospects for smaller retail companies aren't as positive.

A significant fixed cost that most investors don't think about often enough is inventory. Inventory on the balance sheet is a double-edged sword. During good times, high inventory levels are a sign of strength, as long as they're in line with revenue growth. When revenue growth stops (during bad times, most likely), the excess inventory becomes a noose.

This is because companies with high fixed costs typically finance inventory creation or purchases with debt. In bear markets, banks will pay closer attention to loan default rates and if a company cannot service their debt, they'll be forced to liquidate inventory and this drastically reduces margins.

Watch out for signs of high inventories on balance sheets, resulting in low net income figures but high cash flow. A drastic decrease in net margin is also a sign of a company liquidating its excess inventory. While inventories might be listed on the asset side of the balance sheet, it can turn against a company quite quickly.

Accounts receivables (the money that is owed to a company by its customers, also called AR) behave in the same manner. During bad times everyone's going to have trouble paying their bills. A large AR figure on the asset portion of the balance sheet might skew the debt to equity ratio favorably.

However, companies that have the majority of their assets tied up in AR or inventory will be forced to bring cash in by renegotiating the terms of payment and might collect 60 cents on the dollar for them. All this does is boost cash flow while doing nothing for profit margins.

Our point is that AR and inventory are costs as well despite being assets. During bad times, even assets can turn against a company and you should consider them to be the equivalent of fixed costs. Stay away from companies that have excessive inventory levels or AR and are unable to move them.

Discounters

One area of business that does very well during bad times are discount retailers. It doesn't matter what is being sold; if they sell items at a discount more often than not, the company will do well. The reasons for this are pretty simple.

With wallets tightening, people will begin to look for lower prices on essential goods. This means they'll turn to discount operators to get the cheapest prices for a variety of items, whether clothes, food, household items, you name it. Retailers such as Walmart, Costco, Dollar Tree and Ross will witness higher foot traffic and revenues in these times.

All of these retailers do have high fixed costs, but the increase in revenues will decrease the cost per unit numbers. Figuring out the cost per unit is a bit difficult for the investor since most companies don't disclose this. This is because it's tough for them to figure out as well.

However, a good substitute is to look at the sales per square foot of retail space and compare that to the fixed cost per square foot. Companies will disclose the total square footage of retail space they have along with the revenues. Costs can be calculated from the income statement by adding the cash cost items. Divide the revenue and costs by the total square footage to arrive at the cost and sales per square foot.

This method isn't foolproof, but in the case of these companies, it will give you an idea of how well the company is maximizing its retail space. Margins in these industries are typically low and the companies here depend on sales volumes. During bear markets, volumes increase rapidly.

The performance of Wal-Mart, Ross & Dollar Tree vs. the S&P 500 from June 2005 to June 2010. Notice the immediate divergence in mid 2008 as the effects of the financial crisis began taking shape, and the shift in spending habits towards discount retailers began. The returns over the 5 year period were as follows

- Dollar Tree: 173.99%
- Ross: 89.89%
- Wal-Mart: 10.3%
- S&P 500: -7.13%

Companies that have a good economic moat will do well in the long run. An economic moat is an advantage that the company has as part of its business model. In Walmart's case, its sheer size gives it a considerable moat. This allows it to negotiate prices with suppliers to rock-bottom levels, and it allows them to purchase large quantities of stock.

This means items never run out and the shopping experience is always consistent. Smaller retailers cannot compete against this. Amazon employs the same model in the eCommerce sector.

Despite the clear advantages of companies like these, some investors might feel that placing their money in one company might be too risky. Bear markets are unpredictable and analyzing a single company requires investing a lot of time that they don't have. If this is the case, investing in Real Estate Investment Trusts (REITs) are a good option. A REIT is a company that owns real estate properties and earns income by maintaining the property.

For example, a REIT could own a large number of apartment complexes. It earns money by collecting rent from these complexes and its costs include office space and maintenance. An investor that buys shares in the REIT is tying themselves indirectly to the performance of those apartment complexes.

This is an indirect method of owning real estate and is a lot cheaper than having to make a down payment for a property. REITs have a number of concentrations. There are diversified REITs that invest in all kinds of properties and specialized REITs that invest in specific types of properties.

There are REITs that invest solely in real estate leased to discount store operators. The Tanger Factory Outlet Stores REIT (NYSE:SKT) is an example of a company that does this. The company owns 39 outlet centers spread across the US, and considers its business model to be one which thrives in market downturns. CEO Steven Tanger famously stated "In good times, people like a bargain. In tough times, people need a bargain"

What makes these companies good investments is that they tend to fall initially in a bear market thanks to the general selling that the overall retail sector faces. During the initial phase of a bear market pretty much every retail stock nosedives since investors believe that people will spend less money shopping. This leads many unintelligent investors to sell discount retailer stocks as well. These companies therefore end up becoming bargains.

This doesn't mean you should buy every single discount retailer REIT out there! It just means that you're more likely to find a bargain in this sector than in other areas. The best part about REITs is that they are legally mandated to pay out 90% of their profits to their shareholders.

Note that it's 90% of profits, not rent. Rent money represents revenues for REITs. They subtract their office and salary costs before passing on 90% of the rest to you. The dividends that you will receive will make for good supplemental income in bear markets and are a great passive income stream.

There is one thing you should be aware of when it comes to looking at REITs. When you look at them in financial screening software, you'll notice that their payout ratios will seem unsustainable. The payout ratio is calculated by dividing the dividend paid per share by the net income earned per share. You want to see stable payout ratios.

In the case of a REIT, you'd expect it to be around 90% since this is what the law says they must do. However, you'll often see numbers that are above this, even reaching 150%. How can a REIT pay more than what they earn?

The answer lies in the way GAAP treats assets. GAAP mandates that all assets on a balance sheet be depreciated over time. This includes property as well. However, as everyone knows, property appreciates over time, especially if it's well maintained. The depreciation expense that REITs take on their income statement is not real. Sure, there's wear and tear over time, but it hardly occurs on the scale that depreciation expense indicates.

This means the cash flow that a REIT collects is the true net income figure, specifically the free cash flow earned after subtracting capital expenditures from cash flow derived from operations. Both of these are line items in the cash flow statement. Look at the dividend payment with respect to this number instead of comparing it to net income.

Pro tip: If you buy REITs within a Roth IRA, you won't pay any capital gains tax or taxes on dividends. Over time, this is hugely beneficial to your overall profits.

Relaxation and Escapes

When speaking of relaxation and escapes you might think cruises and vacation company operators, but remember we're in a bear market. People don't have the same level of disposable income, and these particular industries will be hard hit as you'll shortly learn.

Given that people need to make do with less, you need to focus on companies that make products that allow people a cheap escape. This means brewery companies such as Anheuser-Busch (EBR:ABI) and Constellation Brands (NYSE:STZ) will see increased consumption of their brands.

You might think that people will reduce consumption of such products in tough times given their relative cost, but remember that this is all about providing an escape. For this same reason, tobacco companies witness a surge in demand in tough times despite the increasingly high costs of their products.

A new entrant into this space is the cannabis industry. While the average cannabis company stock experienced a huge surge upwards thanks to impressive marketing and the novelty factor, you can expect the better-run companies to experience increased demand from the public.

Speaking of escapes, companies such as Netflix (NASDAQ:NFLX) and other streaming device manufacturers such as Roku (NASDAQ:ROKU) will also witness an increase in demand. With less money available for going out to movies or spending a night out, you would expect people to stay at home and stream entertainment.

Keep in mind that there are other business factors to take into consideration. Netflix might witness a surge in demand, but does this mean it will do better than its competitors? It may or may not. It depends on how well the company is run and whether it is able to recover costs. Increased demand isn't the only deciding factor when you are looking to invest in a company. It's merely the starting point for you to begin your research.

A significant competitor to Netflix is Disney (NYSE:DIS), and this company always gets hit hard during bear markets. This is because everyone associates it with Disneyland. While the theme parks do account for a significant portion of revenues, this is hardly the only source of income.

Disney is an entertainment giant. It dominates the world of movies (Marvel, Pixar) television (ABC, Disney channels) and sports (ESPN) over and above children's entertainment. The only industry it hadn't expanded to was streaming, and with the launch of Disney Plus, it's expanded there as well.

In bear markets, the stock gets hammered due to decreased Disneyland visits. However, its vast content library and intellectual trademarks ensure that the cash always flows in steadily. It might be a good prospect to look into in bear markets.

In this category we also have adult entertainment companies such as RCI Hospitality Holdings (NASDAQ:RICK). The name of the company is appropriately boring but it includes brands such as the famous Rick's bar in New York City. There are other companies in this space that deserve a second look as well.

Some investors will have ethical concerns over investing in the majority of the industries profiled here. Remember that it isn't 100% necessary to invest in these industries in order to make money. There are many other options as you've already learned. The key is to stick to what you can analyze.

If you're uncomfortable with a business or find it too complex to fully get a handle on, feel free to skip it. There are abundant opportunities in bear markets for you to take advantage of. Our aim is to merely highlight all of these opportunities that are available.

INDUSTRIES THAT ARE HIT THE HARDEST

From industries that perform the best in a downturn we now turn our attention to the ones that are hit the hardest in a downturn. Stay away from investing in these industries and you'll do yourself a massive favor. A lot of these industries come up with spectacular investment offers during such times.

However, these offers do not provide the investor adequate protection from the poor economics inherent in these businesses.

Airlines

Airlines are curious businesses. They're proof of the fact that high demand alone does not sustain a business. We've highlighted previously the case of Concorde. Passengers were extremely happy with their experience on the plane and the aircraft drastically reduced flight time between two of the major financial centers of the world. Yet it still failed.

The demand for air travel has always been high. In the early days of commercial aviation, this was seen as a buccaneering space with the likes of Howard Hughes' Trans World Airlines and Juan Trippe's Pan American Airways battling for supremacy. In the background were dozens of regional airline companies that also competed for space.

All of these companies are distant memories now, and the American aviation industry is a case of choosing the least bad experience possible. It's as if misery is a given on these flights and the worldwide reputation of America's airline companies is terrible. Having said that, examining the state of the industry worldwide doesn't provide a much better picture.

The space is dominated by airlines that are backed by wealthy governments or those that are subsidized by them. Looking at the list of the best airline companies in the world is instructive. Here are the top five from 2019 (Logan, 2020):

1. Qatar Airways - Backed by the government of Qatar, a natural gas-rich monarchy
2. Singapore Airlines - Backed by the government of Singapore, another rich country

3. ANA - A private airline
4. Cathay Pacific Airways - Privately owned, but the Chinese government owns a significant stake through Air China
5. Emirates - The original government-owned airline, backed by the government of Dubai

In addition to these, recall some of the best-known airline companies in the world. Southwest, Ryanair, Air Asia, British Airways and Air France come to mind. All of these, including the ones in the list above are either budget airlines or are government-owned.

The message is clear here. If you own an airline and aren't a budget operator or backed by the government, you're dead in the water. The economics of the commercial aviation industry are so bad that even during the best of times, airline executives whine about the high cost of business.

They're obsessed over their competition at all times and this by itself is a good indication of how well the business runs. A good business doesn't need to worry about its competition. When was the last time you heard Amazon whining about Facebook, Apple or Google?

However, the likes of Delta (NYSE:DAL), American (NYSE:AAL), and United (NASDAQ: UAL) have repeatedly launched attacks on the "Middle Eastern" (their words, not ours) carriers in an attempt to drum up nationalist sentiment against them (Dastin & Saleem, 2015). They somehow overlook the fact that people don't like to be bodily thrown out of their aircraft and put their failure down to sinister government forces, oil price manipulation and so on.

Some investors view airlines as being cyclical stocks. They fall to low levels during downturns and then rise as the economy gets better. In our view, this is little better than trying to time the market. If you're going to invest like this, you might as well try to trade the daily charts.

Even the best investors are susceptible to the glamor that owning an airline brings. One of Warren Buffett's famous mistakes involved U.S Airways in the early 1990's. Charlie Munger quietly quipped that Buffett hadn't consulted him on that one. More recently, Buffett once again invested in all the major airlines only to have his thesis shattered by the COVID-19 crisis.

The fact that he bought them for low prices even before the crisis hit, is a marker of how terrible airline companies are. We mentioned the economic moat previously. It turns out that airlines have a nonexistent moat. Ask yourself: Unless incentivized by miles, would you ever choose to pick United over any of the other airlines available? What's more, miles redemptions have decreased in value thanks to increased competition and price comparison websites.

Your primary decision is based on the price you receive. Whoever offers the lowest price wins your business. As Buffett once famously said when discussing the operations of Berkshire's textile mills (Green, 2016), "When a management with a reputation for brilliance tackles a business with a reputation for poor fundamental economics, it is the reputation of the business that remains intact."

Hotels

Coming close in second place to airlines in the worst business sweepstakes are hotels. While the margins of most hotels aren't as bad as the ones airlines face, the hotel industry is a tough business. It is a business that relies on discount pricing but has to maintain the facade of luxury nonetheless.

Much like airlines, the hotel businesses that do well tend to have a lot of history or backing behind them. The hotel industry is dominated by a small number of conglomerates, such as Hilton (NYSE:HLT) and Marriott (NASDAQ:MAR). There are a few regional brands that displace them, but these are the major players.

All of them have similar business models in that they lease their name to facilities around the world and collect royalties on the brand name. This means these brands have reduced their operational expenses significantly and have removed the risk of having a failed property on their portfolio.

Understanding this decision is a good way of figuring out the economics of the business. If someone approached you with an offer to start a great business with your name on it in another part of the world, you'd most likely jump at the offer.

This is assuming the business is in your circle of competence and you've conducted your research into the area.

For example, McDonald's owns all of its restaurant locations. By owning the property, it commits itself to creating a great business wherever it goes. Hotel operators don't do this. Why would they choose to avoid it? Why would you choose to avoid such opportunities from the example in the previous paragraph?

It's probably because the cost of failure and the probability of failure is too high. You'd avoid a deal that is a terrible one. However, hotels have to keep running their business, and as a result they franchise themselves. From the franchisee's perspective, assuming the costs of running a restaurant is a lot lower than assuming the costs of running a 100-room hotel.

The poor economics of running a hotel can be better understood by looking at the work involved in running an Airbnb business. We're not referring to letting out your own property on the platform. Instead, we're talking about offering a handful of owner-owned properties and collecting profits on the price difference in rent you get paid versus the rent you pay.

It is a full-time business to say the least. Your fixed costs are going to be extremely high and you'll have to carry out constant maintenance of the property. You'll need to deal with empty premises and have to market the property to ensure a good flow of tenants. You'll have to pay the rent to the landlord no matter what or else you'll lose the property and your source of income.

Now imagine having these problems multiplied by 100 and having to bear staff salaries and increased marketing costs thanks to competition. You'll also have to deal with regulation since you can't offer just any room as a hotel room for rent. It's little wonder that hotel operators have constantly lobbied governments against platforms such as Airbnb.

As we mentioned in the previous section, a reliable indicator of a business with terrible economics is one where the major executives are either asking for handouts all the time or are engaged in lobbying to pass laws that cripple their competition. The hotel industry doesn't have as poor a reputation as airlines do, but their actions speak loudly.

One particular offer that all hotel operators come up with during tough times is to offer "investment" opportunities in their properties. The marketing material typically highlights the amazing chance to own a room in a five-star property, fully serviced. What's more, the owner can earn rent thanks to the room being rented out. Maintenance is fully taken care of, and the owner can occupy it whenever they wish.

What's worse is you'll be tying yourself to one particular location and will be at the mercy of the hotel's business. Don't even think about such offers.

Both airlines and hotels are ideal condition industries, in short. They need a lot of things to line up in their favor in order to make money. If even one of these things goes slightly off-balance, they lose money. Given the volatility that bear markets introduce to the system, you can bet that these businesses will be the first ones to feel the pinch.

Casual Dining

The casual dining sector is a no man's land. It isn't upscale enough to warrant high prices (think Ruth's Chris) and neither is it cheap enough like fast food to justify repeated visits. A lot of these mid-range dining options incorporate the worst of both worlds.

You pay a higher price to be seated at a table only to be delivered potentially microwaved food. During good times, it's a decent option for a night out and you don't have to spend too much money for family entertainment. During bad times, the negatives of these establishments comes to mind and consumers stay away.

A good example of how badly these companies get hit is Red Robin Gourmet Burgers (NASDAQ:RRGB). The company is in the same space of operations as Chili's, Applebee's and Olive Garden. Once the lockdowns that were prompted by the COVID-19 crisis began, the stock price fell from $30 to $5 over the course of two weeks.

The majority of this price drop was caused by investors overreacting to bad news, to be certain. However, the price as of this writing has barely recovered to $12. These mid-range restaurants have the fixed costs of their higher-priced counterparts in terms of kitchen, real estate and employee salaries. However, their margins are much lower due to the items on their menus being priced lower.

They don't have much brand recognition and struggle to separate themselves from one another. Nor do they have huge fan followings. In order to entice customers to visit them over another brand, they need to offer discounts or special promotions. Olive Garden is particularly famous for this.

Unlimited breadsticks are a promotion that the company uses to lure patrons in. However, these breadsticks don't get them spending more. After all, anyone who eats a large amount of bread before their meal isn't going to spend much on entrees or desserts. Then there's the fact that abusing the breadstick policy at Olive Garden is a cult topic.

Stories abound of people hiding them in their bags and entire threads on Reddit are dedicated to instructing people in the art of maximizing breadsticks. The chain also runs yearly promotions such as bottomless salads and unlimited pasta bowls. These usually attract college students who are unlikely to be repeat patrons.

While Olive Garden's promotions are the most famous example, other chains run similar promotions all the time. Thanks to their menus failing to make any impact with patrons, these companies need to reinvest money to upgrade or change them every few months.

It makes for a tough time if you're an executive of the company. As an investor, you'll constantly be on the lookout for the next downturn so that you can exit as quickly as possible. Some investors might believe these stocks are cyclical, but not every single company adheres to this pattern.

They usually bounce back only when things are going really well and the bull market is already well established. If the bull market happens to be short, then these companies will be stuck in a seemingly perennial rut.

Landlords

What happens the minute people begin to lose jobs? They stop paying rent and other bills. This hits landlords and landlord-related businesses the hardest. The number of vacancies increases and foreclosures increase. Rents might drop, but this depends on how bad the economy gets.

This is a second order effect of a bear market or economic downturn. The real estate cycle doesn't move in the same one as the stock market does. However, it does get affected. Residential real estate is usually hit the hardest and it follows more of a boom and bust cycle than its commercial counterpart.

Residential real estate depends heavily on average consumers having enough money to make mortgage payments and down payments. With money scarce, home purchasing hits record lows. As a result, home builders slow down the pace of development and this hits their business hard.

Recovery is also questionable when it comes to home building companies. They tend to experience the worst of both the stock market and real estate cycles. From the market peak of 2007 till 2020, not a single home building company's stock outperformed the market except for NVR, Inc. (NYSE:NVR)

This has a knock-on effect on companies that are suppliers to home builders. Building materials suppliers such as Caterpillar (NYSE:CAT) and Sherwin Williams (NYSE:SHW) face problems. Other home builders such as Pulte group (NYSE:PHM) and D.R. Horton (NYSE:DHI) also face headwinds.

These days, real estate has moved online and there has been a lot of talk of how the realty industry has been disrupted. This isn't true. The likes of Zillow (NAS-DAQ:ZG) front themselves as being technology companies but are realtors at heart. The technology angle allows them to push a narrative that gets them valued at higher earnings in the stock market. However, Zillow is still affected by the same cycle as these other companies, regardless of how disruptive it claims to be.

Big box retailers also suffer, especially those catering to home maintenance and contracting. Home Depot (NYSE:HD) and Lowe's (NYSE:LOW) are examples of these.

Despite residential real estate being hit the hardest, commercial real estate gets hit as well. While it does not follow the same boom and bust cycle of residential property, commercial properties tend to get hit hard. REITs that focus on commercial properties especially suffer.

Companies such as Brookfield Group (NYSE:BAM), Simon Property Group (NYSE:SPG) and Macerich (NYSE:MAC) absorb the impact of a slowing retail sector. Less spending means less rental payments made on time. Office space leasing also slows down thanks to the prospect of layoffs and bankruptcies.

A good way to take advantage of these downturns is to purchase an inverse ETF or short the individual stocks. You could also short ETFs that track a commercial real estate index. Whatever method you choose to employ, remember to conduct thorough research into the instrument and understand what you're gaining exposure to.

Delayed Purchase Eligible Products

These products cover a wide range of industries, but their underlying theme is the same. All of them can be bought down the road if money is tight. They aren't products that are necessary and can be considered luxuries. Don't let the word luxury fool you. This doesn't mean companies such as LVMH or Ferrari will struggle.

Truly luxurious items will always have a market since there will always be people with enough money to afford them. Besides, those products do not depend on the bull and bear market cycle anyway. By luxuries, we meant products that are "wants" as opposed to "needs."

A smartphone is a need, but is an iPhone one? If money is tight, even the most rabid Apple fanboys will reconsider their decision to spend money on them. They will either delay the purchase of a new phone for a year or will borrow money through a payment plan to finance the purchase. This may not be the smartest of decisions, but this isn't a book about personal finance.

The companies that make these products will feel the pinch since there's less revenues coming in, even if products are being shipped. The other factor that affects these purchases is that credit card delinquencies typically rise during a bear market.

The pandemic has currently created a bear market and right on cue, credit card delinquencies have risen to their highest point since 2013 ("Delinquency Rate on Credit Card Loans, All Commercial Banks", 2020). Meanwhile, household debt reached record levels in February, when things were still relatively stable (Marte, 2020)

Combine this with an economic recovery over the past decade that was a sham, and you have a perfect situation for spending patterns to change in the coming years. Households will seek to save more money moving forward in anticipation of the next shock.

USING SECTOR SPECIFIC ETFS AS A HEDGE

Capitalizing on bear markets will require you to expand your circle of competence. In some cases, you will find that the instruments in question will be difficult for you to understand fully. In such situations one option for you to utilize would be to invest in ETFs that provide you with exposure to that sector or opportunity.

This will help you stay away from instruments that are too complex or from sectors whose economics you aren't intimately familiar with. The ETFs highlighted in this section will help you hedge against the falling market. You can also use them as long term investments that will remain stable.

Treasury Bills, Notes and Bonds

We've explained what T-bills are previously. These are bonds that are issued by the U.S. Government and form one of the most secure forms of debt in the world. The word "bill" in the name indicates that their maturity is less than a year. These bills have a few quirks to them, and it's worth taking the time to understand how they work.

Bonds are a form of debt. The issuer of the bond borrows money from you when you buy the bond. For example, if company X issues bonds worth $5 million, they're looking to borrow that amount from investors. An investor buys one of these bonds and earns an interest rate that will be paid by the issuer. This interest rate is referred to as the coupon.

The price of a bond fluctuates since it can be traded in the open market. This is true of T-bills as well. This means the bond's yield fluctuates. A bond's yield is a measure of the return the investor will receive if they purchase the bond at the current price. For example a bond that costs $1,000 and pays $10 in annual coupon payments is yielding one percent.

It's important to note that the face value of a bond can be different from its price. The bond from the previous example might be trading currently at $1,000, but it could have a face value of $1,500. When the bond matures, or reaches its expiry date, the issuer returns the face value of the bond to the current owner.

This means investors can earn significant capital gains from speculating on bond prices as well. In practice, this is tough to do and the average investor is best off staying away from such speculation due to the risks involved. T-bills work slightly differently from regular bonds.

For starters, since their maturities are just for one year at most, they don't pay coupons. The government sells them at a discount from their face value and promises to repay the face value upon maturity. The yield is calculated as being the difference between the face value and the discounted value.

The government lists the current T-bill rates at https://www.treasury.gov/resource-center/data-chart-center/interest-rates/Pages/TextView.aspx?data=billrates. Currently, the one-month T-bill is selling at a 0.1% discount to its face value and the one-year bill is selling at a 0.18% discount. As you can see, the returns aren't exactly earth-shattering. However, that's not the point of a T-bill.

As a creditor to the American government, you're backing the most transparent and robust financial system on the planet. Despite rising debt levels, it's unlikely that the American government is going to default on these payments anytime soon.

You can purchase these bills directly from the government at published rates or you can enter a competitive auction. The most common and practical way for a retail investor to purchase T-bills is through an ETF. You buy shares in the ETF and the fund holds previously issued T-bills.

T-notes, or Treasury notes, are bonds that have maturity dates between one and 10 years. These function like normal bonds as detailed previously. The investor receives a coupon payment every year. Typically, the government issues notes with maturity terms of two, three, five, seven and 10 years (Chen, 2020).

T-bonds, or Treasury bonds, have maturities that are above 10 years and run up to 30 years. Currently the 30-year T-bond is yielding 1.44% while the five-year note is yielding 0.34%. All of these instruments are safe havens and are considered to be a safe place to hold cash while the rest of the market declines.

The noteworthy point about all of these instruments is that the gains on them are not taxable. After all, you're funding the government by buying them. Something to keep in mind when buying bonds is the relationship between interest rates and bond prices. They move in opposite directions from one another.

As interest rates rise, bond prices fall. Here's why this happens. Let's say you buy a T-note that is paying you a 0.12% coupon. It's paying you this much because that's the rate fixed by the U.S Federal Reserve Bank (the Fed). During tough economic times, interest rates are slashed to low levels, as you've learned already.

Once times get better, interest rate levels are raised. This means the new T-notes that are issued will pay higher coupons, perhaps 0.2%. Holders of the older notes are therefore losing out. This makes the old notes unattractive and everyone will buy the new notes.

If you hold on till the maturity of the note, you will realize a yield equal to the coupon rate since you'll receive the face value back. Unless you plan on selling the bond before maturity, you don't have anything to worry about. However, you should be aware of this phenomenon.

Like with T-bills, you can gain exposure to bonds and notes through ETFs. There are three ETFs in particular that have proven themselves to be reputable. Keep in mind that by owning these ETFs you're not owning any bonds or fixed-income instruments. Instead, you're gaining exposure to the yield curves of these instruments.

If the interest rate scenario explained previously happens, the price of the ETF will fluctuate depending on what the manager decides to do. If they dump the old notes in favor of the new, prices will rise. However, if they sell too much, they'll take too large a capital loss and the ETF price will fall.

This makes it imperative for you to choose ETFs that have been run by experienced managers who have a proven track record. The three ETFs below satisfy this criteria:

1. TLT
2. SHY
3. EDV

TLT is the iShares 20+ Year Treasury Bond ETF. The ETF tracks the performance of an index tied to U.S. Treasury Bonds with maturities of greater than 20 years. The fund has returned 9.46% over the past 10 years.

It currently has over $18 billion in assets and is one of the largest ETFs that is currently listed on the NASDAQ. Investors will have to pay 0.15% of their capital invested in the fund as fees every year. This is called the expense ratio. Currently, the fund holds a 99.3% exposure to U.S. Bonds with the remaining 0.7% held as cash.

SHY is the iShares 1-3 Year Treasury Bond ETF. As the name suggests, the fund invests its money in T-notes with a maturity of one to three years. It has returned 1.31% over the past 10 years. The underlying index it tracks is the ICE U.S. Treasury 1-3 Year Bond Index and it has lagged behind this benchmark slightly over the past decade.

It currently has over $23 billion under management. Like the previous ETF, SHY also has an expense ratio of 0.15%. It currently holds a 98.48% exposure to T-notes with the rest held in cash.

EDV is the Vanguard Extended Duration Treasury ETF. Given that this fund is a Vanguard product, it functions as a pure index fund. The underlying index it tracks is the Bloomberg Barclays U.S. Treasury STRIPS 20-30 Equal Par Bond Index. That's quite a mouthful, but the index simply tracks the yields of 20-30 year T-Bonds.

It currently holds over $3.2 billion in assets and has returned 12.57% over the past decade. It has the lowest expense ratio of the trio with just 0.07%. It currently holds 100% of its funds in U.S. Bonds.

None of the above returns are particularly groundbreaking, but that's not the point. The point is that these funds should give a better return than merely holding cash during an economic downturn. Once market conditions begin to improve, then you can sell your holdings in these funds and move more of them into traditional stocks and ETFs.

Consumer Staples

Consumer staples are products that are essential household goods. Groceries, hygiene products and beverages come under this category. As their name suggests, they'll always be in demand no matter what is going on with the economy. The rationale behind buying shares of discount retailers is that cheap consumer staples will always face increased demand during tough times.

Despite the demand for consumer staples remaining constant, there is the danger of prices not matching consumer expectations. If store A stocks a product at $5 and store B stocks it for $6, A will receive the bulk of the business. This makes consumer staples an extremely price-sensitive segment.

The danger for the investor is that they might end up investing in a store or retailer that doesn't offer the lowest prices. This opens them up to huge levels of risk should the underlying economics of that business change. It's far less risky to instead gain exposure to consumer staples as a whole instead of concentrating holdings in one particular company.

This is where the XLP ETF comes into the picture. The underlying index it follows is the Consumer Staples Select Sector Index. This index is a collection of all the consumer staples companies listed in the S&P 500. The companies retail products that range from grocery stores to beverages, other food products, tobacco, personal hygiene products and household products.

It currently has over $14 billion in assets under management. This money is spread over 33 stocks. The highest weighted stock in its portfolio is Procter & Gamble, which is 15% of the overall portfolio, with PepsiCo, Coca-Cola and

Wal-Mart also making up a large proportion of its holdings. It has an expense ratio of 0.13% and has returned 10.72% over the past decade.

Healthcare

Healthcare is something that people will always need. From pharmaceutical companies to hospitals to pharmacies, healthcare is a massive sector. Recently, healthcare has been evolving from a person-to-person model to an online model. Teleconsultations have been on the rise over the past decade and the sector is rapidly changing.

Given the large number of companies that operate in the sector, it can be tricky to get your portfolio allocation right. This is where the XLV ETF comes into the picture. Much like the ETF highlighted when we looked at consumer staples, XLV offers the investor exposure to 61 companies in the healthcare field.

The fund has over $26 billion in assets under management and has returned a healthy 14.4% over the past decade. It has an expense ratio of 0.13% and pays a quarterly dividend. Its underlying index is the Health Care Select Sector Index which comprises the biggest stocks in the healthcare sector.

The dividend yield is currently 1.39%, which puts it on par with most common stocks. It has exposure to companies such as Johnson & Johnson, Pfizer, Merck etc.

Safe Dividend Yield

Earning a stream of passive cash flow is pretty attractive for most investors. Dividend paying stocks are sought after for a variety of reasons. Historically, they've outperformed the rest of the market during bear market declines. Their ability to produce income sometimes indicates a core business that is stable.

For example, companies such as Coca-Cola pay steady dividends thanks to their large balance sheets and well-established earning advantages. The downside of investing in a single common stock is that you're gaining exposure to the economics of that particular company. We saw the results of this in Q2 of 2020 as many companies, including Royal Dutch Shell, Dunkin' Brands and General Motors, cut or suspended their dividend due to the COVID-19 pandemic.

In bear markets, ETFs come to the rescue once again if you wish to capture the advantage of steady dividend payouts without having to run the risk of downside exposure in common stocks.

SDY is a famous ETF that offers investors exactly this advantage. The ETF tracks the S&P Dividend Aristocrats Index. This index is composed of companies that have large market size and have paid increasing dividends for at least 25 years. Some companies in this index, such as Coca-Cola and Kimberly Clark, have paid dividends stretching back over 50 years.

It currently has over $15 billion in assets under management and has an expense ratio of 0.35%. It is currently yielding a healthy 3.09%. It has returned 9.87% over the past decade and has distributed its assets across 119 companies. SDY usually sells for prices that place its yields around one to two percent. The current bear market has provided investors a great opportunity to enter.

The US Dollar

We've discussed assets ranging from equities to fixed income thus far. Currencies are another asset class, but they tend to be highly speculative. This is why the average investor is best served by staying away from them. Currencies don't have any value by themselves.

They derive their value in relation to other currencies. When traders speculate in the forex markets, it is the exchange rate they're betting on. Typically, currency investments require huge degrees of leverage because the underlying exchange rates move so little.

Betting directly on currencies, not the exchange rates, is an expensive prospect for the average investor. The amount of capital needed to do this is exorbitant. However, if you have a view on the U.S. dollar, there is a way for you to bet on its strength.

UUP is an ETF that allows you to do just this. The underlying index this fund tracks is a bit complex, but the gist of it is that it tracks the strength in the U.S. dollar (and weaknesses). If the dollar grows stronger, UUP rises in value and if it grows weak, UUP falls.

It currently has $868 million under management and has a high expense ratio of 0.79%. Over the past decade it has returned 1.45%. Keep in mind that the prior decade witnessed a strong bull market and the dollar held its value throughout this. A bear market might result in other currencies weakening, and given the dollar's position as the world's preferred trade currency, one might witness an upswing in prices.

This fund is not a long-term hold since over the long term equities outperform currencies by some distance. However, for periods of three years and under, UUP is a good bet should you want to add US dollar exposure to your portfolio.

Volatility

Another way to protect your portfolio during uncertain times is by profiting from an increase in market volatility. The Chicago Board Options Exchange (CBOE) created an index which tracked the volatility of the overall market, known as VIX. This index tracks the market's expectation for volatility in the next 30 days.

We've previously discussed how bear markets often move more sharply than bull markets. During these times, VIX tends to spike. Which means VIX is inversely correlated with equity prices.

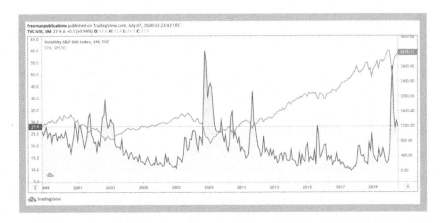

From this chart you can see how VIX spikes as equity prices decrease. March 2020 saw VIX hit an intraday level of 82.69, a level not seen since 2008. As prices climbed from 2012 to the beginning of 2020, VIX remained relatively low, with short spikes during market corrections.

You cannot directly access the VIX index, however one way to profit from this volatility is to use an Exchange Traded Note (ETN) which trades in a similar pattern to VIX. ETNs operate in a similar manner to ETFs, however the main difference is that they do not own the underlying asset.

One such ETN is iPath S&P 500 VIX Short-Term Futures ETN, which trades under the symbol VXX. This product consists of 1 month and 2 month VIX futures contracts, and trades in line with the VIX itself. Which means that in bear markets, as VIX increases, the price of VXX increases. For example, between February 22nd and March 18th 2020, VXX was up by more than 300% due to the huge spike in volatility caused by COVID-19.

Using an ETN like VXX can be an effective way to hedge against your long-term portfolio and protect your downside during a bear market. You would not want to hold VXX long-term as there is no upside to holding it in a bull market when volatility tends to be low. Like any futures based product, ensure you understand how the instrument works, as well as the risks involved with a product which tracks volatility, because you can lose a significant portion of your investment in a short period of time.

CRYPTOCURRENCY

Cryptocurrencies are the latest sexy asset class that everyone wants to get into. However, this doesn't mean that you automatically should. A majority of attention around this asset class occurred when the price of Bitcoin hit over $19,000 and everyone rushed in to invest in it.

The price now sits at $9,000 and is still subject to extreme volatility. However, the growing acceptance of Bitcoin and other alternative currencies has led to them becoming more mainstream, and as a result they've come to be viewed as safe hedges from fiat currencies.

A fiat currency is paper money. It has no value of its own. For example, the paper that the dollar is printed on is worth nothing. However, it gains value because everyone accepts the use of money as a means to trade goods with one another. Cryptocurrency enthusiasts cite this as an example of how paper money and the currencies attached to it is worthless.

All cryptocurrencies, the good ones at least, seek to achieve a purpose. In the case of Bitcoin, the idea was to create a universal currency that could be used across borders and one that was secure. These aims are now inherent in every cryptocurrency that has been launched. Given that Bitcoin was the first to the scene, these aims were revolutionary when it was first launched.

As an asset class, there is a lot of evidence to suggest that a basket of cryptocurrencies is a great hedge against traditional investments. The long-term evidence of such an investment thesis working out is questionable, though. Many Governments worldwide vehemently oppose cryptos and many have enacted laws that make it impossible to trade with them, even if exchanging them for fiat currencies is allowed.

This has turned crypto into a speculative space, and apart from the initial investors, many currencies attract people hoping to make a quick buck thanks to what they've heard on social media. There is an intelligent way to invest, but this requires the investors to put in some work up front.

For starters, the cryptocurrency's whitepaper is to the currency what the 10-K is to a company. It details everything to do with the currency and, most importantly, the function it is trying to implement. Understanding this process is critical if you're looking to invest in any currency.

This throws up quite a few barriers to the average investor. First there is the technical jargon one needs to understand. Whitepapers are fertile ground for discussion of the technical aspects of blockchain and its enhancements. Some cryptos are even tied to specific platforms and are not meant to be freely traded. For example, there are currencies that are tied to specific computing platforms.

Each coin translates to a certain number of hours that can be used on the computing platform by developers. Such a coin is hardly a good investment for the average investor. The second problematic aspect for the average investor is the culture surrounding the asset class. As things currently stand, no cryptocurrency has utility in our economies.

Even Bitcoin is not traded with any kind of significant volume compared to more traditional financial instruments. This means all currency prices are heavily tied to its price since no one knows which number represents good value. The average market player in this space is a speculator and they're not concerned with the long-term utility aspect of the asset.

The other type of major player in this space is the crypto evangelist who believes that the asset class represents a new paradigm for the world. They may or may not be right in this regard. That's beside the point. The issue is that such people don't care about the money that is present in cryptos. They're investing in something bigger.

The average investor is thus faced with a difficult situation if they aren't an evangelist. A basket of cryptocurrencies might hold some value against the dollar, but it's tough to predict. The evangelists do have a point and cryptocurrencies seem to be here to stay. Even if they don't replace fiat currencies, the online nature of our world means that they'll have some function moving forward.

Given these risks, we recommend investing no more than five percent of your total capital in Bitcoin while leaving the other cryptocurrencies alone unless you are a more experienced investor. The highly speculative nature of Bitcoin will move the value of your portfolio to extremes if it exceeds this limit. Taking a small position is a smart move though, as the potential for 500-1000% gains is still there, and this could prove to be a portfolio-saver if there is a collapse in traditional assets.

7

PROTECTING YOUR PORTFOLIO & GENERATING EXTRA MONTHLY INCOME WITH RISK-AVERSE OPTIONS STRATEGIES

You might have heard of options if you've dabbled in the markets previously. Options are a derivative instrument and have been called many things in the past. One description that has been applied to them has always been "complicated." This is far from the truth.

Options are a little bit more complex than common stock purchases, but this hardly means you can't understand how they work. What's important for you to grasp is that it isn't the instrument itself that is complex, but the strategy applied that can be complicated.

These instruments lend themselves very well to both simple and highly convoluted strategies. In this chapter, we're going to highlight two simple strategies that you can use to earn steady monthly income. Before we do that though, we have to ask, what are options, and how do they work?

Derivative instruments are identified as such because they derive their value from something else. Options derive their value from what is called the underlying. The underlying could be a stock (it usually is), a bond, an index or a currency pair. Bond options are highly complex and will not be available for you to trade. Most brokers won't offer you currency options either.

This leaves us with stock options, and there are two kinds of them: *calls* and *puts*. *Calls* give you the right but not the obligation to buy the underlying stock at a specified price before a specified date. While *puts* allow you to sell the underlying at a specified price before a specified date.

In plain English: If you own a call, you can choose to buy a stock and if you own a put you can choose to sell it. The price at which you buy or sell is called the strike price and the date before which you can do this is called the expiration date. Like futures, options are also contracts that expire monthly.

Options can be bought and sold in the open market like common stock. The price of an option is called its premium (like an insurance policy). Options pricing is a complicated topic since there are two components to it: the prospects of the underlying and the time left to expiration. To illustrate how complex it is, the professors who developed the model to price options ended up winning the Nobel Prize.

When you buy an option, you cannot earn back the premium. Your profit on the trade is whatever you earn from it minus the option premium.

However, you don't need to understand these intricacies to trade options in simple strategies. What's more important is for you to understand calls and puts and what they signify. You make money on a call when the underlying price increases. With puts, you make money when the underlying price falls.

Here's an example. Let's say you buy a call on Walmart. Below is the relevant information:

Underlying price: $120

Call premium: $10

Call strike price: $130

Call expiry date: One month from purchase date (today)

If the price of Walmart hits or exceeds $130, your call option gives you the right to buy the stock at $130. Let's say it goes up to $145 a week after you buy it. You can now exercise your option and buy Walmart for $130 and sell it back into the market for $145. You've made a profit of $5 per share. (Sale price - Buy price - Call premium = 145-130-10 = 5)

Similarly, here's an example of a put.

Underlying price: $120

Put premium: $10

Put strike price: $110

Put expiry date: One month from purchase date (today)

If the price of Walmart dips below the strike price to say $95, you can sell WMT at $110 (put strike price) and cover your position by buying it back at $95. You've sold at $110 and bought at $95 and this gives you a $5 profit (110-95-10 = 5)

In addition to exercising your option, you can buy and sell the option itself. When the underlying price moves up and down as in the examples above, the option premium moves along with it. This is because the value of the premium changes depending on how close or far away the underlying is from the strike price, as well as the time remaining before the option expires.

If the underlying moves past the call strike price, the call premium is going to rise in value. You can sell the call and collect a profit.

Every options contract covers 100 shares of the underlying. This means you'll need to multiply the option premium by 100 to figure out what you'll have to pay to purchase it. This means options are a leveraged instrument. By purchasing a single option you've gained exposure to 100 shares.

If you don't fully understand your strategy, options can be a dangerous tool. It's a bit like handing the keys to a powerful car to someone who hasn't driven before. In the hands of an experienced driver, the car is capable of performing brilliantly. In the hands of someone who's a poor driver or a novice, it'll end up causing harm to its occupants.

Having said that, the options strategies highlighted here are easy to understand. If you can comprehend sixth grade math, you'll be able to understand how they work. The key to making options work for you is to understand the role time plays.

Options decrease in value drastically when they enter the 30 days before expiration time frame. This means any strategy that you implement needs to run for at least 31 days. If you go long within this timeframe, you're probably not going to capture the fullest extent of the increase in premium prices. This means you're not going to buy any options that are going to expire within a few days. Unless the underlying moves massively, the odds of you making a profit are slim to none.

Let's look at the first options strategy.

PROTECTIVE PUTS

Given that prices will be dropping like flies in a bear market, the first step you can take to secure any long positions is to use protective puts. These will cover your downside risk better than a stop loss order.

A stop loss order is prone to being jumped by the market. In other words, you might set a stop loss order at $35 (after having purchased the stock at $50). If the market experiences huge volatility and if the only prices available in the market are $20 and $25, your broker will sell your order at one of these two prices.

This is despite your stop loss level being defined at $35. It isn't the broker's fault that market prices behaved this way. The stop loss level is just a trigger. It tells your broker to liquidate if the market sinks below that price. It doesn't say that the broker has to execute at the trigger price.

Options give you the ability to fix the price you receive upon exit. If you purchased a put at $35, you now have the right to sell the stock at this price. If the market price dips below this level you can exercise your option and the person who sold you the option has to honor the strike price.

Thus, you sell the underlying for $35. Since you've already bought the stock (for $50), you don't need to cover your position. The protective put isn't a money-making strategy. It's something that ensures your downside is properly protected. Stop loss orders get jumped quite often in bear markets since volatility spikes massively.

The second strategy is a money-making one but requires you to carry out some preliminary prep work.

CASH-SECURED PUTS

Since options can be freely traded in the markets, you can go ahead and sell a put without owning the underlying stock. Selling an option is also referred to as writing one. If you sell/write/short a put, you're betting on the stock price to rise and remain above the put's strike price.

Let's say you see Walmart at $50 and think that it isn't going to dip below $35. You write a put at $35 that expires one month from now. When you write or sell a put, you receive the option premium upfront. This is because the person who bought the put from you pays you this amount.

The option premium also represents your maximum profit from the trade. You might be wondering: If you feel that Walmart won't dip below $35 and will rise, why not buy a call? You could do this. However, the call option is likely going to be expensive. You'll need the stock to rise pretty high in order to clear a profit. Remember, you need to earn the option premium to break even on your trade.

There's no way of predicting how high the stock will rise. If all you know is that the stock won't dip below $35, selling a put is a much simpler way to make money. It removes the pressure of having to predict the degree of the rise. What's more, you earn your profit up front and this is a good way of earning income.

However, since you've sold a put without owning the underlying stock, you're naked. If the price dips below $35, you'll have to deliver the underlying to the buyer. This means you'll have to buy the stock at whatever price it's selling in the market and sell the stock to the option buyer at the strike price.

If Walmart falls to $10, you've just made a loss of $25 per share. On a single options contract that's a loss of $2,500.

Given this risk, many brokers will not allow you to write naked puts. Instead, they will insist on you securing it with either stock or cash. Securing the put with stock means you'll have to buy it and this might not appeal to you. Instead, you can secure it with cash.

The amount of cash you'll need to have on hand to do this is equal to the strike price multiplied by the number of shares you own via the options contract. In our example of Walmart, the strike price is $35 and you own a single option. This means you'll have to have at least $3,500 as cash in your account to cover the maximum potential loss.

The secured put strategy is a great strategy when you think that a stock has hit its lowest point and is now poised to rise higher. Bearish sentiment will be high and put premiums will be overpriced. This means you'll earn a lot more than in normal circumstances. As the put expires, worthless, you get to keep the premium earned.

COMPLEXITY

Options strategies get complicated when you introduce multiple legs into it. Strategies such as vertical spreads use two or even four legs to take advantage of a situation. It's best for you to stay away from them since these strategies require a much deeper understanding of the way options work.

Use puts in a protective fashion or apply the secured put strategy to take advantage of bear markets.

If you'd like a deeper understanding of options, including video examples then we've prepared a free introductory guide called *Options 101* inside our bonus resources section which you can find at:

https://freemanpublications.com/bonus

8

HOW TO PREPARE FOR THE ABSOLUTE WORST

This chapter is aimed at helping you prepare for an absolute worst-case scenario. We don't believe this is likely to happen anytime soon, but it never hurts to be prepared. In case a crisis does unfold, it's better to have and not need certain items as opposed to not having them and needing them.

STOCKING UP ON ESSENTIAL ITEMS

Supermarkets and grocery stores typically stock two to three days' worth of items in-store. If demand for these essential items runs high, then you're likely going to face empty shelves. It's important to stock up on these items since they run out quickly during times of crisis.

Generators

Backup sources of power are invaluable during tough times. These sell out first. The downside to generators is that they need fuel to run and will make a noise. If this bothers you too much, you can opt for an inverter or even use the battery in your car.

Canned Goods

If you're unlikely to have power, then canned goods are a great source of nutrition. They last long and usually don't need too much cooking to deliver a good meal.

Radios

When the power goes out, you won't have access to the internet or television. Old-fashioned radios will be the only source of communication. Instead of opting for battery-powered radios, buy hand-cranked ones.

Candles

You can stock up on batteries, but they will likely run out at some point. In such situations, candles are great to stock up on. While they don't have to be your primary source of light, they are good backups.

First Aid and Medicine

You'll need to have a first aid box well prepared. Stock it with necessities such as antiseptics, gauze and cotton. You'll also need basic medicine such as paracetamol tablets and ibuprofen. You can opt for generic brands for such medicines since they do the job well.

Make sure you stock up on vitamins too.

Flashlights

Flashlights and headlamps can be your primary light source. Make sure they're solar-powered instead of battery-operated.

Non-Perishable Food and Drinking Water

Stay away from frozen food since you might not have power. Opt for canned food as mentioned previously or food that can be cooked over a grill or a simple stovetop. This will change your purchasing options, so think this through carefully.

Stove

You'll need something to cook your food over. Opt for a propane stove since these are the most practical and safe.

FOOD STORAGE BEST PRACTICES

When it comes to food, storage is extremely important. Start small by storing enough food for three days. Most households will already have enough food for that length of time. Then slowly build up to three weeks and then scale up to three months. Most preppers eventually manage to store enough for a year.

Consider the shelf life of the food you store when buying it. White rice and pasta might not be as healthy as their brown varieties, but they tend to last longer. Foods such as dairy products and vegetable oil will not last long, so it's pointless to store these. Examples of foods that pretty much last forever include:

- Apple cider vinegar
- Cornstarch
- Clarified butter/ghee
- Hard liquor
- Hardtack - made from a mixture of flour and water and is a hard cracker
- Honey
- Salt
- Soy sauce
- Sugar
- White rice

Have a Grab Bag Ready

You never know when an emergency might strike and will force you to leave your home. Having a grab bag of essential items ready at all times is a good idea.

In this, you should have:

- A three-day supply of non-perishable food and a manual can opener
- 2 liters of water per person per day for at least three days
- Phone charger or battery bank
- Hand crank radio
- Hand crank flashlight

- First aid kit
- Extra batteries
- Additional pairs of eyeglasses or contacts
- Copies of important documents along with originals. Passport, certificates, insurance, title deeds etc.
- Garbage bags and moist towelettes
- Seasonal clothing
- Whistle
- Pen and notepad
- Local map

In addition to this you should also have an amount of cash in small bills at home equivalent to your weekly spend. Cash is still king in a worst case scenario, and you will have an easier time bartering with cash than you will precious metals or ammo.

9

PREPARING FOR THE NEXT TIME— WHAT TO DO AT THE END OF A BULL MARKET

Make it a point to re-read this book five years from now when the economic outlook is different. People get used to existing conditions pretty quickly and tend to forget that the opposite set of conditions might exist as well. In bear markets we forget that bull markets can exist.

In bull markets, euphoria cons us into thinking that bear markets will never exist. Keep looking out for the signs of overextended markets as we described when talking about the stages of a market. The fact is that bull and bear markets end, and at some point they'll begin as well.

ANTICIPATING CAUSES

As we mentioned earlier, trying to anticipate a single cause for a bear market is futile. Bear markets begin when there are enough reasons built up for the market to fall. All it needs is a catalyst and everything comes tumbling down. Many investors get caught up in trying to find these catalysts.

This is no different from trying to time the market and enter it at an optimal point. Note that all bear markets in the past have been caused by seemingly innocuous things.

1901

This was the first stock market crash that attracted widespread media attention. It began as a soap opera. E.H. Harriman and Jacob Schiff aimed to assume control over the Union Pacific Railroad and were opposed by J.P. Morgan and James Hill. It was a bit like two colossal walls of money clashing against one another.

Given the fact that both sides were trying to gain control of the important railroad, investors piled into railroad stocks and borrowed money heavily to do so. This led to railroad stocks rising to absurd levels. As all smart investors do, Harriman and Schiff (who would win this battle) had amassed their holdings at far lower levels.

Viewing the extremely high valuations, they sold a portion of their holdings without relinquishing control of the company. Word spread that both men were now selling and this caused a colossal crash in railroad stocks that cleaned many market participants out. This precipitated a wave of margin calls that led to sell-offs in every other company listed on the exchange.

Who would have thought a single railroad company could cause such a huge crash? Jesse Livermore, whom we mentioned before, managed to call this crash correctly even though he didn't anticipate that the struggle over Union Pacific would cause it (Lefèvre, 1994).

1906

The cause for this crash was the great earthquake that rocked San Francisco. Initial reports suggested that the fire was contained early on and that there wasn't significant damage. However, as reports kept trickling in, the damage was a lot larger than imagined.

This caused a panic in certain stocks that spread like wildfire to every other stock in the market. You must keep in mind that the telegraph was the only reliable source of communication back then. This made the market extremely susceptible to misinformation.

Jesse Livermore once again managed to call this market. Bizarrely, he did so when vacationing with a friend and wandering into a broker's office. He saw

Union Pacific's stock (the railroad was based out of San Francisco) behaving oddly and decided to short it on a hunch (Lefèvre, 1994).

2000

Livermore was long gone by the time the year 2000 rolled around, but the underlying emotions that the market produced were still the same. Internet stocks were all the rage and these were promoted thanks to the advent of online trading. "Online" back then simply meant a real-time feed of prices on broker software, not what we think of today.

The euphoria leading up to the crash was fueled by IPOs from companies who were claiming to eliminate the efficiencies from certain industries, while simultaneously hemorrhaging money themselves. Priceline.com was one of the best examples of this. The company went from $16/share to $88/share on its IPO day, and was valued at $9.8 Billion. At the time this was the largest valuation of a public internet company on its IPO day. This was despite Priceline's core business (allowing consumers to bid on airline tickets at a discount) being a money loser, with no signs of ever becoming profitable. This led to the CEO of rival website CheapTickets famously stating "We've got a policy here at CheapTickets. We need to make money." Many of these overvaluations were caused by Venture Capital firms driving prices up as much as possible, because this is when they got paid. After the initial IPO period, the VC investors would cash out their gigantic profits, and leave retail investors holding the bag.

Perhaps no single statistic was more damning than Mary Meeker's analysis of Internet Stocks in October 1999. Meeker discovered that the market cap of the 199 internet stocks was a whopping $450 billion. But the total annual sales of these companies came to only about $21 billion. And their annual profits? A collective loss of $6.2 Billion.

To paraphrase, Benjamin Graham, the market eventually went from a voting machine to a weighing machine. Company after company declared bankruptcy and the market went into freefall. The Nasdaq peaked at 5,048.62 on March 10th 2000, it would be 15 years before it reached that figure again (McCullough, 2018).

2001

There was a brief bear market towards the end of 2001 that followed 9/11. This was a classic case of an external shock that the average investor could never have foreseen happening.

2008

This one was building up for years, if not decades. Everyone forgot that home prices could go down as well as up. Lending standards collapsed. Strawberry pickers were given money to buy million-dollar homes. The ratings agencies abdicated responsibility and a few Wall Street banks managed to get out of the burning house before locking the door behind them.

2020

This one was also a decade in the making. Cheap money caused high levels of leverage and papered over cracks in the economy. Everyone knew the party would come to an end at some point. It eventually did when a bat infected a pangolin that ended up being eaten by someone in Wuhan, China.

The virus spread and the fragile market came crashing down. No one could have foreseen that a virus would bring things down before it occurred. There have been a few investors who acted swiftly once they heard of the virus.

Bill Ackman from the previous Herbalife story is one of them. He was one of the first American voices to warn against the lackadaisical attitude of the American government and he was proven right. Some sources estimate Ackman has cleared over a billion dollars acting on his convictions (Winck, 2020).

LESSONS

The point of this history lesson is to show that there is no limit to the number of things that can prompt a bear market. In the five stages of the economic cycle that we referenced earlier in this book, you must remember that it doesn't matter *what* the shock is. All that matters is that there is one. And the underlying causes of all shocks are the same. Euphoria and complacency are present throughout. While many think the markets have become even more unstable these days, the fact is that the early 1900s were far more unstable.

This was due to the lack of regulation. The formation of the SEC led to an era of relatively stable markets before technology introduced the lack of regulation right back. Will we see an era of better regulation governing technology? Or will instability continue?

There's no point trying to predict this. All the investor can do is look for the tell-tale signs and act accordingly. We previously mentioned the death cross technical indicator in chapter 6. This is one of the tools you can use to be prepared for a potential crash. Do not be hesitant to move your holdings into cash if you spot the signs of an overvalued market. Remember that holding cash is a position in itself. This is especially true if you are closer to, or currently in retirement.

10

HOW TO IDENTIFY FRAUDULENT OPERATIONS

The start of bear markets typically brings to light a variety of fraudulent behavior. Many companies that were coasting along during the good times get exposed and an almighty ruckus ensues. The popular media comes up with quotes about how the signs were there for everyone to see.

They carefully sidestep the fact that they were amongst those that missed the signs. Despite all of this, there are a few telling markers that reveal instances of fraudulent activity.

SMARTER THAN EVERYONE ELSE

Appearing to be smarter than everyone else is a tried and tested con artist strategy. Our brains are extremely susceptible to appearances and as long as something looks right, we ignore other rational evidence. Someone wearing a fancy suit must be wealthy while the guy riding the bus must be poor.

This bias triggers our confirmation bias and with the blinders firmly on we grow hostile towards information that contradicts our opinion. The "too smart for common folk" technique has been used by financial frauds repeatedly.

Enron and its incomparable CEO Jeff Skilling were famous for this attitude (McLean & Elkind, 2004). Skilling famously created an atmosphere of intellectual intimidation at Enron and repeatedly used words like smart and complex to describe Enron's strategies. At the end of the day, all he was doing was making things up as he went along.

Another example was Bernie Madoff (Arvedlund, 2008). Madoff used a childishly simple options strategy to supposedly earn 15% returns every year like clockwork. Veteran options traders, even retail ones, wondered how that strategy could earn such astronomical returns. Madoff's constant refrain was that his methods were more sophisticated and that others didn't understand his genius.

Complexity by itself isn't a problem, but it is a red flag when the creator of the complexity cannot seemingly explain it in detail. This was amply evident with Madoff. Add to the fact that everyone was raving about him, and you have a scenario that screams fraudulent activity.

NOTHING CAN GO WRONG

Another key component of fraudulent investment opportunities is that they have an air of nothing possibly going wrong. Real investment opportunities always have risks attached to them. Smart investors understand that risk needs to be correlated to reward in order to justify an investment decision. Anyone who claims you can make 20% per month or 200% per year, every year, is either outright lying or is not explaining the huge amount of risk involved in such a strategy.

While every investment opportunity carries risk, assuming this risk is justified if the reward on offer is large. If you don't have money for college, you could assume student loan debt. This might be a good decision if you can find a high-paying job after school. It's a terrible decision if you decide to study art history.

Every investor's risk appetite is different and this is why there's no such thing as a can't-miss opportunity. If you don't have the mindset to handle the risk inherent in an opportunity, you will screw it up. Most investors don't want this to happen. They want to be comfortable at all times and want money to flow in easily. They don't want to work for it.

Frauds latch onto this and exploit it at every turn. What's more, they charge exorbitant amounts of money or nothing at all for this "system." Skilling charged his investors huge amounts through stock options and dumped his stock when he saw the writing on the wall. Madoff famously never charged anything for his money management services.

The zero-fee ploy is seemingly a polar opposite to the high-fee ploy, but both have the same psychological effect. They lead you to believe you've found a gold mine and confirmation bias kicks in.

Internet companies that went bust in the dotcom crash employed similar tactics. By being technology companies, they couldn't fail (at least that's what they said). They used stock options to reward their executives since they didn't have enough cash to do so. They used their stock prices to borrow heavily from banks who had a history of lending to exactly the kind of people who shouldn't be given money.

The presence of buzzwords cause FOMO to manifest and the next thing you know people have placed their life savings into such companies. The use of sophisticated phrases and words by themselves are signs of fraud. This perpetuates the theme that the investor or person in charge of the opportunity is a genius.

LUCK VERSUS COMPETENCE

Every so often an incompetent person manages to make tons of money. Even broken clocks are right twice a day. Spotting whether money was made due to sheer luck or due to competence is a tough task. Keep in mind that even the best investments need some luck in order to work out.

The proportion of luck versus skill is what you want to look at. In every investment opportunity, you want to be siding with skill as much as possible since this is a more repeatable process. Relying on luck is a bit like investing your money in lottery tickets and hoping that they'll pay out someday.

A great way to spot whether an investment manager is relying on skill is to look at their circle of competence and match that to the investment opportunity. If Steve Jobs came up to you and told you to invest in Apple back in 2004, you would have done well to follow that advice.

If he came up to you and told you to invest in the Segway, that would have been a dumb decision. Even Steve Jobs was subject to the circle of competence. Jobs was one of the investors who famously placed money in the Segway along with a number of other luminaries. The company was founded by a famous inventor who had a brilliant track record.

The only issue was that every single one of them were well outside their circle of competence. The inventor hailed from a medical device background and there wasn't a single person from anything remotely resembling transportation devices on board. In hindsight, the Segway might be thought of as being ahead of its time.

However, people who understand their circle of competence usually manage to time their products right. We're not suggesting in any way that the Segway is an example of fraud. It's just that even great opportunities backed by highly trustworthy people can end up relying on luck instead of skill.

In the annals of corporate fraud in America, Elizabeth Holmes comes a close second to Skilling purely because her company Theranos was a private operation. If it was public, there's no doubt she would have surpassed him easily.

Holmes checked all the right boxes of fraud. She was intelligent sounding, had the right pedigree (Stanford dropout which in the entrepreneurial world is immediately equated to genius), a complex solution to a complex problem, used heavy-sounding terms and ran a company that practiced absurd levels of secrecy.

She had the right people around her too. Former statesmen, U.S. Armed Forces generals and former CEOs littered her board of directors. She was pals with Chelsea Clinton, which meant Hillary was close by. Henry Kissinger was involved too, which satisfied the Republican crowd (Carreyrou, 2011).

Everything was perfect! Except it wasn't. Holmes had zero competence in the medical field. She was a chemical engineering major and dropped out after freshman year. She played the technology disruption card. Her patent was all she leaned on, but that was just a piece of paper. Investors forget that a patent without a working prototype is useless.

When it came crashing down, there was disbelief followed by "we knew it all along" reporting. Holmes is trying to raise money for her next company despite facing the prospect of spending the rest of her life in jail. Given her skill set, she might even succeed.

Con artists use charisma and the previous two points to obscure the fact that everything depends on getting lucky. Holmes started off as an idealist teenager trying to do good but somewhere along the way her inner con artist asserted itself. She never had competence to begin with and began relying on luck. Naturally, this doesn't work over and over as a strategy.

She got lucky a few times and resorted to fraud moving forward when she couldn't replicate it.

ALWAYS HAS AN ANSWER

The smartest of people understand that there are many things they don't know. The dumbest among us are fully convinced that they know everything. What's more, they're so sure of it that they end up convincing the intelligent ones too. Life can be ironic like that.

Be very careful of an investment adviser or principal who seems to know the answer to everything or has an inability to say "I don't know." You obviously don't want someone who says this all the time. This merely indicates that they're well outside their circle of competence.

However, a field such as investing has so many variables that it is impossible for someone to know everything. Ask Warren Buffett about the global economy and the first thing he says is that he doesn't know. Ask George Soros about the prospects of a particular company and he responds by saying he doesn't know.

Intelligent investors know what they don't know. By avoiding a reliance on such matters they ensure the odds are on their side. It's only the unknowns they need to worry about.

How to Adopt this Process in the Next 18-24 Months

If there was an apt slogan for bear markets, it would be: Keep Calm and Carry On. Our emotional biases make it seem as if bear markets and bad times will persist forever, but this is just an illusion. The truth is that everything ends, even bear markets.

Capitalizing on bear markets requires a different skill set from the ones that allow you to thrive in bullish conditions. In bear markets, there is no place to hide, and it will seem as if everything is close to collapse. The place to begin is to evaluate the stage the bear market is in.

Different stages call for different strategies and we've highlighted a number of these. For example, the cash-protected put option is a great strategy for phase five of the economic cycle. The biggest challenge you will face will be presented by your own mindset. We're naturally conditioned to value the good times and be extremely fearful of the bad.

This causes us to shun bear markets and sit them out. However, intelligent investors realize that bear markets are the ones that provide huge entry opportunities in great companies. Investors overreact to bad news, and as a result everything gets sold. This means perfectly good companies with strong businesses end up being priced at bargain levels.

Transforming the way you view bear markets is crucial to your success. Uncertainty equals opportunity in such times. The media and social media will push the narrative that markets will never recover from the current crisis. Every little rally in the market will be celebrated joyously.

People will rush into the markets, believing in them, and will promptly get burned. As an intelligent investor, your job is to remain as rational as possible, and the best way to do this is to examine the layers related to the company from the inside out. The best place to begin is the 10-K, and we've broken down how you need to go about looking at the important points in this filing.

Company press releases and earnings calls contain factual information, but this is often wrapped in a heavy degree of spin. Social media and your neighbor are the last places you should think of when it comes to collecting information.

Tweet-happy CEOs and press departments manipulate perception of companies and you should stay away from this as much as possible.

We carry a large number of biases within us, and these cloud our judgment. We've highlighted the most important ones in this book. While it might be close to impossible to get rid of all of them, it pays to remain aware of them. By bringing awareness, you'll be able to avoid some of the huge problems that these biases create.

Avoid traps such as forming narratives tied to investment and looking for quick riches. This will cause you to jump into poor investments that will cost you money. Before jumping into the market make sure you have a healthy amount of cash in the bank. Invest only the money that you can afford to lose.

Gold and silver are examples of asset classes that do well in turbulent times. In this age of quantitative easing and money printing, the case for these assets gets better by the day. You could short the industries that perform poorly. Airlines and hospitality companies tend to be hit the hardest during tough times. Their business economics are poor and there are telltale signs to spot such companies.

You could also invest in sector-specific ETFs to hedge your investments against a declining market. Lastly, cryptocurrencies are also a good hedge, but these bring their own risks to the table. You can also use options strategies to protect your investments as well as bring additional income every month.

While the worst-case scenario might be far away, it helps to be prepared. We've provided you with brief guidelines on how you can go about doing this. Stop looking for reasons the market might fail and instead learn what you need to do. Spot fraudulent activity before you fall for it and you'll do just fine.

Bear markets are tough, but with the right process and mindset, you will get through them and thrive. We wish you the best of luck with your investments and hope you've learned to view bear markets differently thanks to reading this book!

One final word from us. If this book has helped you in any way, we'd appreciate it if you left a review on Amazon. Reviews are the lifeblood of our business. We read every single one, and incorporate your feedback into future book projects.

To leave an Amazon review go to https://
freemanpublications.com/leaveareview

"THE MOST SUCCESSFUL PEOPLE IN LIFE ARE THE ONES
WHO ASK QUESTIONS. THEY'RE ALWAYS LEARNING.
THEY'RE ALWAYS GROWING. THEY'RE ALWAYS PUSHING."

- Robert Kiyosaki

CONTINUING YOUR JOURNEY

Like Robert Kiyosaki said on the previous page, "The most successful people in life are always learning, growing, and asking questions."

Which is why we created our investing community, aptly named **How To NOT Lose Money in the Stock Market.**

So that like-minded individuals could get together to share ideas and learn from each other.

We regularly run giveaways, share wins from our readers, and you'll be the first to know when our new books are released.

It's 100% free, and there are no requirements to join, except for the willingness to learn.

You can join us on Facebook by going to

http://freemanpublications.com/facebook

REFERENCES

Arvedlund, E. (2008). What We Wrote About Madoff. Retrieved 29 May 2020, from https://www.barrons.com/articles/SB122973813073623485?tesla=y

Banton, C. (2020). Trading the Gold-Silver Ratio. Retrieved 29 May 2020, from https://www.investopedia.com/articles/trading/09/gold-silver-ration.asp

Beattie, A. (2019). Silver Thursday: How Two Wealthy Traders Cornered The Market. Retrieved 29 May 2020, from https://www.investopedia.com/articles/optioninvestor/09/silver-thursday-hunt-brothers.asp

Bernstein, R. (2018). Retrieved 29 May 2020, from https://www.rbadvisors.com/images/pdfs/toward_the_sounds_of_chaos.pdf

Brook, D. (2016). How Dubai Became Dubai. Retrieved 29 May 2020, from https://nextcity.org/daily/entry/how-dubai-became-dubai

Burry, M. (2010). I Saw the Crisis Coming. Why Didn't the Fed? Retrieved 17 June 2020, from https://www.nytimes.com/2010/04/04/opinion/04burry.html

Carreyrou, J. Bad blood.

Chamaria, N. (2018). Why This Struggling Silver Stock Rocketed 51% in November | The Motley Fool. Retrieved 29 May 2020, from https://www.fool.

com/investing/2018/12/05/why-this-struggling-silver-stock-rocketed-51-in-no.aspx

Chen, J. (2020). Understanding Treasury Notes. Retrieved 29 May 2020, from https://www.investopedia.com/terms/t/treasurynote.asp

Chen, J. (2019). Sir John Templeton. Retrieved 29 May 2020, from https://www.investopedia.com/terms/s/sirjohntempleton.asp

Cheng, E. (2017). $24 million iced tea company says it's pivoting to the blockchain, and its stock jumps 200%. Retrieved 29 May 2020, from https://www.cnbc.com/2017/12/21/long-island-iced-tea-micro-cap-adds-blockchain-to-name-and-stock-soars.html

Colarusso, D. (2020). Mirror Mirror on the Wall, Explain for Me a Put and Call. Retrieved 29 May 2020, from https://www.thestreet.com/investing/options/mirror-mirror-on-the-wall-explain-for-me-a-put-and-call-964257

Dastin, J., & Saleem, N. (2015). Dubai airline Emirates rejects Delta apology over 9/11 comments. Retrieved 13 June 2020, from https://www.reuters.com/article/us-emirates-airlines-delta/dubai-airline-emirates-rejects-delta-apology-over-9-11-comments-idUSKBN0LN1S320150219

Delinquency Rate on Credit Card Loans, All Commercial Banks. (2020). Retrieved 29 May 2020, from https://fred.stlouisfed.org/series/DRCCLACBS

Emspak, J. (2020). Why Is the Price of Gold More Than Just Supply and Demand?. Retrieved 29 May 2020, from https://www.investopedia.com/articles/active-trading/031915/what-moves-gold-prices.asp

Floyd, D. (2019). Buffett's Bet with the Hedge Funds: And the Winner Is …. Retrieved 29 May 2020, from https://www.investopedia.com/articles/investing/030916/buffetts-bet-hedge-funds-year-eight-brka-brkb.asp

Garret, O. (2017). 3 Reasons Why Investors Should Avoid Gold ETFs. Retrieved 29 May 2020, from https://www.forbes.com/sites/oliviergarret/2017/03/09/3-reasons-why-investors-should-avoid-gold-etfs/#2c535f754dd8

Green, T. (2016). This Warren Buffett Quote Describes Twitter Perfectly | The Motley Fool. Retrieved 29 May 2020, from https://www.fool.com/investing/2016/11/30/this-warren-buffett-quote-describes-twitter-perfec.aspx

Guide to Analyst Recommendations. (2020). Retrieved 29 May 2020, from https://www.marketwatch.com/tools/guide.asp

Han, W. (2020). Investors Sip the Bitter Taste of the Luckin Coffee Scandal. Retrieved 19 June 2020, from https://www.caixinglobal.com/2020-04-20/in-depth-investors-sip-the-bitter-taste-of-the-luckin-coffee-scandal-101544557.html

Hayes, A. (2019). History of the Dutch Tulip Bulb Market's Bubble. Retrieved 29 May 2020, from https://www.investopedia.com/terms/d/dutch_tulip_bulb_market_bubble.asp

Heaton, C. (2016). Retrieved 29 May 2020, from https://moneyweek.com/430541/bill-gross-is-still-bearish

Iacurci, G. (2020). Unemployment is nearing Great Depression levels. Here's how the eras are similar — and different. Retrieved 29 May 2020, from https://www.cnbc.com/2020/05/19/unemployment-today-vs-the-great-depression-how-do-the-eras-compare.html

Kagan, J. (2020). Maintenance Margin Definition. Retrieved 29 May 2020, from https://www.investopedia.com/terms/m/maintenancemargin.asp

Kettleman, J., & Schultz, K. (2020). Modi Orders 3-Week Total Lockdown for All 1.3 Billion Indians. Retrieved 29 May 2020, from https://www.nytimes.com/2020/03/24/world/asia/india-coronavirus-lockdown.html

Koster, J. (2018). Jim Chanos on primary research and peeling the onion... Retrieved 29 May 2020, from https://www.valueinvestingworld.com/2018/04/jim-chanos-on-primary-research-and.html

Lefèvre, E. (1994). Reminiscences of a stock operator. New York: Wiley.

Lewis, M. (2008). The Big Short.

Logan, B. (2020). The world's 20 best airlines for 2019. Retrieved 29 May 2020, from https://www.businessinsider.com/best-airlines-in-the-world-2019-skytrax-rankings-2019-6

Marte, J. (2020). U.S. household debt tops $14 trillion and reaches new record. Retrieved 29 May 2020, from https://www.reuters.com/article/us-usa-fed-household-debt/u-s-household-debt-tops-14-trillion-and-reaches-new-record-idUSKBN20521Z.

McLean, B., & Elkind, P. (2004). The smartest guys in the room. London: Penguin.

McCullough, B. (2018). An eye-opening look at the dot-com bubble of the 2000 – and how it shapes our lives today. Retrieved 18 June 2020, from https://ideas.ted.com/an-eye-opening-look-at-the-dot-com-bubble-of-2000-and-how-it-shapes-our-lives-today/

Mercer, C. (2020). EBITDA's "Naughty 11" Problems and What to Do About Them. Retrieved 29 May 2020, from https://chrismercer.net/ebitdas-naughty-11-problems-and-what-to-do-about-them/

Monica, P. (2018). Bill Ackman's Herbalife disaster is finally over. Retrieved 29 May 2020, from https://money.cnn.com/2018/03/01/investing/herbalife-bill-ackman-carl-icahn/index.html

O'Brien, M. (2012). John Maynard Keynes Was the Warren Buffett of His Day. Retrieved 29 May 2020, from https://www.theatlantic.com/business/archive/2012/04/john-maynard-keynes-was-the-warren-buffett-of-his-day/255356/

Parrish, S. (2020). How Darwin Thought: The Golden Rule of Thinking. Retrieved 29 May 2020, from https://fs.blog/2016/01/charles-darwin-thinker/

Ponzio, J. (2007). Enron: Accounting Scandal or Bad Business | Joe Ponzio's F Wall Street. Retrieved 29 May 2020, from https://www.fwallstreet.com/article/54-enron-accounting-scandal-or-bad-business

Schroeder, A. (2008). The snowball. London: Bloomsbury.

SEC.gov | Facebook to Pay $100 Million for Misleading Investors About the Risks It Faced From Misuse of User Data. (2019). Retrieved 29 May 2020, from https://www.sec.gov/news/press-release/2019-140

Segal, T. (2020). Enron Scandal: The Fall of a Wall Street Darling. Retrieved 29 May 2020, from https://www.investopedia.com/updates/enron-scandal-summary/

Summers, J. (2020). Bloomberg. Retrieved 29 May 2020, from https://www.bloomberg.com/news/articles/2020-03-30/oil-etf-seen-as-tourist-trap-with-crude-trading-in-the-20s

Tesla Q1 2020 Vehicle Production & Deliveries. (2020). Retrieved 29 May 2020, from https://ir.tesla.com/news-releases/news-release-details/tesla-q1-2020-vehicle-production-deliveries

Tesla. (2020). 10-K. New York: Tesla Inc.

The Voting and Weighing Machines. (2020). Retrieved 29 May 2020, from https://news.morningstar.com/classroom2/course.asp?docId=142901&page=7

Tuovila, A. (2020). Generally Accepted Accounting Principles (GAAP). Retrieved 29 May 2020, from https://www.investopedia.com/terms/g/gaap.asp

When Did Concorde First Fly to North America?. (2020). Retrieved 29 May 2020, from https://www.historyhit.com/concorde-opens-london-new-york-route/

Who Benefits From Loaning Shares in a Short Sale?. (2020). Retrieved 29 May 2020, from https://www.investopedia.com/ask/answers/05/shortsalebenefit.asp

Winck, B. (2020). Billionaire investor Bill Ackman turned $27 million into $2.6 billion by betting that the coronavirus would tank the market | Markets Insider. Retrieved 29 May 2020, from https://markets.businessinsider.com/news/stocks/bill-ackman-hedge-profits-billions-coronavirus-tanks-stock-market-economy-2020-3-1029035562

Winck, B. (2020). Gold prices will nearly double to a record $3,000 as central banks fuel 'financial repression,' Bank of America says | Markets Insider. Retrieved 29 May 2020, from https://markets.businessinsider.com/news/stocks/gold-price-target-record-central-bank-stimulus-bank-america-double-2020-4-1029113912